AF594532

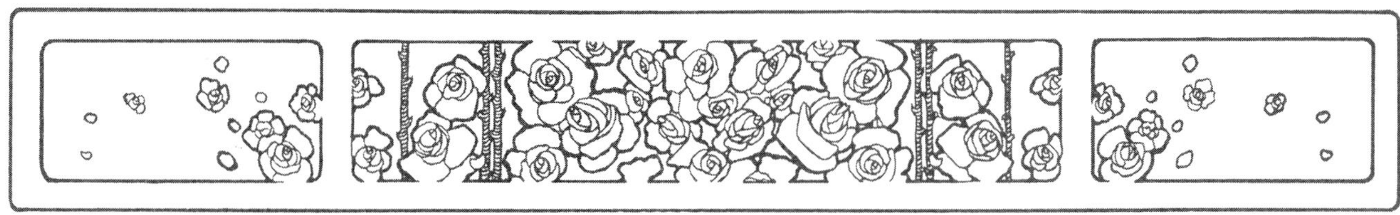

VINTAGE Typography & Signage

FOR DESIGNERS, BY DESIGNERS

FRANK H. ATKINSON,
CHARLES J. STRONG AND L. S. STRONG

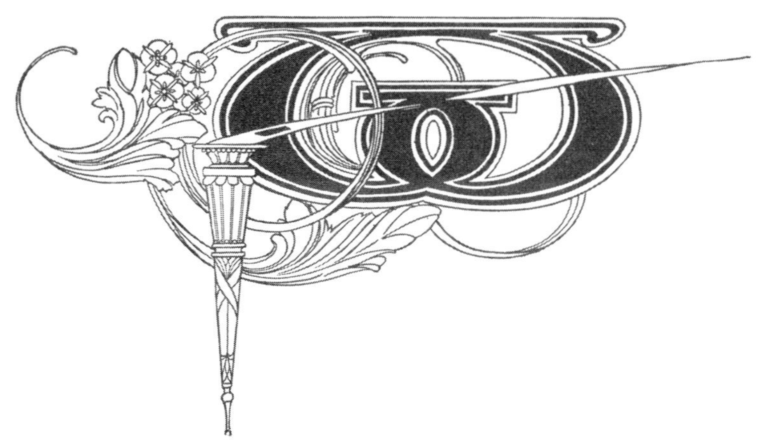

DOVER PUBLICATIONS, INC.
MINEOLA, NEW YORK

Bibliographical Note

This Dover edition, first published in 2011 as *Vintage Commercial Art and Design*, and reissued by Dover in 2018, contains a selection of images from *Sign Painting* by Frank H. Atkinson (1915) and *Strong's Book of Designs* (1917), both originally published by Frederick J. Drake & Company, Chicago. The CD-ROM from the original Dover edition has been removed, and a new black-and-white image has been added on page 89.

International Standard Book Number

ISBN-13: 978-0-486-82497-0
ISBN-10: 0-486-82497-7

Manufactured in the United States by LSC Communications
82497701 2018
www.doverpublications.com

Note

This exquisite collection of commercial signs, illustrations, and fonts are from two rare, early-twentieth-century sources that were used as a reference for sign painters and lithographers. This valuable resource includes more than 1,400 eye-catching signs and design elements—including 25 different fonts and over 100 full-color images. Ranging from simple and graceful to complex and bold, the designs in this treasury will inspire artists, craftspeople, and graphic designers looking to add a classic vintage accent to their work.

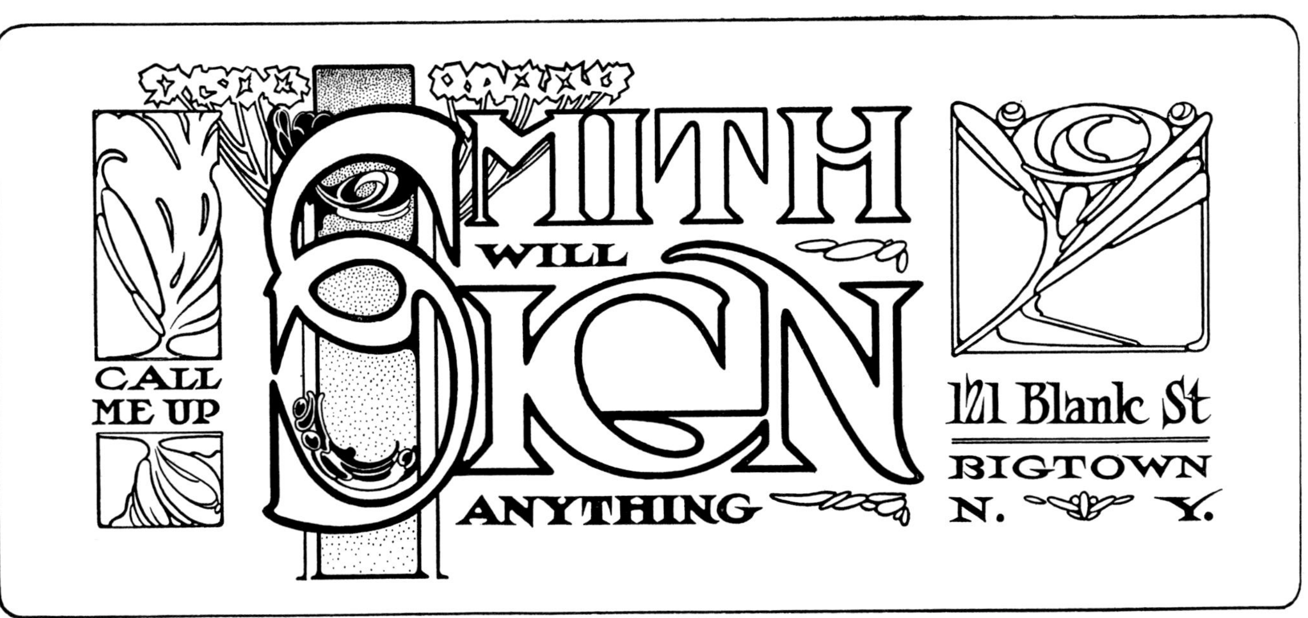
SMITH
WILL
SIGN
ANYTHING
CALL
ME UP
121 Blank St
BIGTOWN
N. Y.

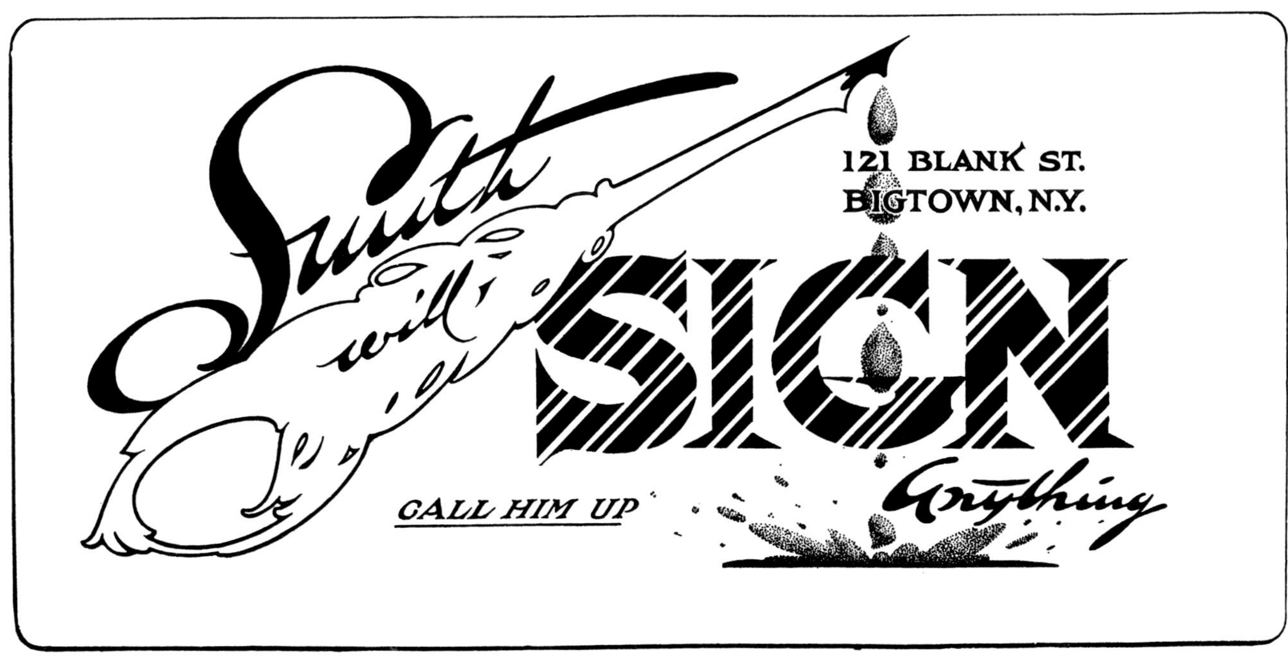
Smith
will
SIGN
Anything
121 BLANK ST.
BIGTOWN, N.Y.
CALL HIM UP

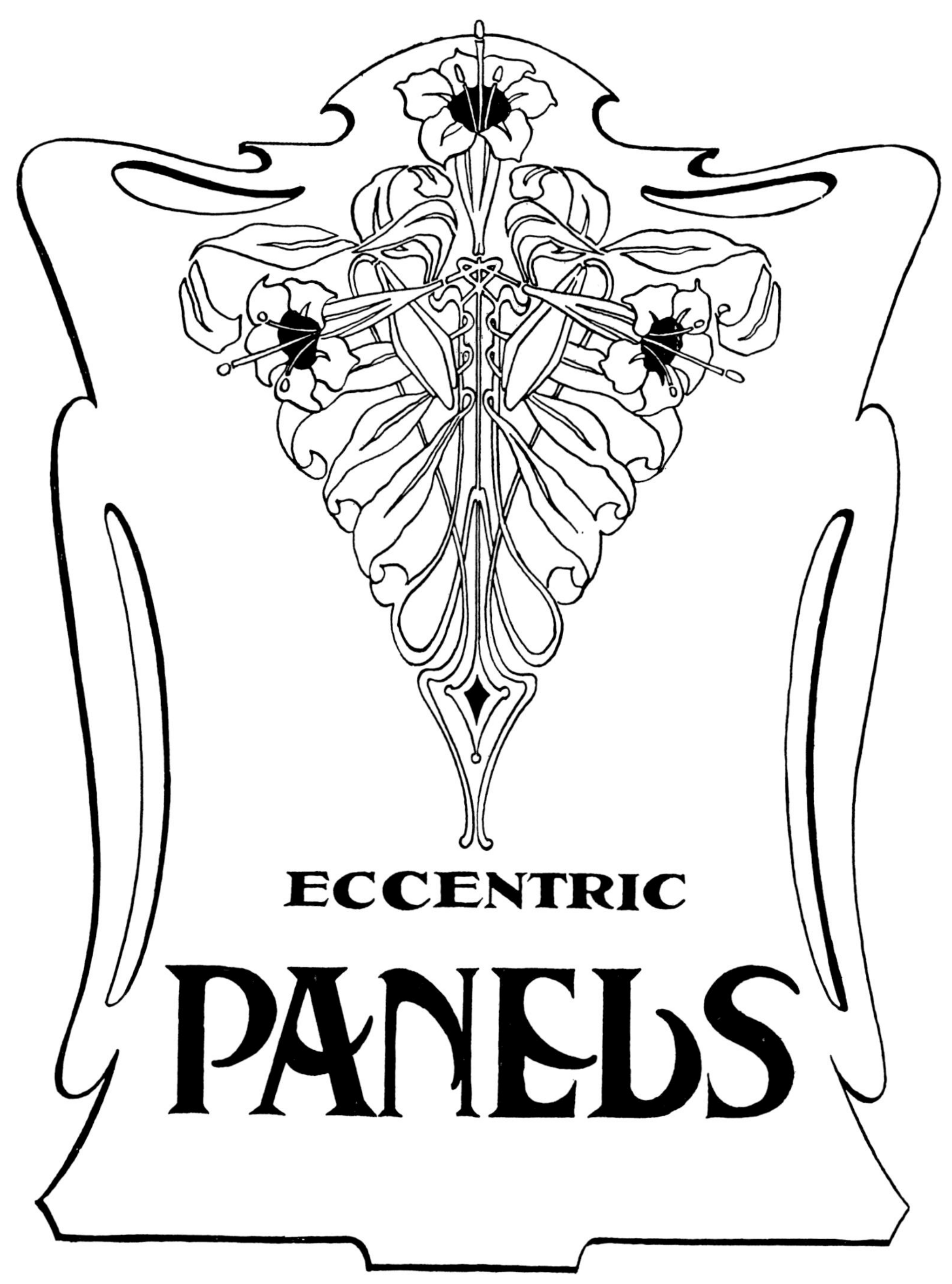
ECCENTRIC
PANELS

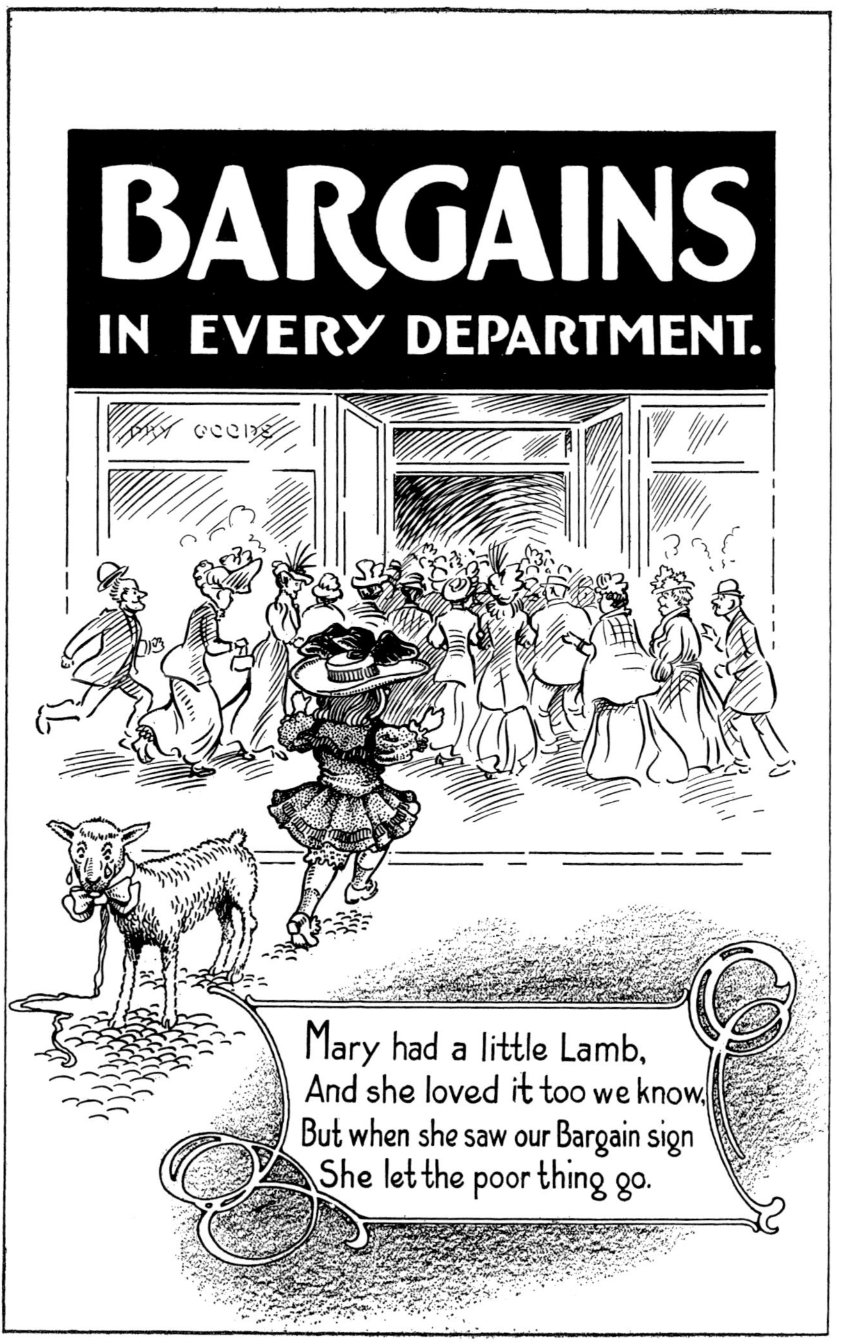
BARGAINS
IN EVERY DEPARTMENT.
DRY GOODS
Mary had a little Lamb,
And she loved it too we know,
But when she saw our Bargain sign
She let the poor thing go.

A
customer that
gets the
"BUTT-END"
of a deal
goes
straight up
and
NEVER
COMES
BACK!

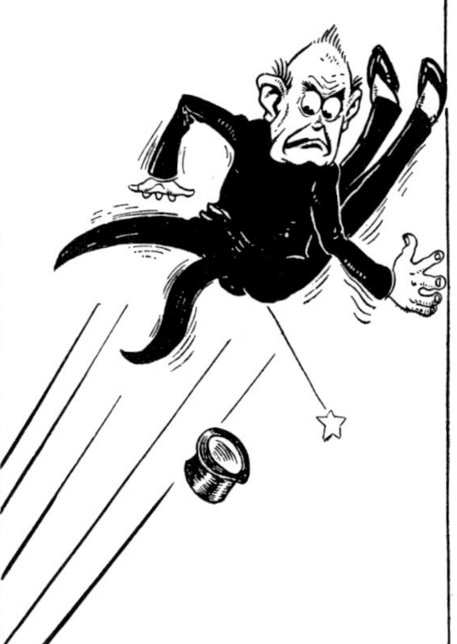

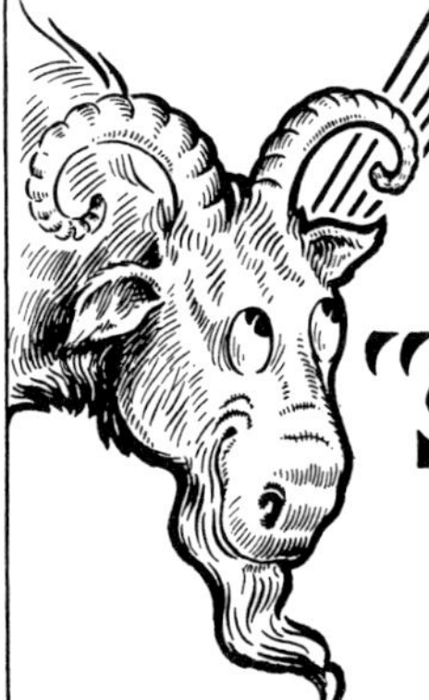

WE HAVE
NO
"STRONG
BUTTER"

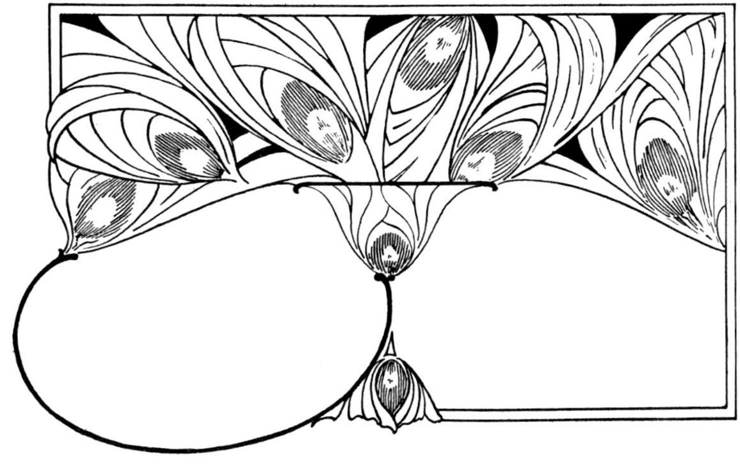

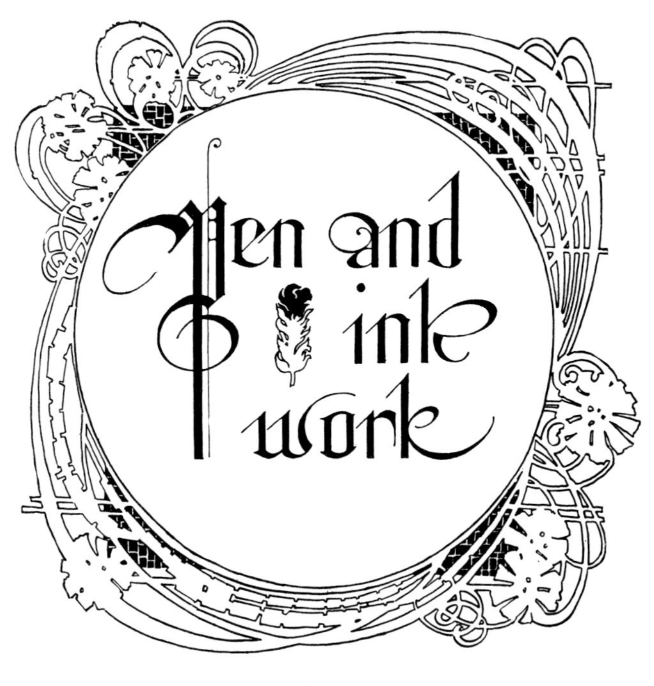
Pen and
ink
work

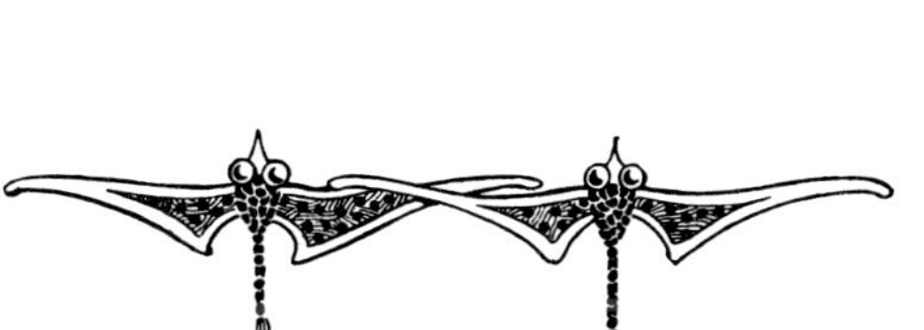

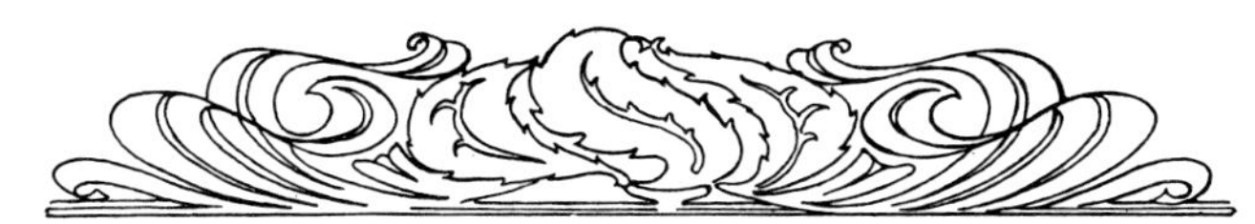

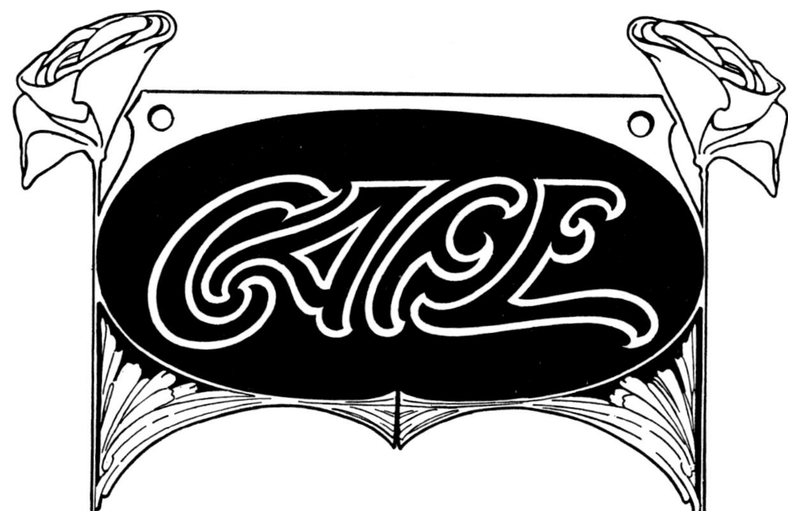

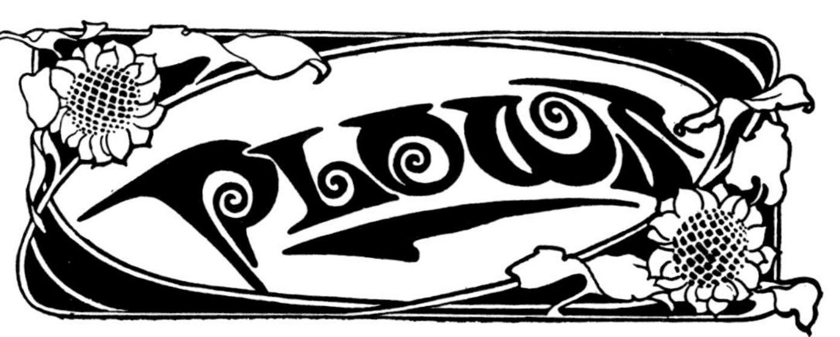

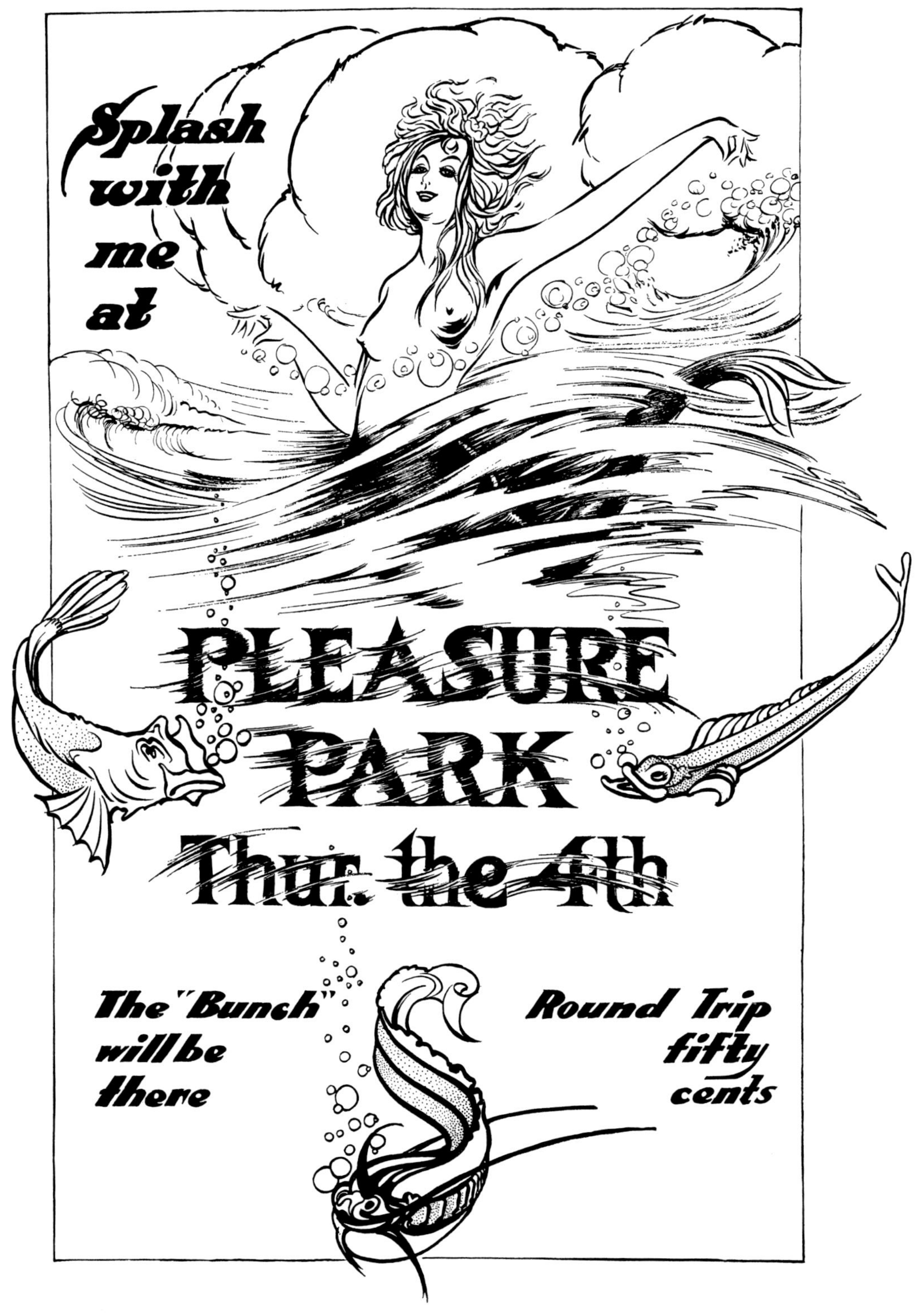
Splash
with
me
at
PLEASURE
PARK
Thur. the 4th
The "Bunch"
will be
there
Round Trip
fifty
cents

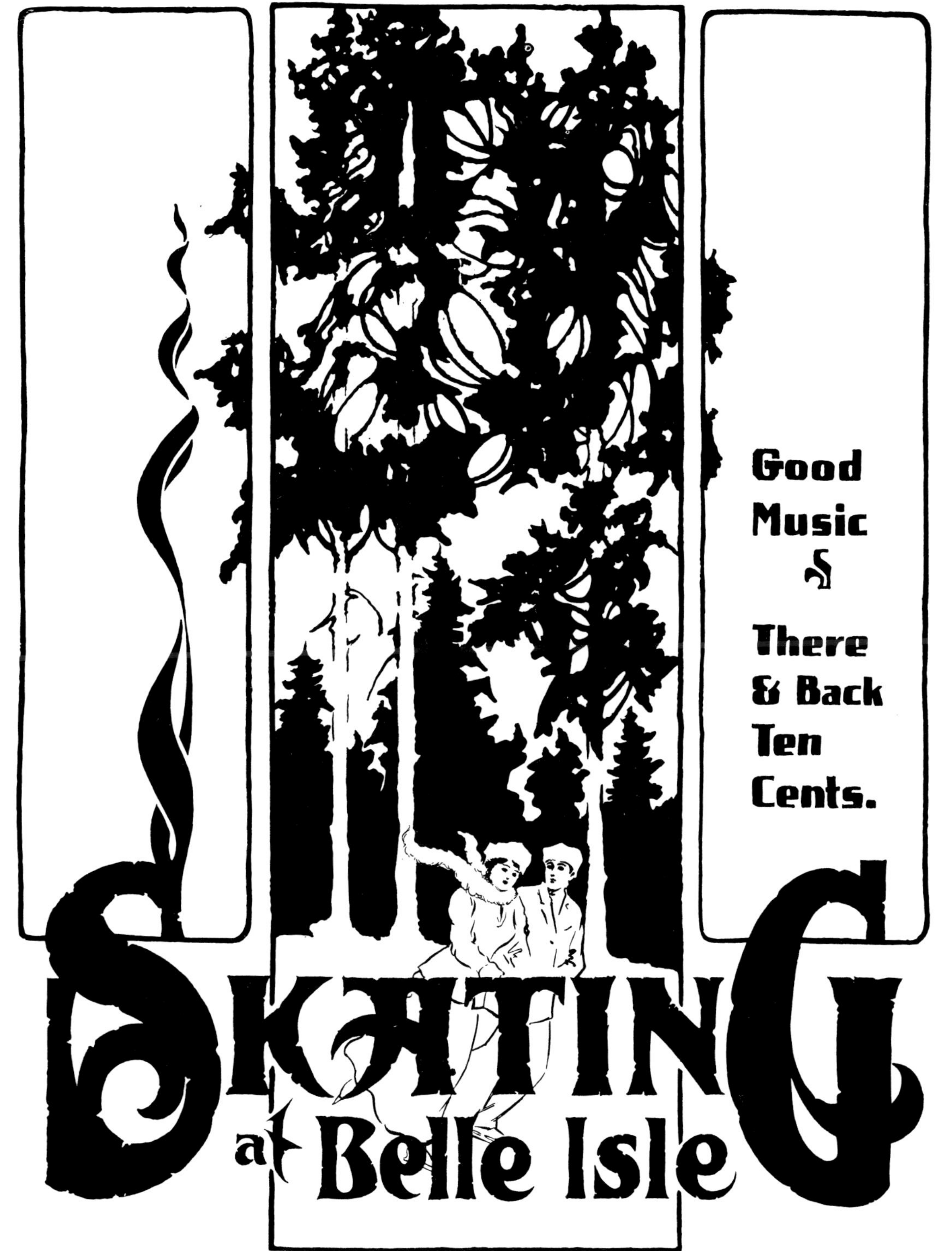
Good
Music
&
There
& Back
Ten
Cents.
SKATING
at Belle Isle

BULLETIN & DESIGNS

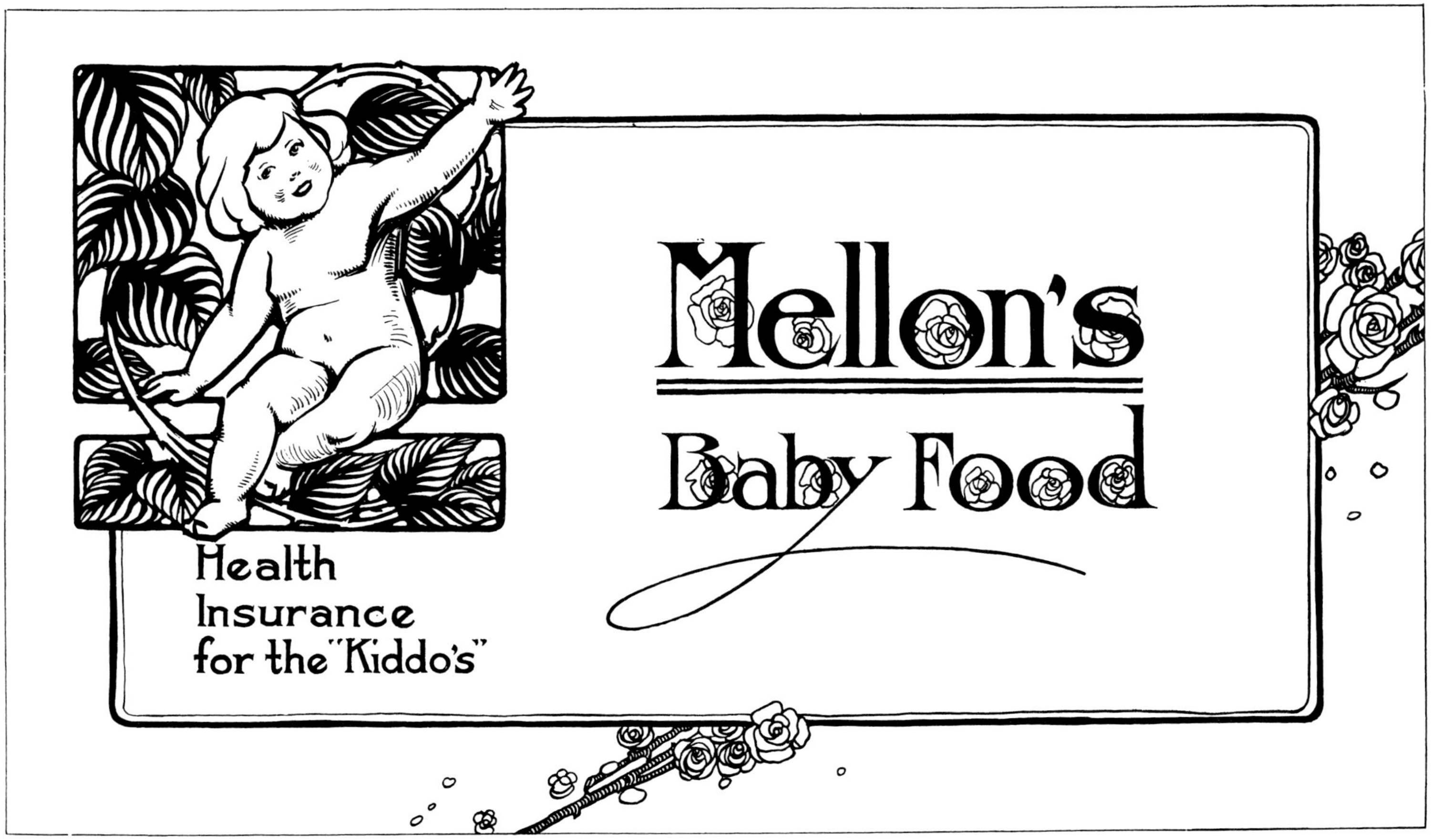

Mellon's

Baby Food

Health
Insurance
for the "Kiddo's"

ABC
DEFGHI
JKLMNOPQ
RSTUV
WXYZ

ABCD

EFGHIJKL

MNOPRST

UVWXYZ

ABC

DEFGHIJ

KLMNOP

RSTUV

WXYZ

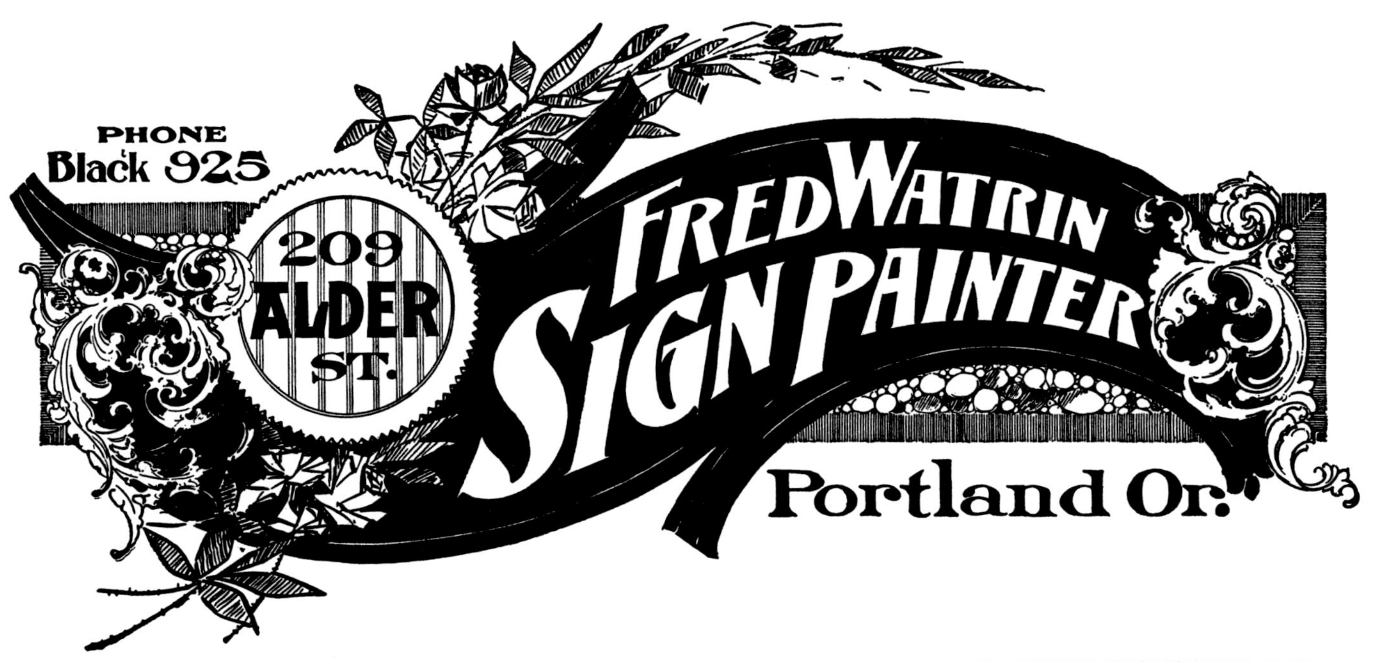
PHONE
Black 925
209
ALDER
ST.
FRED WATRIN
SIGN PAINTER
Portland Or.

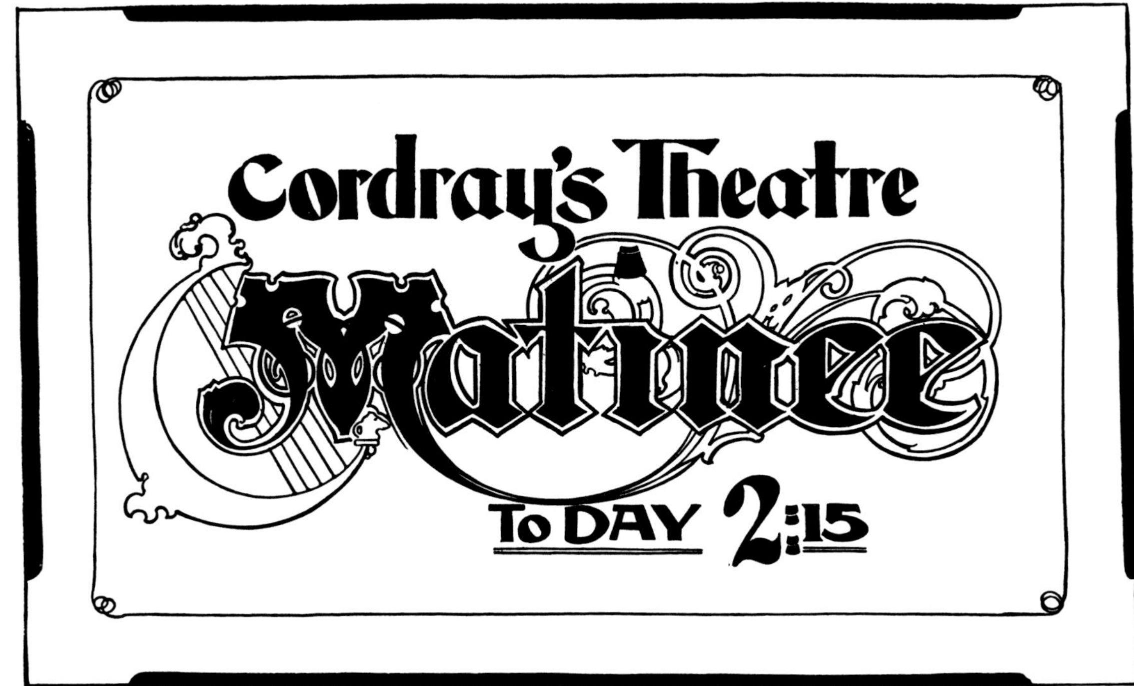
Cordray's Theatre
Matinee
To DAY 2:15

ABCD

EFGHIJKL

MNOPQRST

UVWXYZ

ABCDEFG
HIJKLMN
OPQRSTUV
WXYZ
123456789

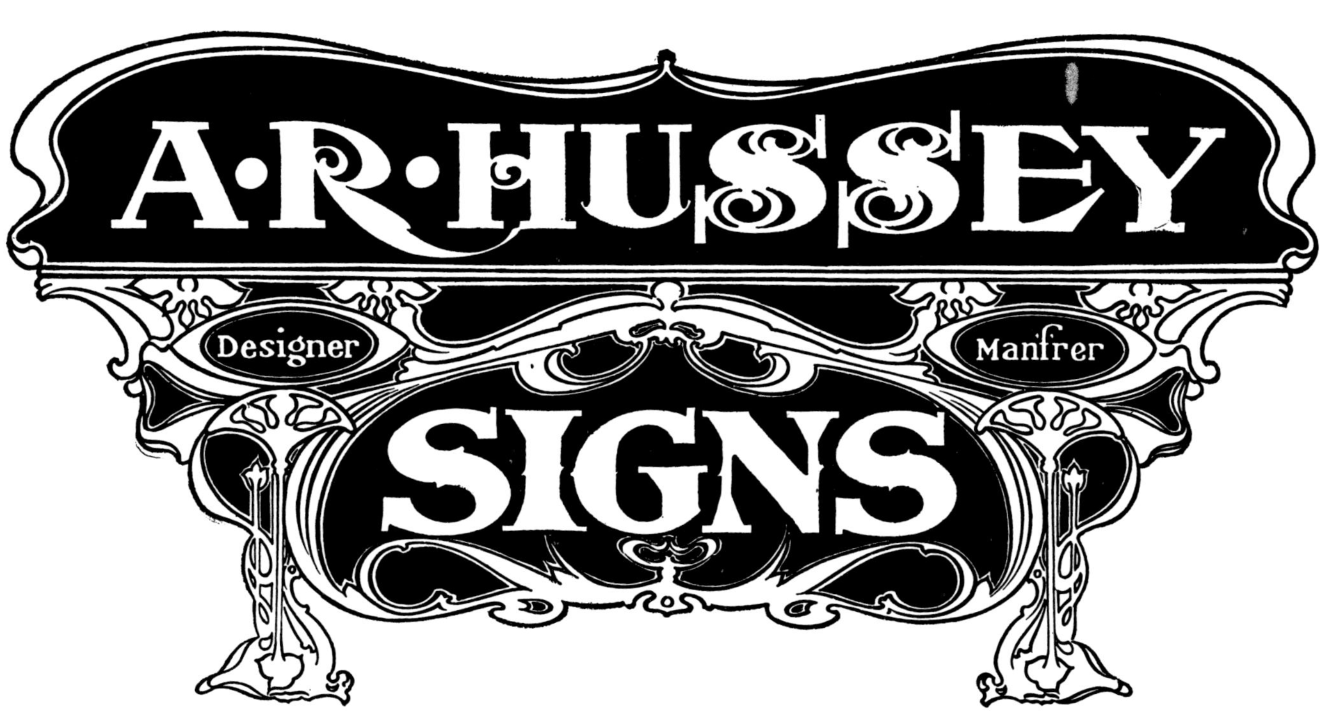
A·R·HUSSEY
Designer
Manfrer
SIGNS

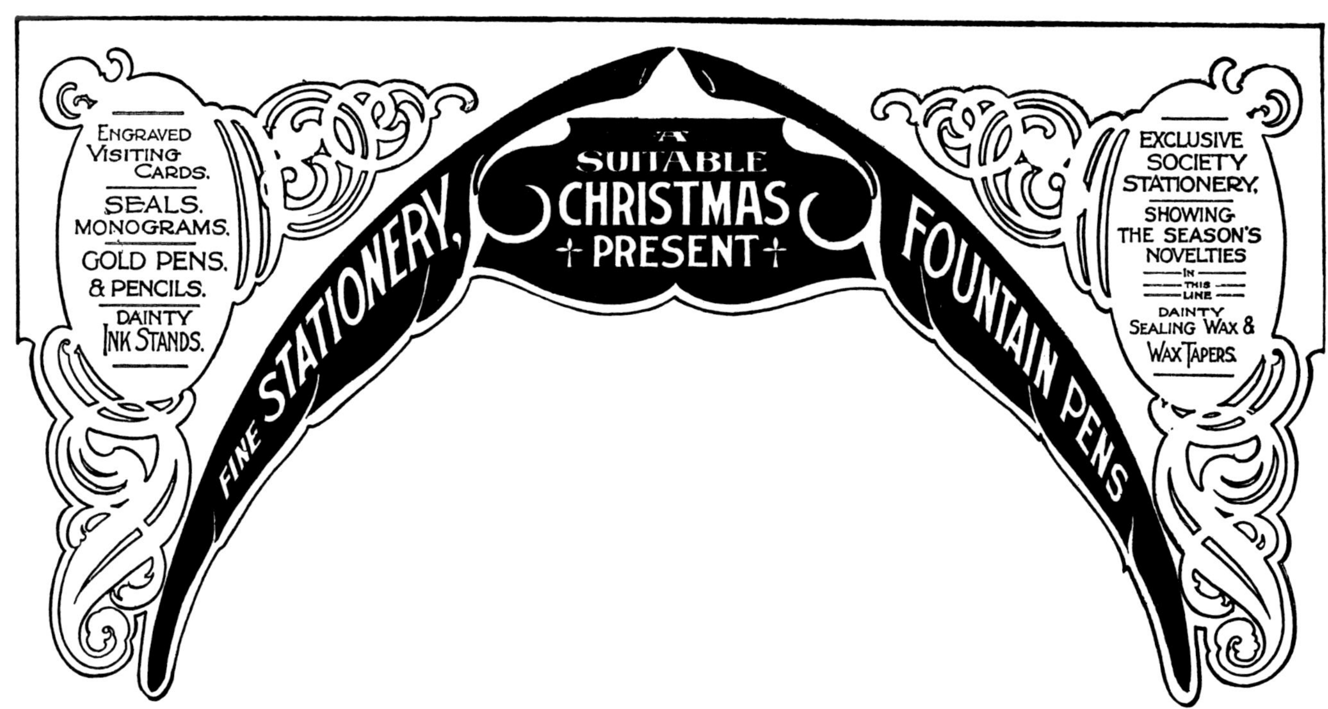
ENGRAVED VISITING CARDS.
SEALS. MONOGRAMS.
GOLD PENS. & PENCILS.
DAINTY INK STANDS.
FINE STATIONERY,
A SUITABLE CHRISTMAS PRESENT
FOUNTAIN PENS
EXCLUSIVE SOCIETY STATIONERY,
SHOWING THE SEASON'S NOVELTIES
IN THIS LINE
DAINTY SEALING WAX & WAX TAPERS.

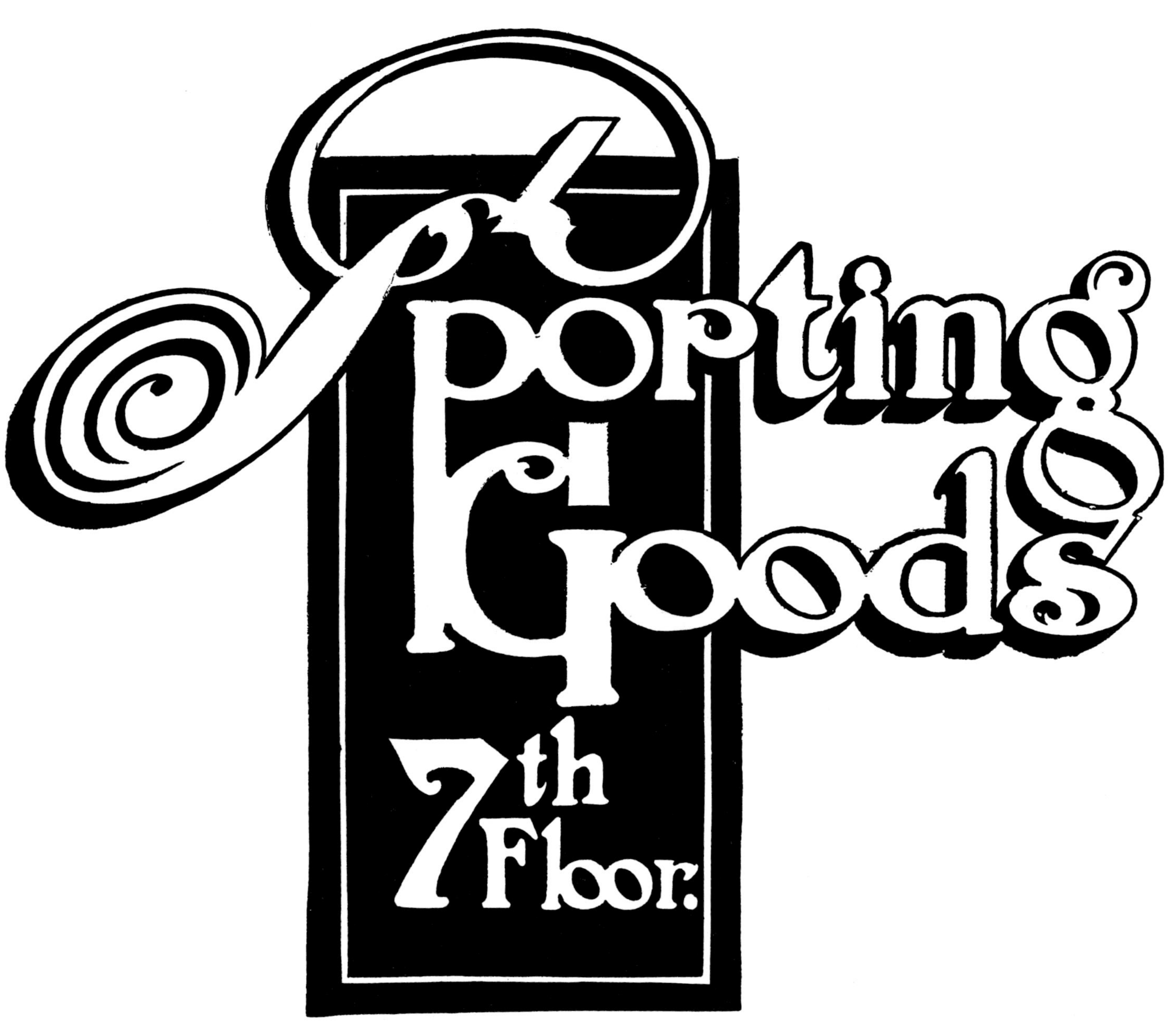
Sporting
Goods
7th
Floor.

ABCD

EFGHIJKL

MNQPRST

UVWXYZ

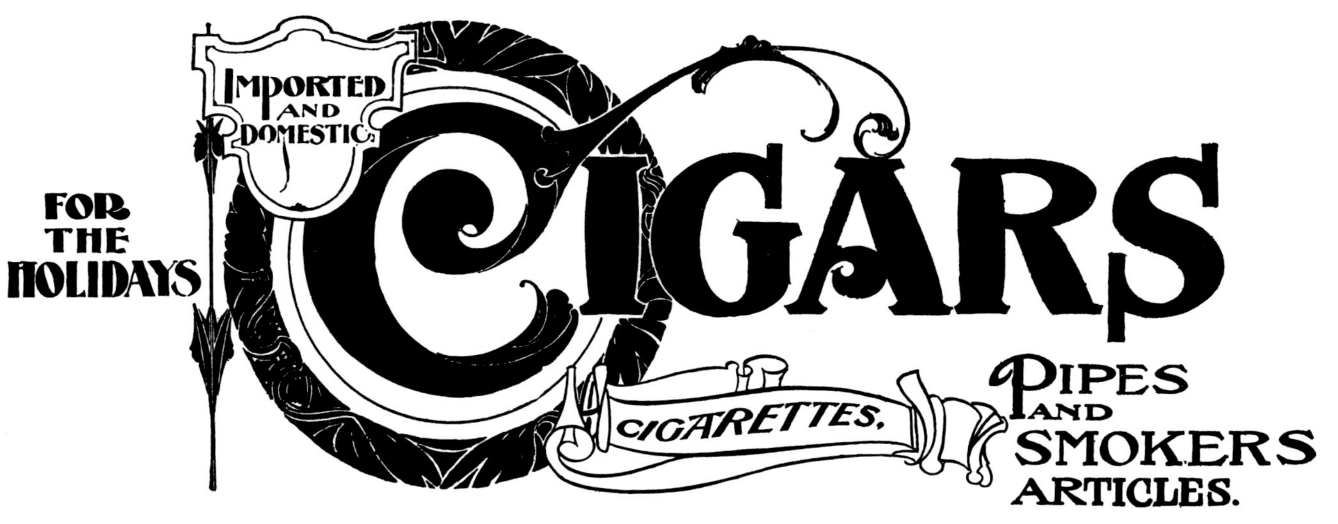
FOR THE HOLIDAYS
IMPORTED AND DOMESTIC
CIGARS
CIGARETTES,
PIPES AND SMOKERS ARTICLES.

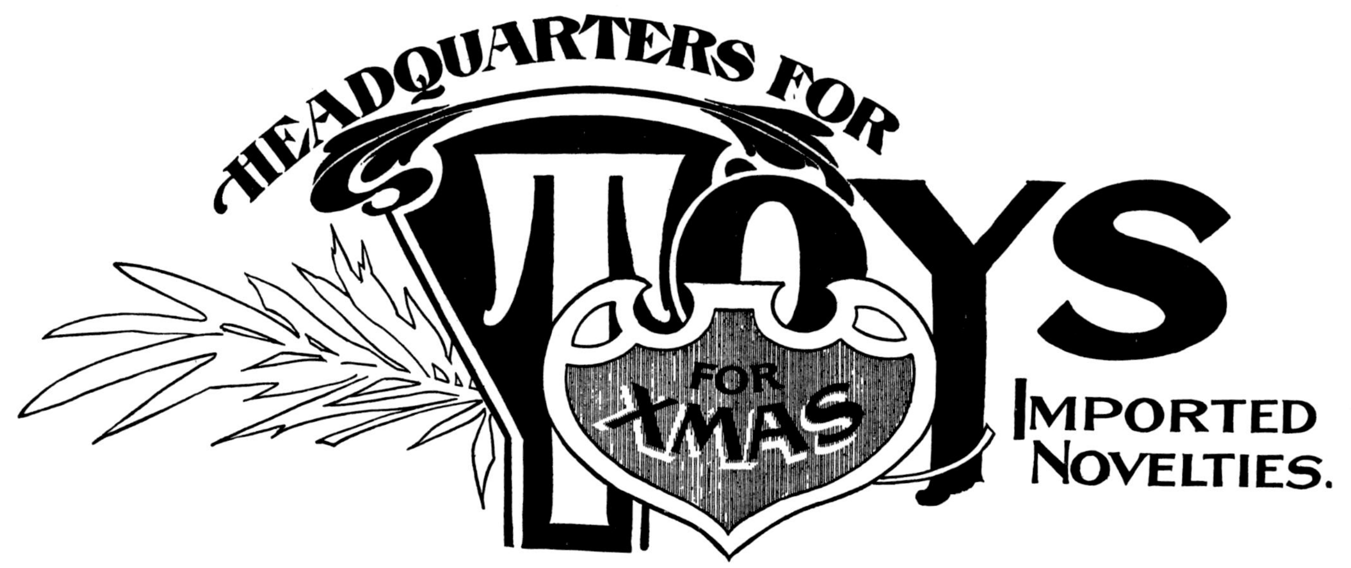
HEADQUARTERS FOR
TOYS
FOR XMAS
IMPORTED NOVELTIES.

ABCD

EFGHIJKL

MNQPRST

UVWXYZ

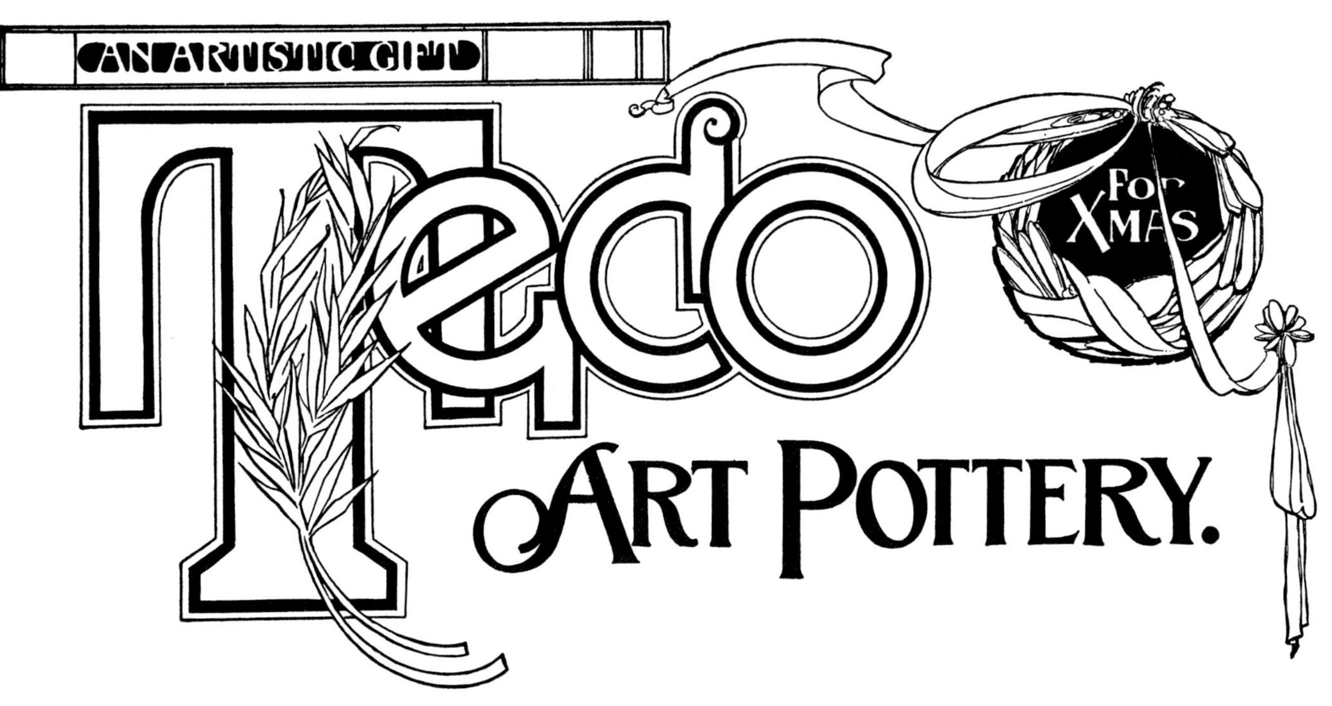
AN ARTISTIC GIFT
Tedo
For Xmas
Art Pottery.

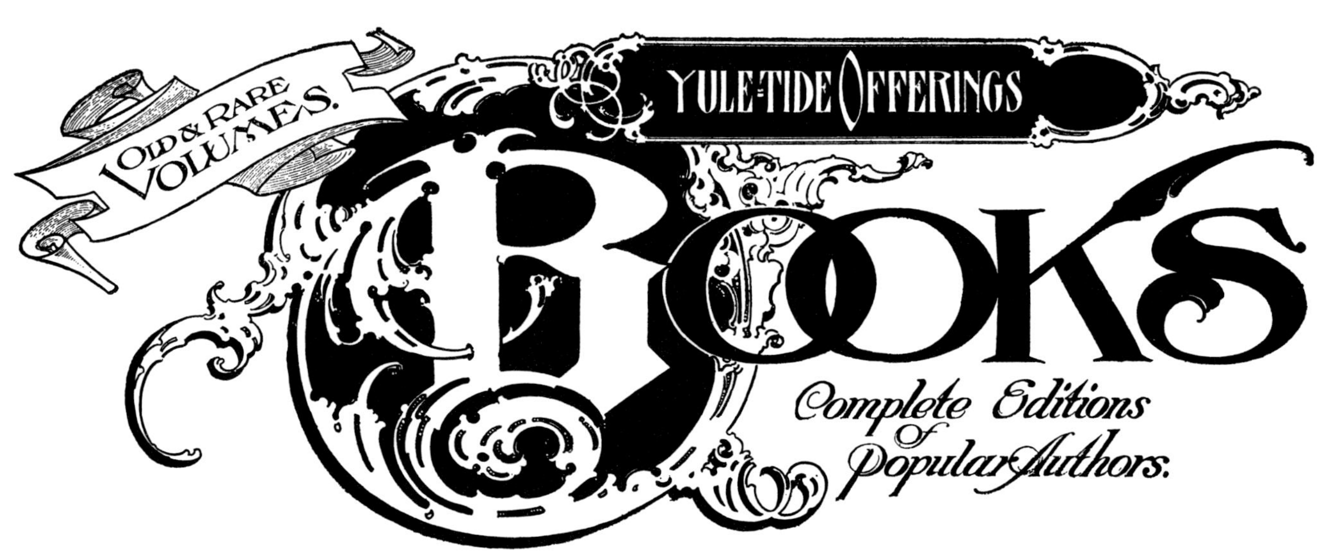
Old & Rare Volumes.
Yule-Tide Offerings
Books
Complete Editions of Popular Authors.

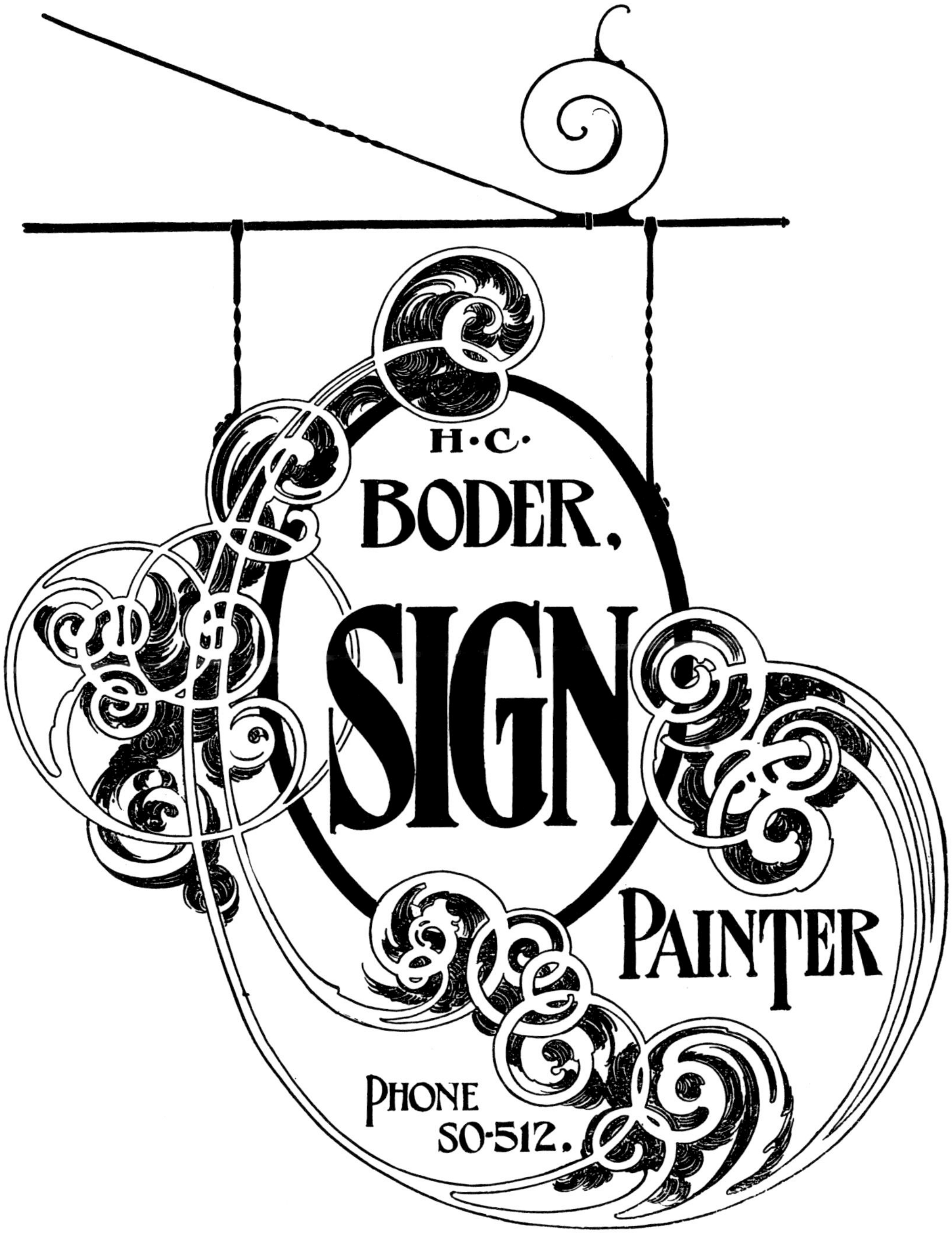

H·C·
BODER,
SIGN
PAINTER
PHONE
SO-512.

Business Cards

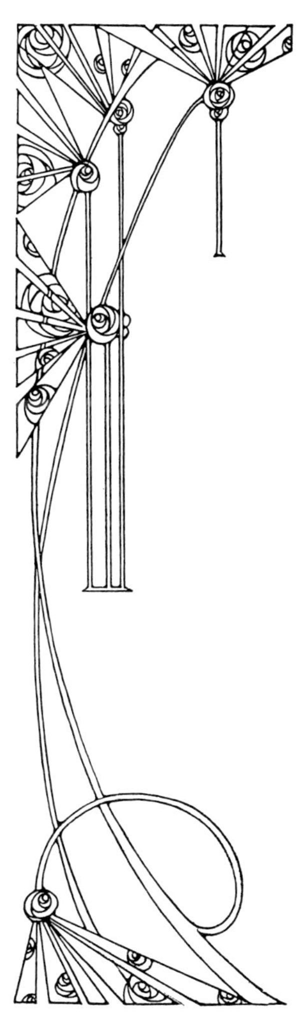

ABCD

EFGHIJKL

MNQPRST

UVWXYZ

A B C D E F

G H I J K L M N

O P Q R R S S T

U V W X Y Z

a b c d e f g h h i j k l m n

o p q r s t t u u v w x y z z

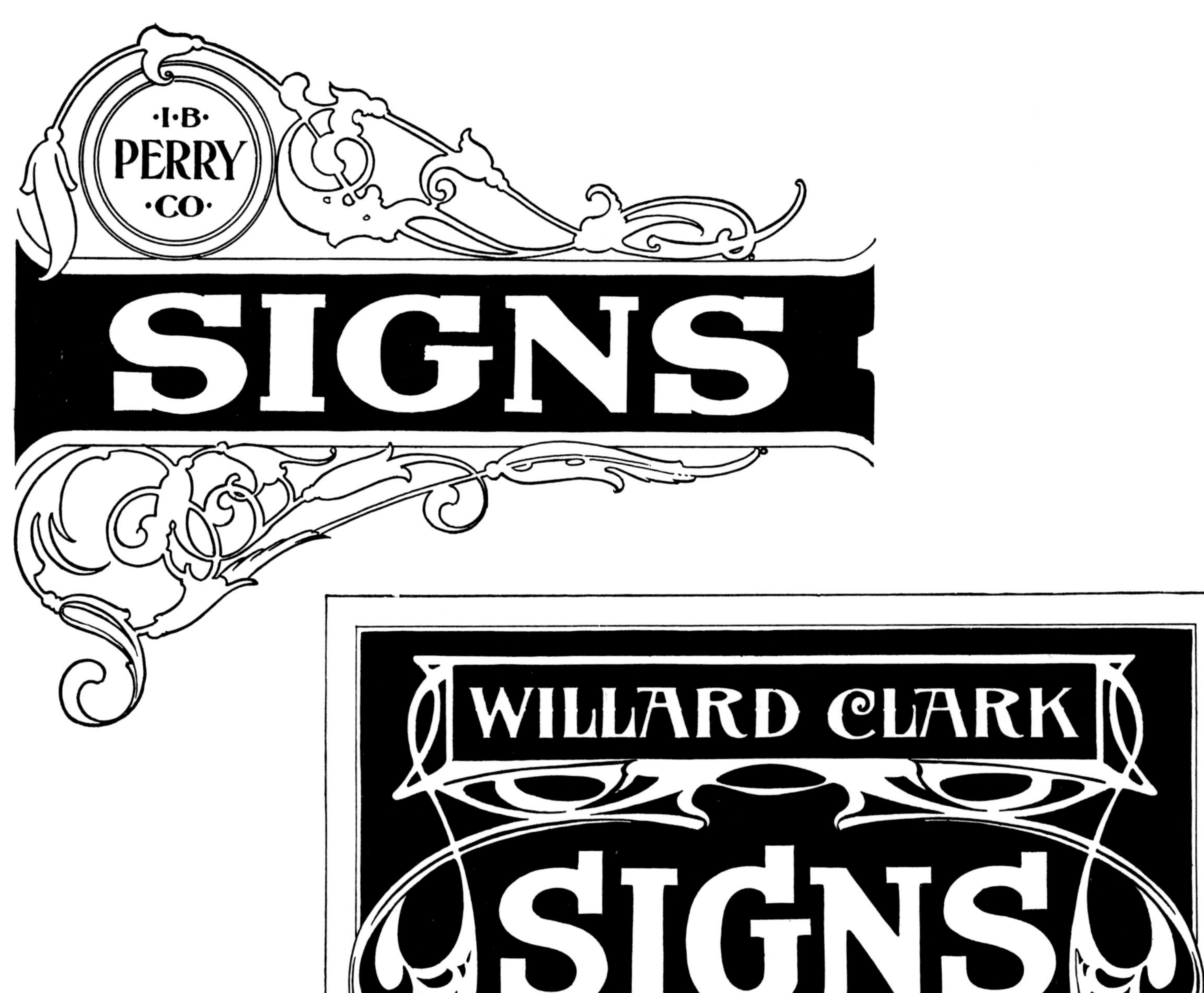
·I·B·
PERRY
·CO·
SIGNS
WILLARD CLARK
SIGNS

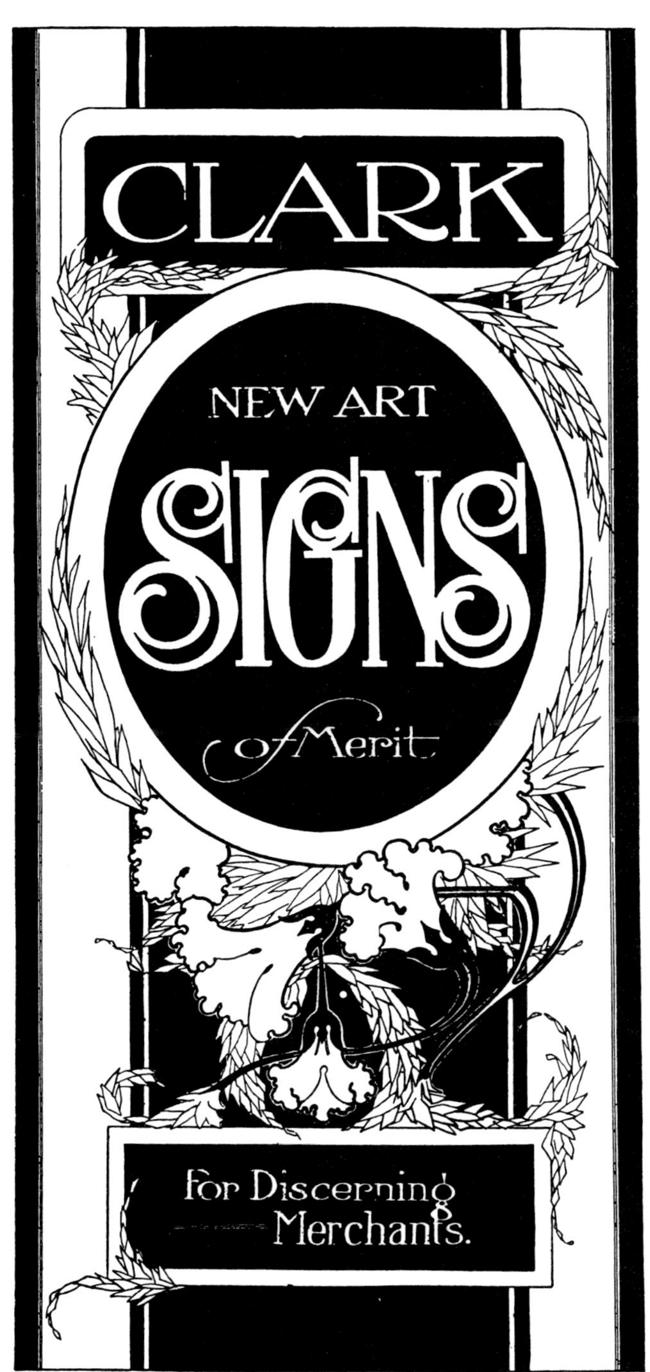
CLARK
NEW ART
SIGNS
of Merit
For Discerning
Merchants.

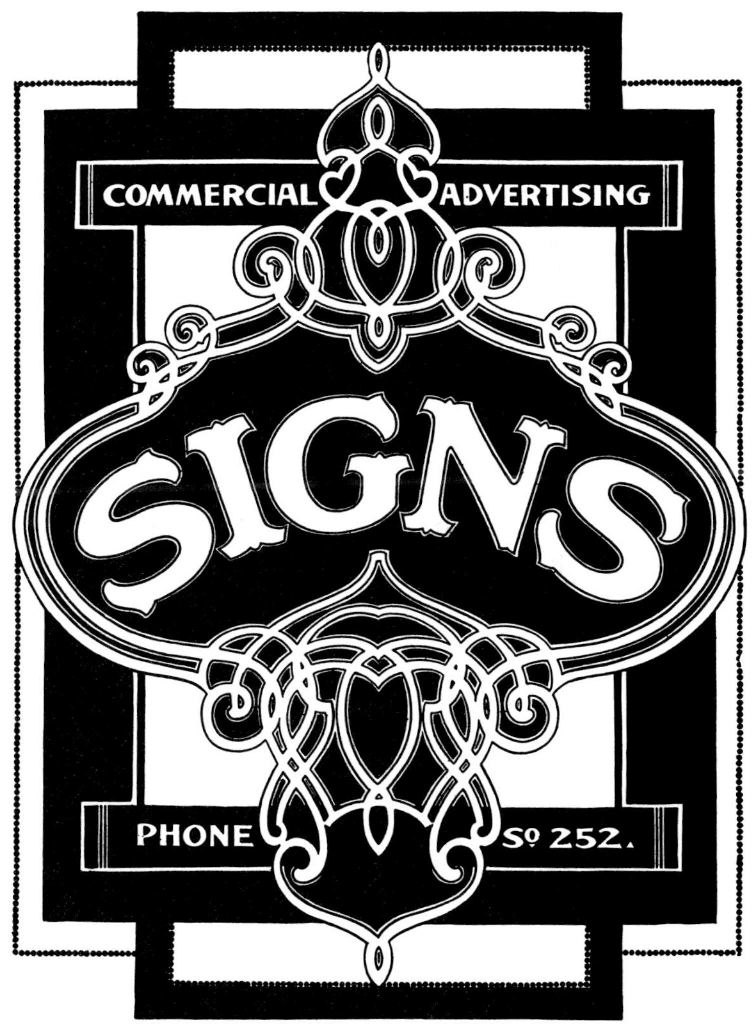
COMMERCIAL
ADVERTISING
SIGNS
PHONE
Nº 252.

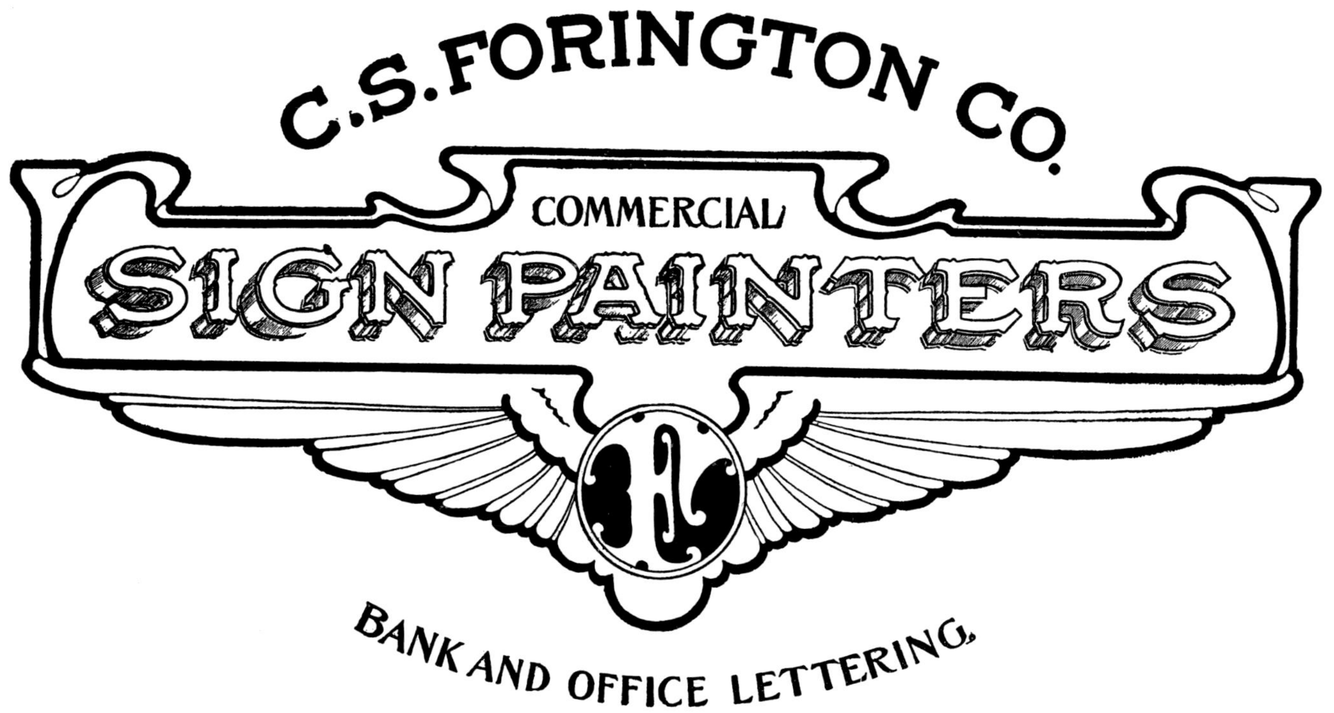
C.S. FORINGTON CO.
COMMERCIAL
SIGN PAINTERS
BANK AND OFFICE LETTERING

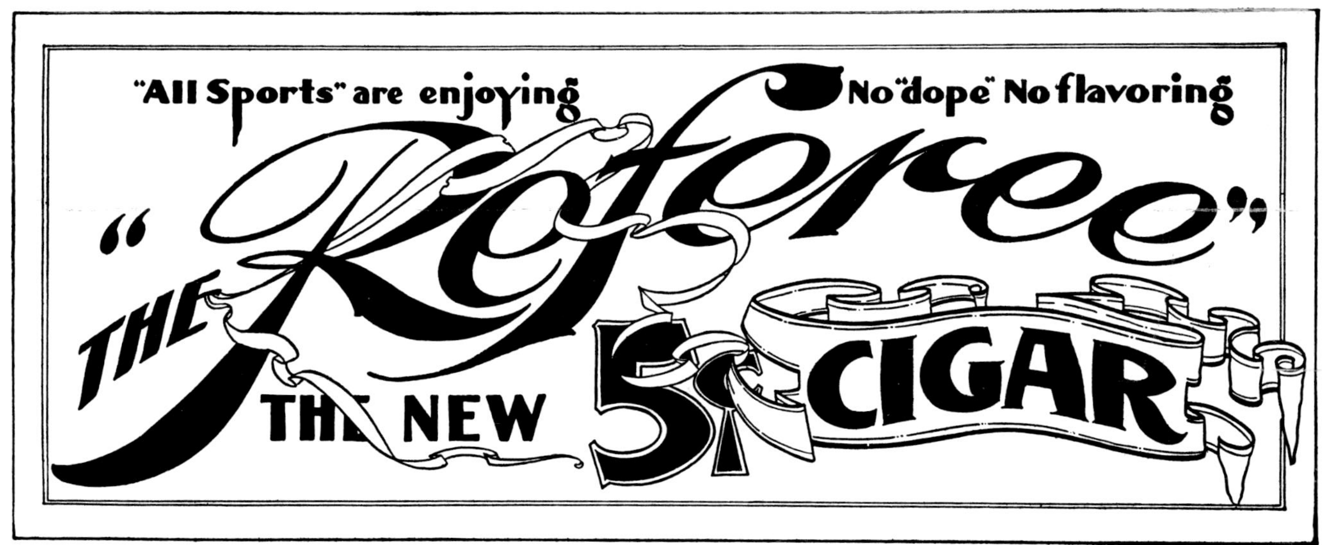
"All Sports" are enjoying
No "dope" No flavoring
THE "Referee"
THE NEW 5¢ CIGAR

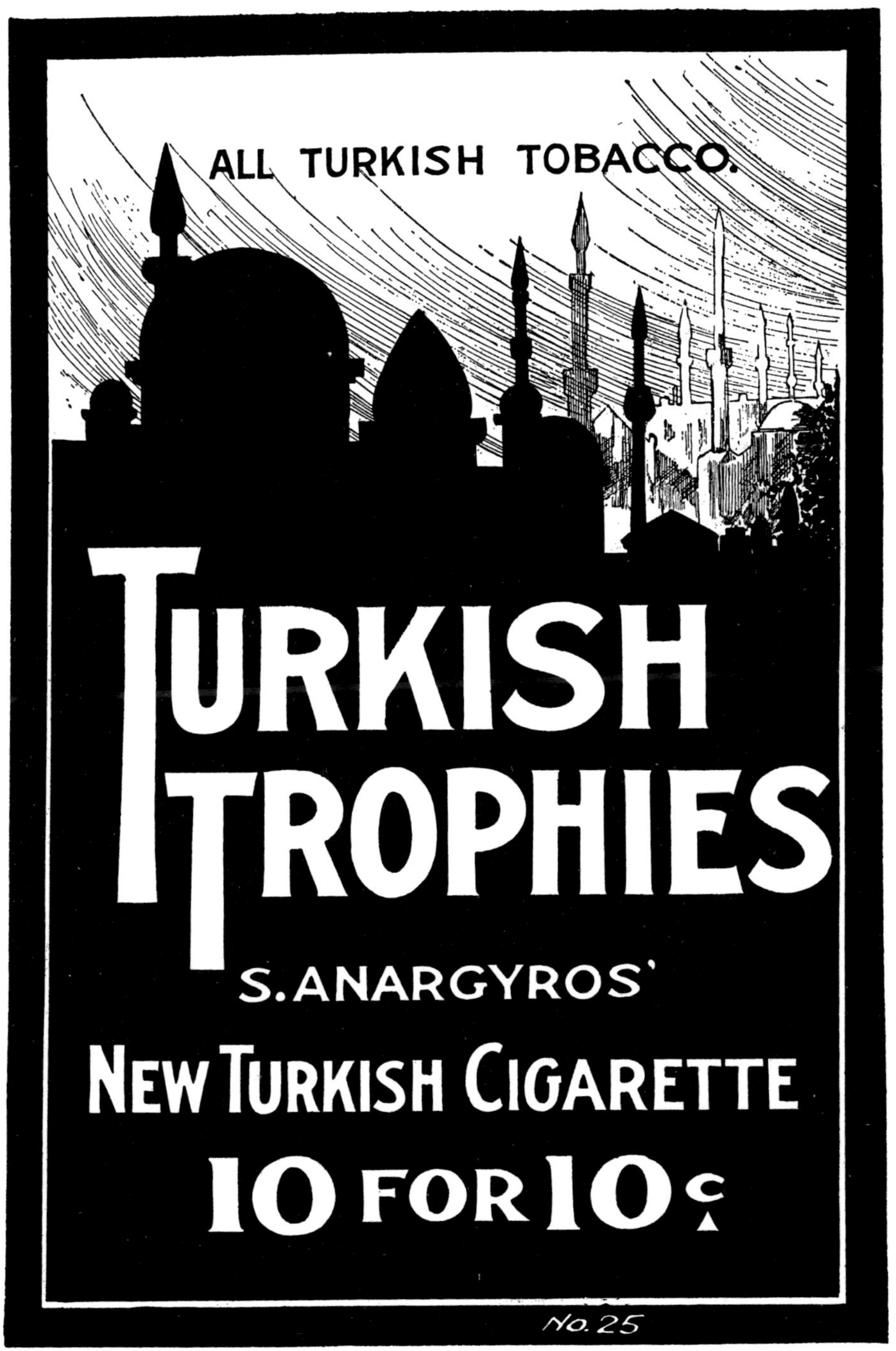
ALL TURKISH TOBACCO.
TURKISH
TROPHIES
S. ANARGYROS'
NEW TURKISH CIGARETTE
10 FOR 10¢
No. 25

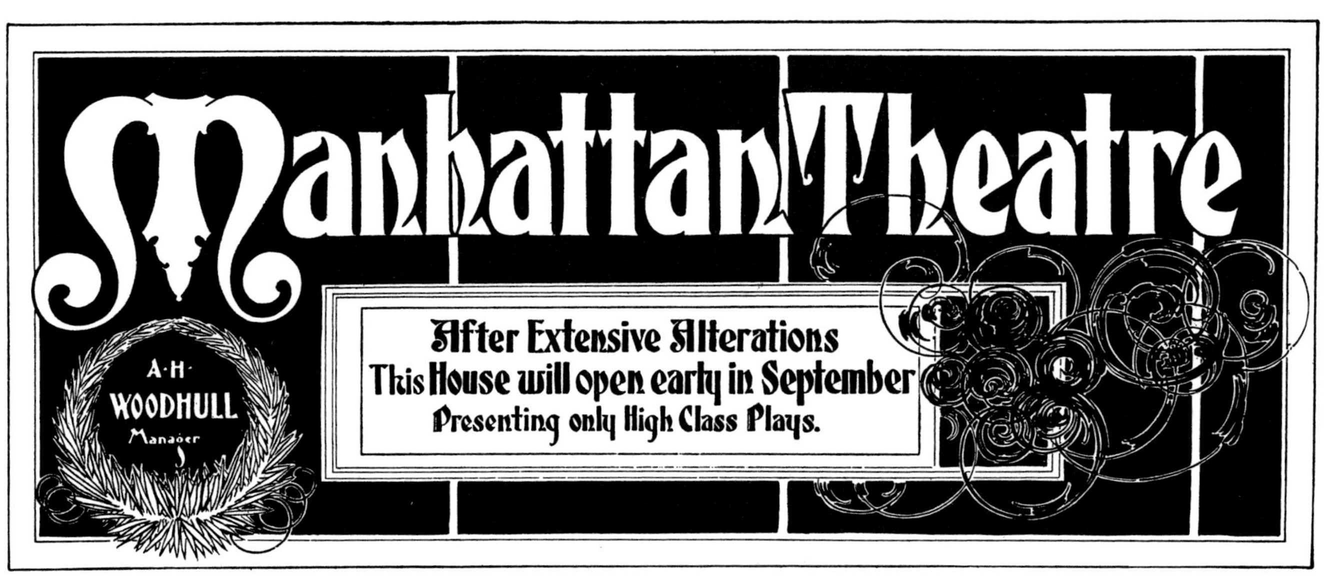
Manhattan Theatre
After Extensive Alterations
This House will open early in September
Presenting only High Class Plays.
A·H·
WOODHULL
Manager

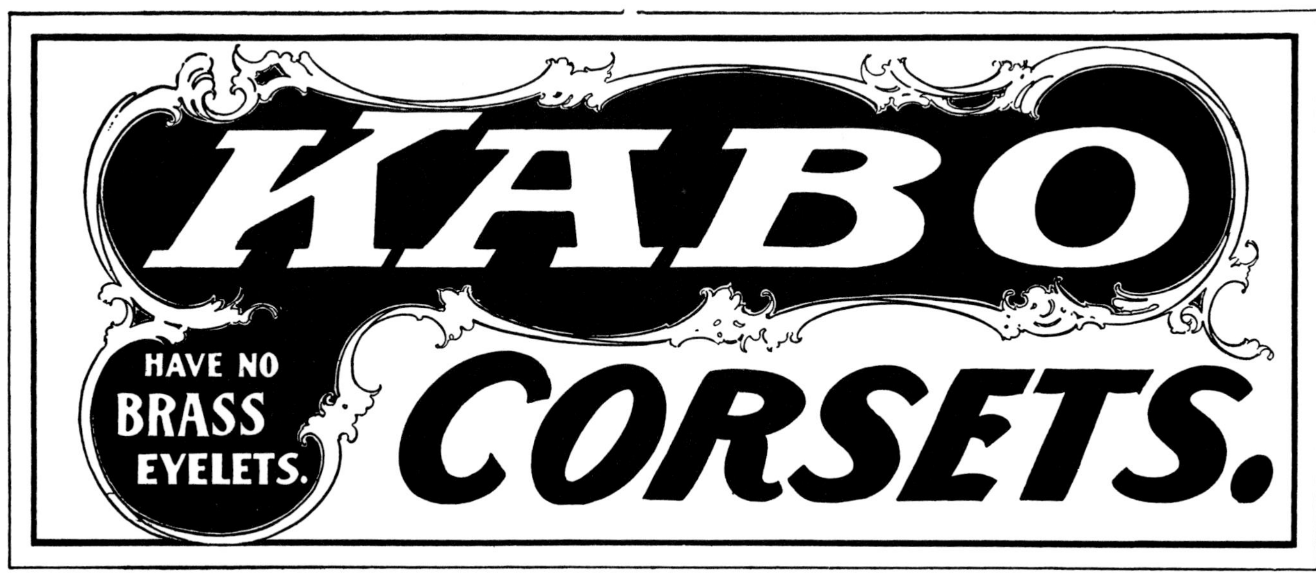
KABO
HAVE NO
BRASS
EYELETS.
CORSETS.

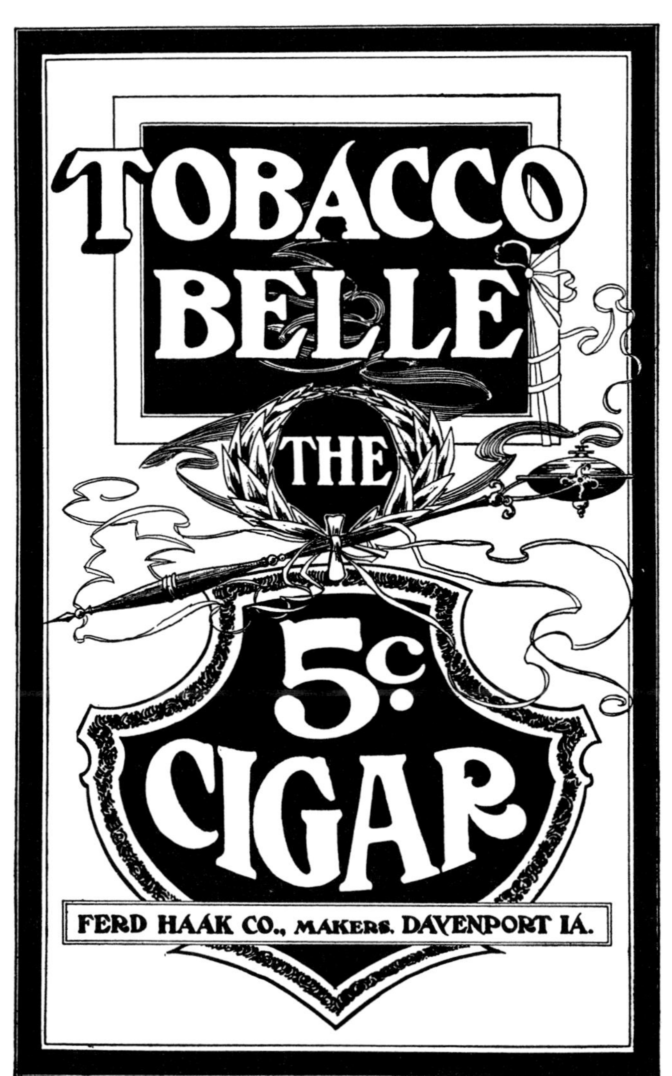
TOBACCO
BELLE
THE
5c
CIGAR
FERD HAAK CO., MAKERS, DAVENPORT IA.

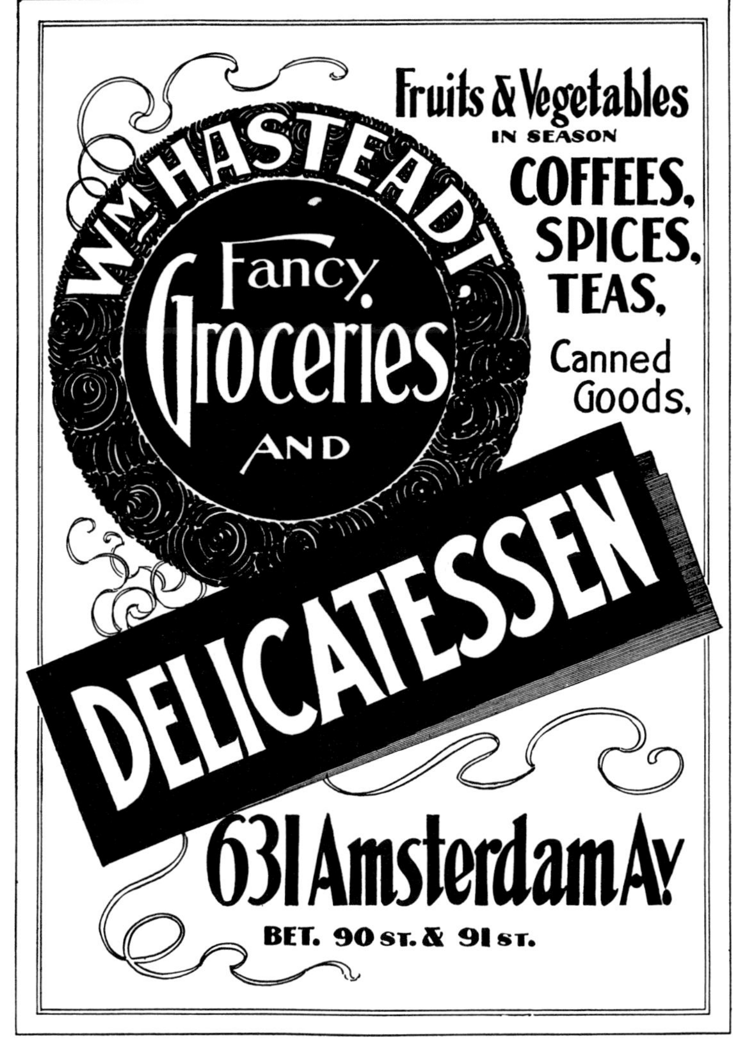
Fruits & Vegetables
IN SEASON
COFFEES,
SPICES,
TEAS,
Canned
Goods,
Wm HASTEADT,
Fancy
Groceries
AND
DELICATESSEN
631 Amsterdam Av.
BET. 90 ST. & 91 ST.

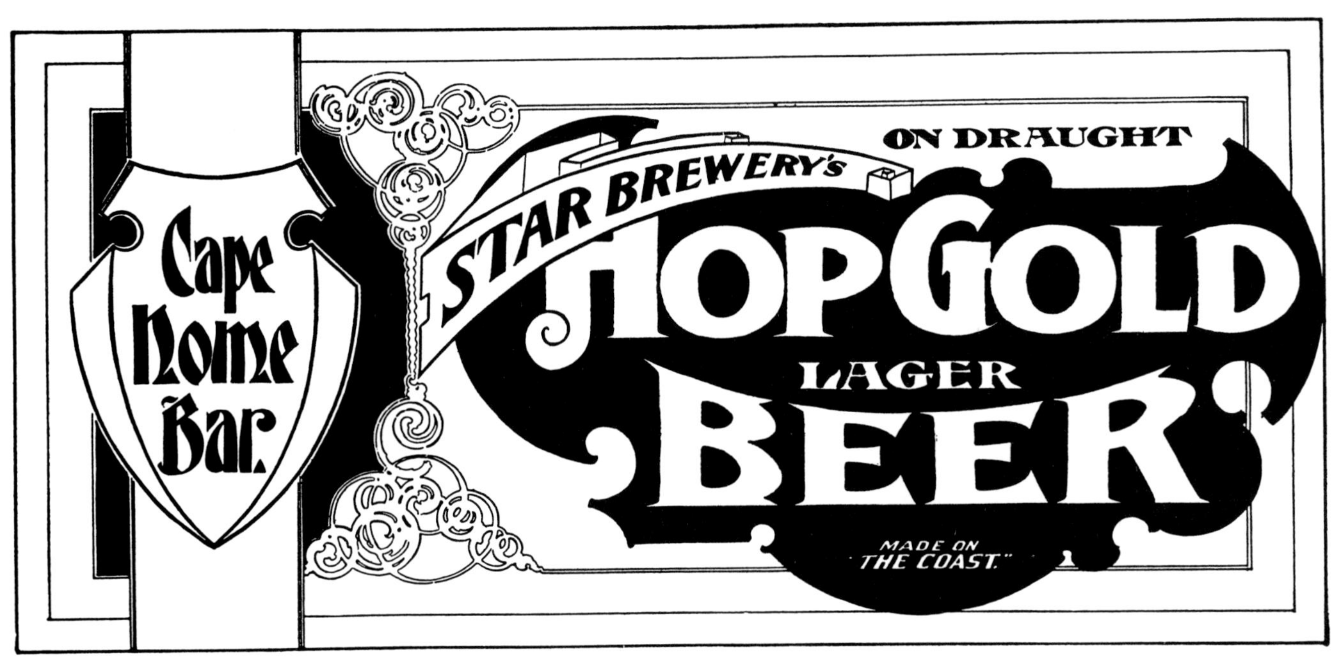
Cape Nome Bar.
STAR BREWERY'S
ON DRAUGHT
HOPGOLD
LAGER
BEER
MADE ON
"THE COAST."

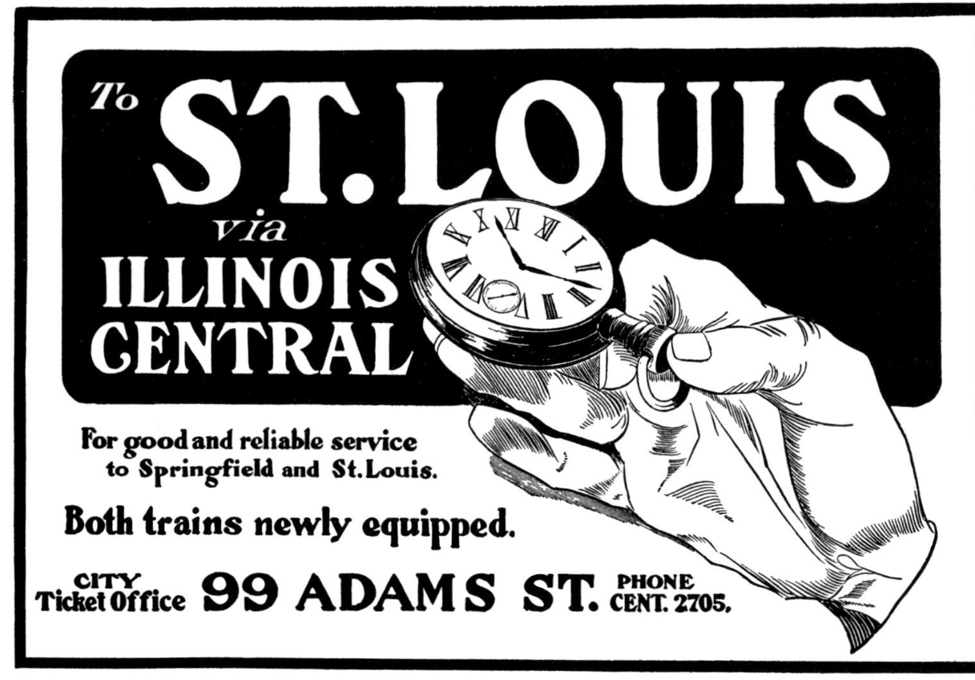
To ST. LOUIS
via
ILLINOIS CENTRAL
For good and reliable service
to Springfield and St. Louis.
Both trains newly equipped.
CITY Ticket Office 99 ADAMS ST. PHONE CENT. 2705.

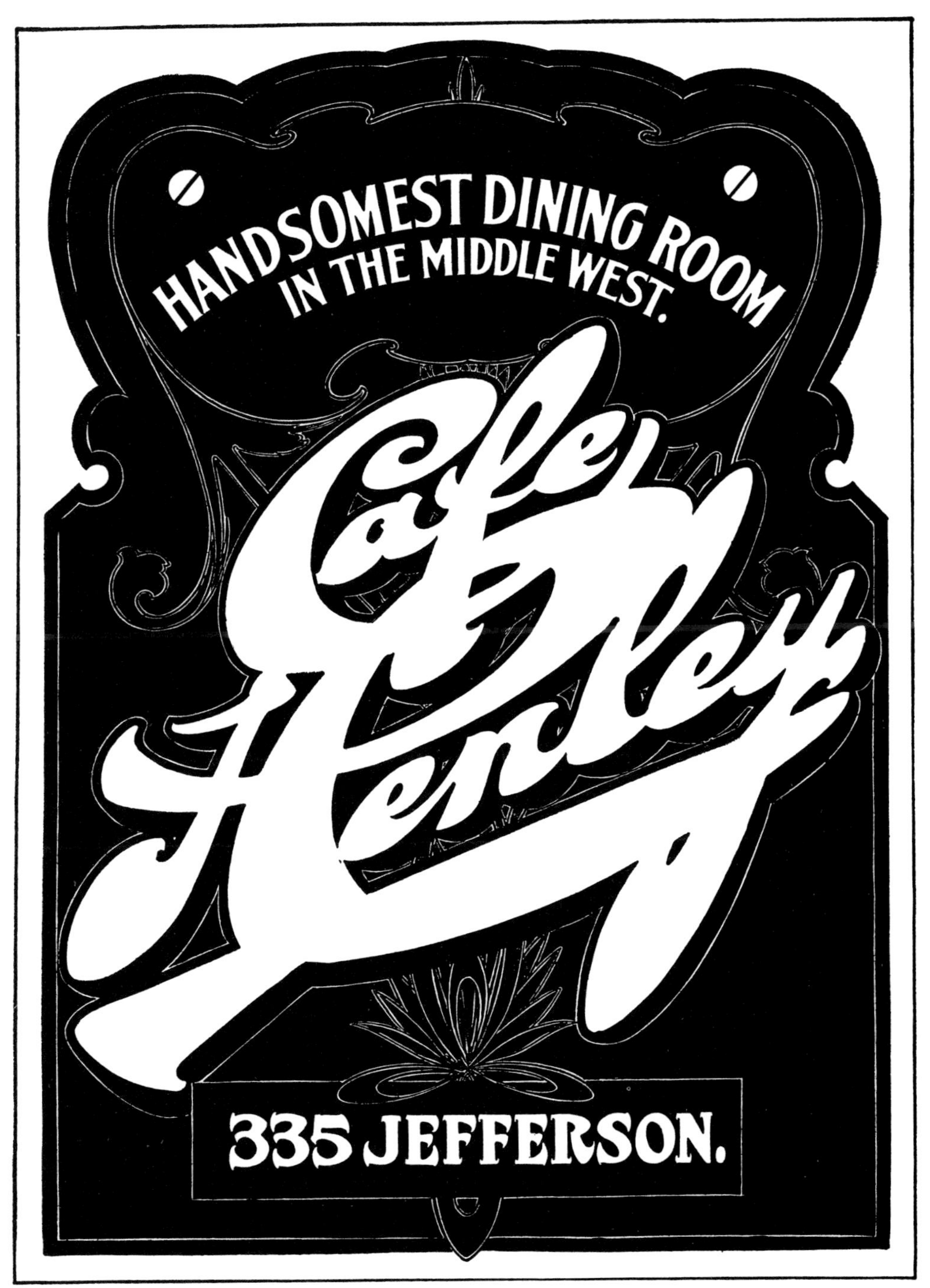
HANDSOMEST DINING ROOM
IN THE MIDDLE WEST.
Cafe Henley
335 JEFFERSON.

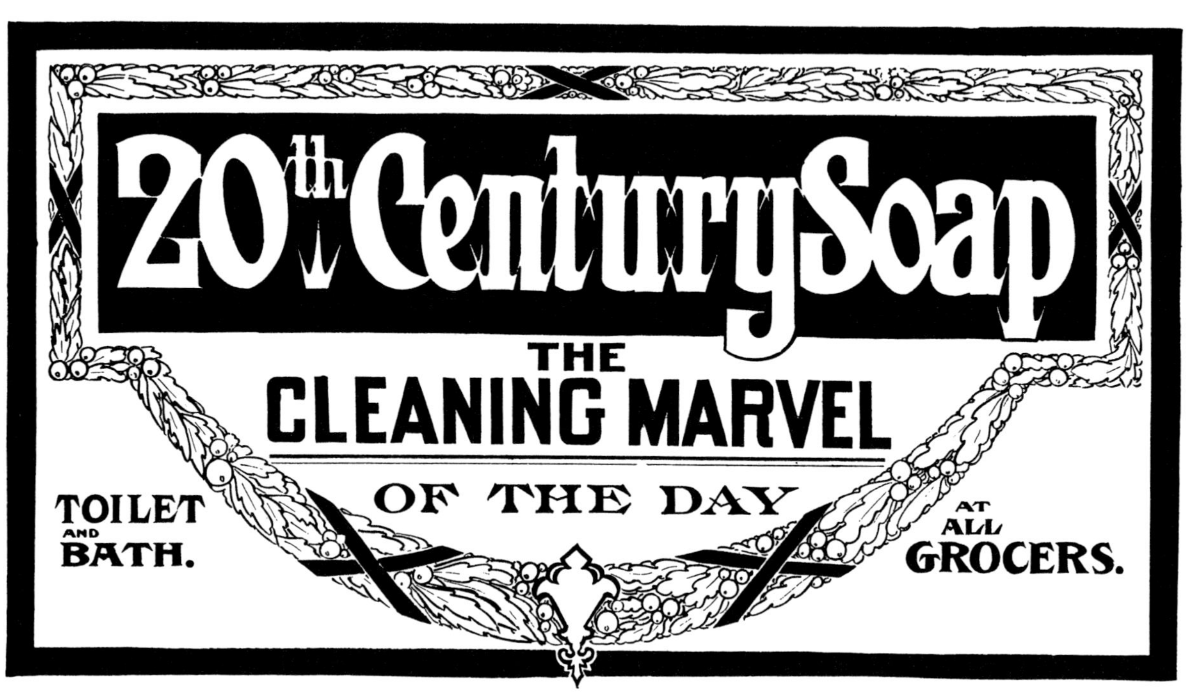
20th Century Soap
THE
CLEANING MARVEL
OF THE DAY
TOILET
AND
BATH.
AT
ALL
GROCERS.

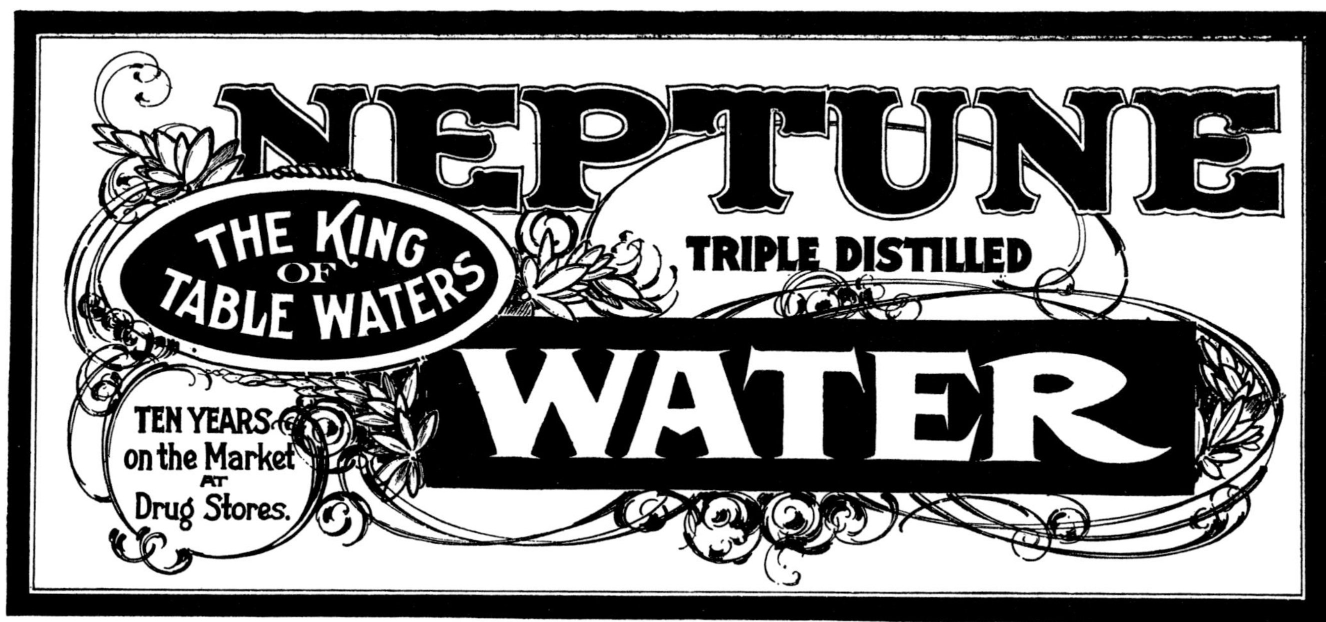
NEPTUNE
THE KING OF TABLE WATERS
TRIPLE DISTILLED
WATER
TEN YEARS
on the Market
AT
Drug Stores.

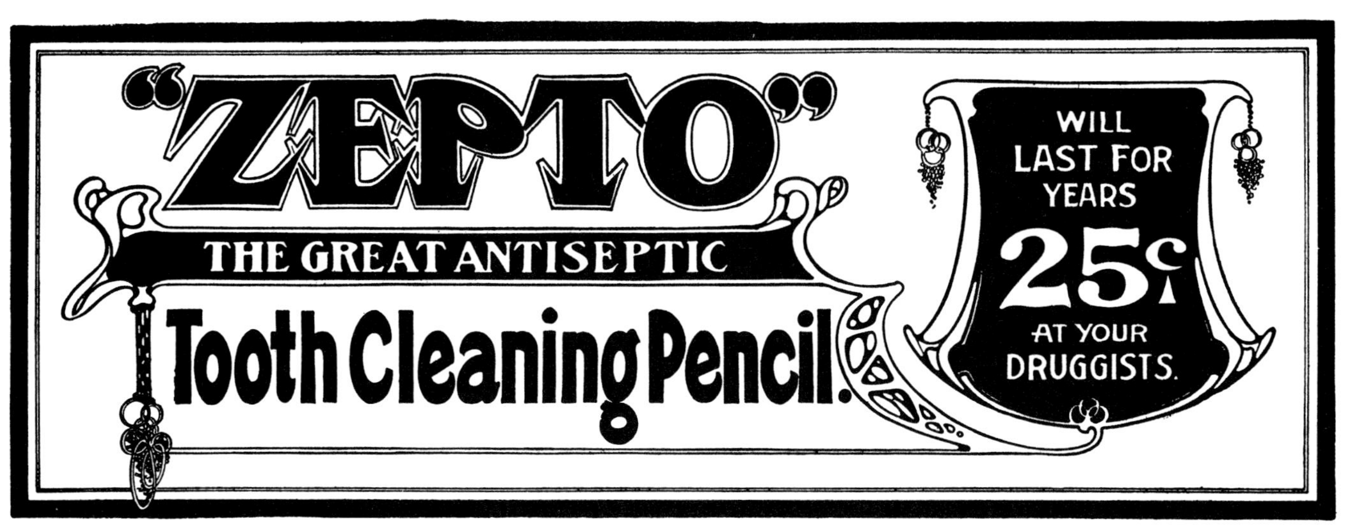
"ZEPTO"
THE GREAT ANTISEPTIC
Tooth Cleaning Pencil.
WILL
LAST FOR
YEARS
25¢
AT YOUR
DRUGGISTS.

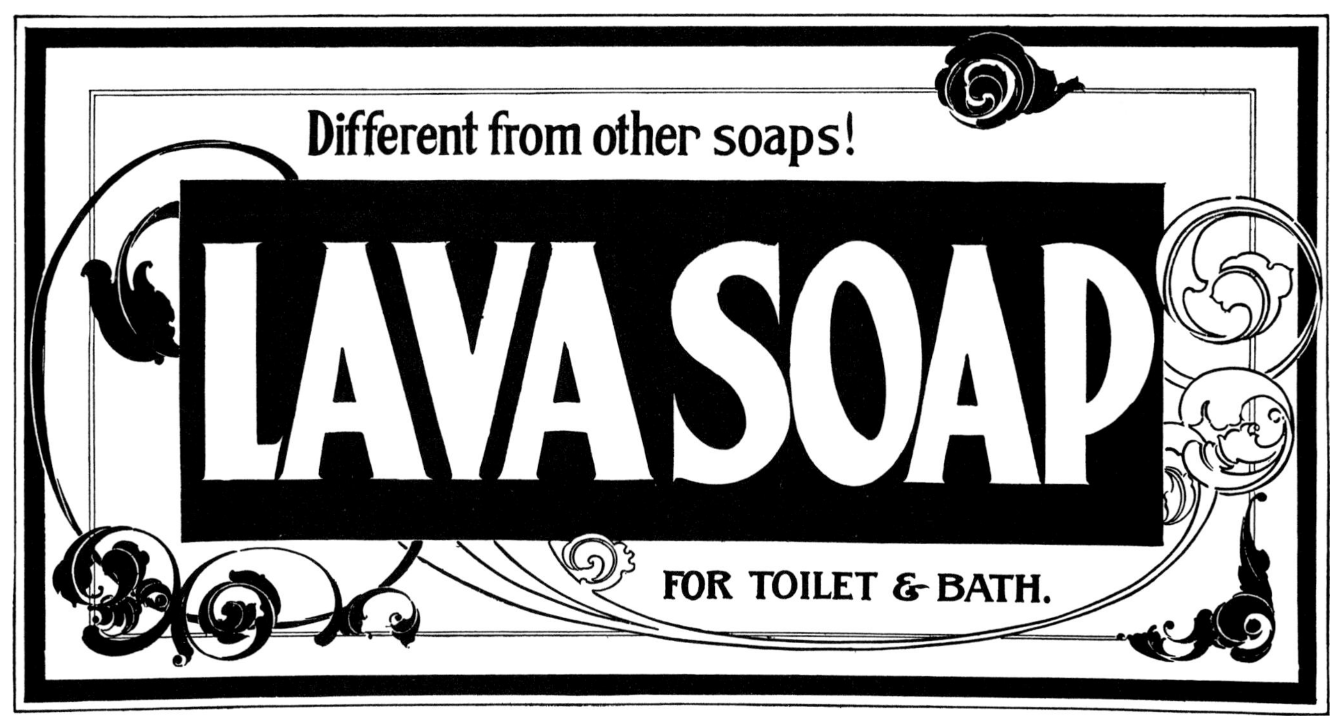
Different from other soaps!
LAVA SOAP
FOR TOILET & BATH.

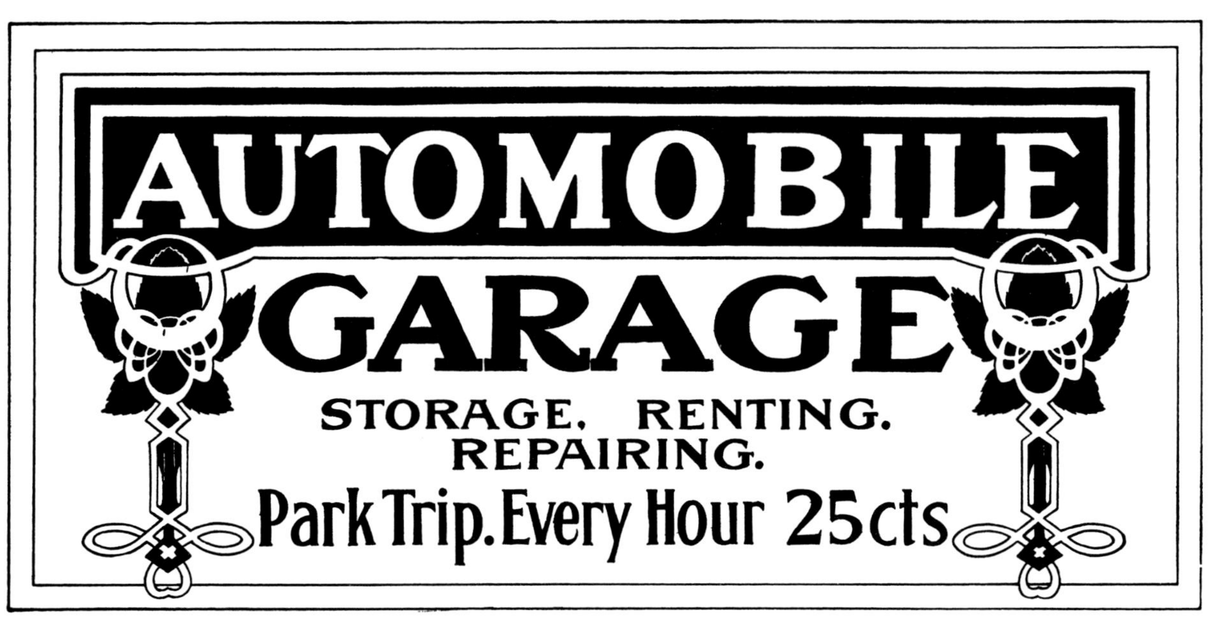
AUTOMOBILE
GARAGE
STORAGE. RENTING.
REPAIRING.
Park Trip. Every Hour 25cts

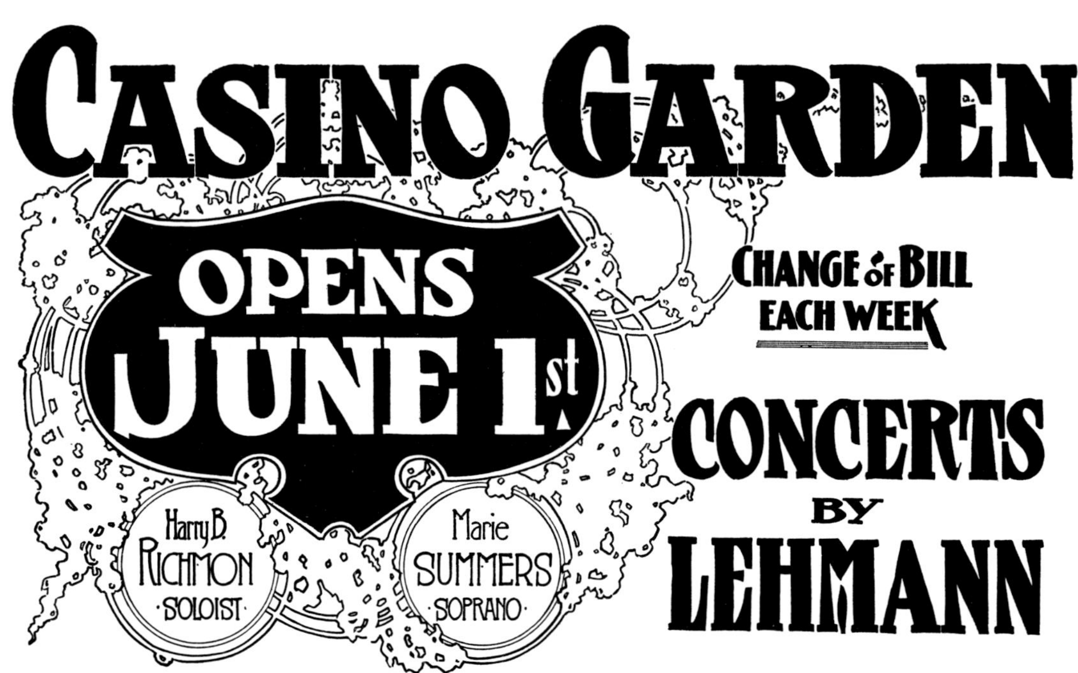
CASINO GARDEN
OPENS
JUNE 1st
Harry B.
RICHMON
SOLOIST
Marie
SUMMERS
SOPRANO
CHANGE OF BILL
EACH WEEK
CONCERTS
BY
LEHMANN

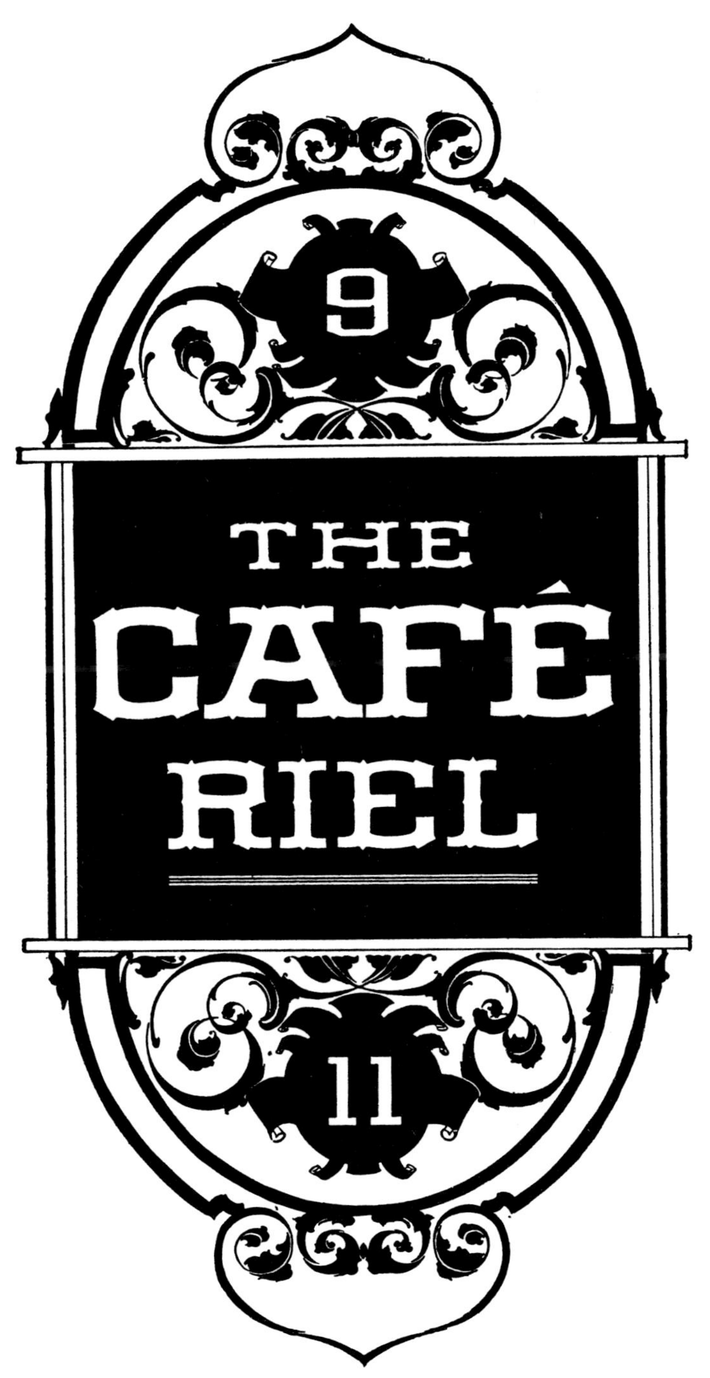
9
THE
CAFÉ
RIEL
11

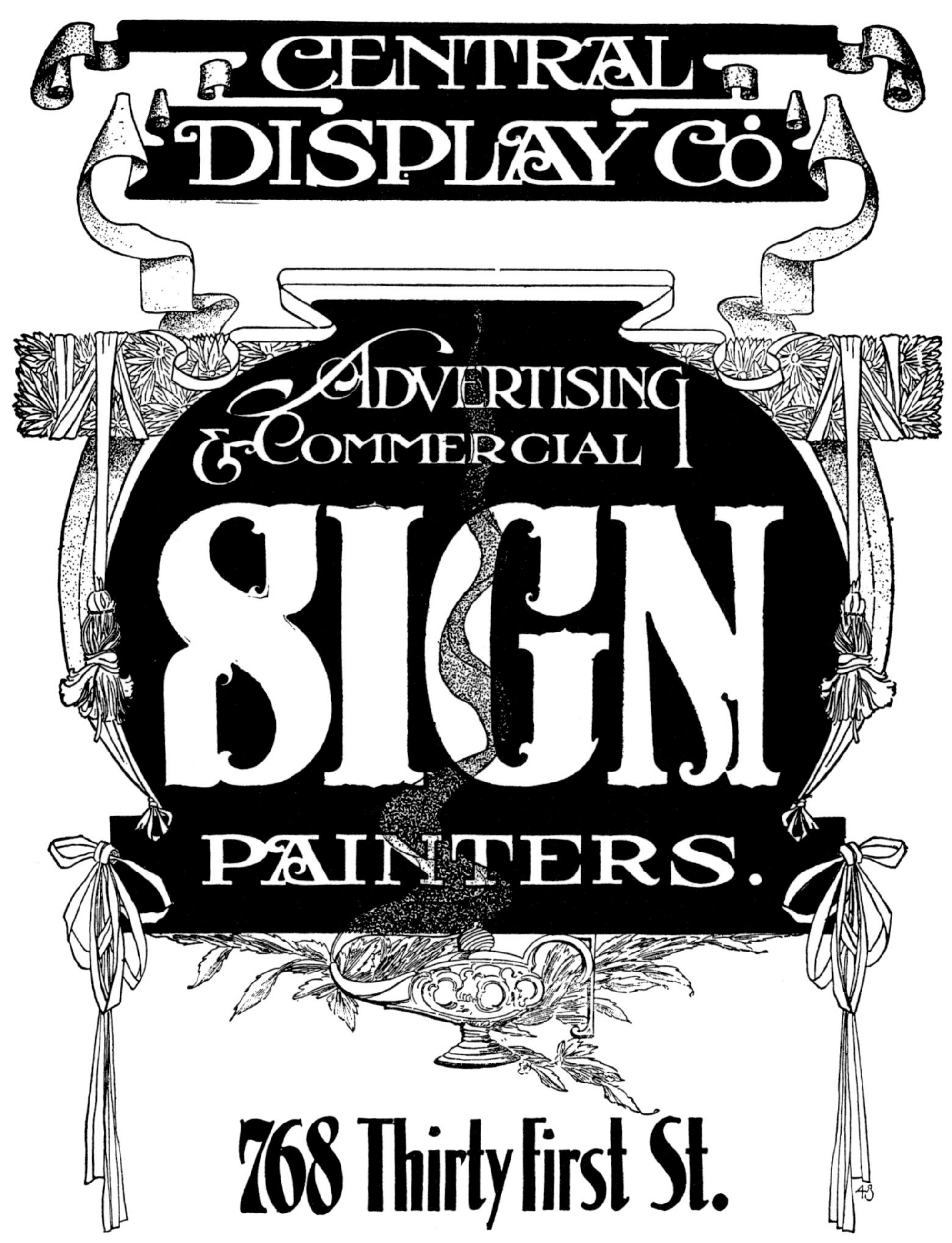
·PHONE YARDS 1306·
CENTRAL
DISPLAY Co
ADVERTISING
& COMMERCIAL
SIGN
PAINTERS.
768 Thirty First St.

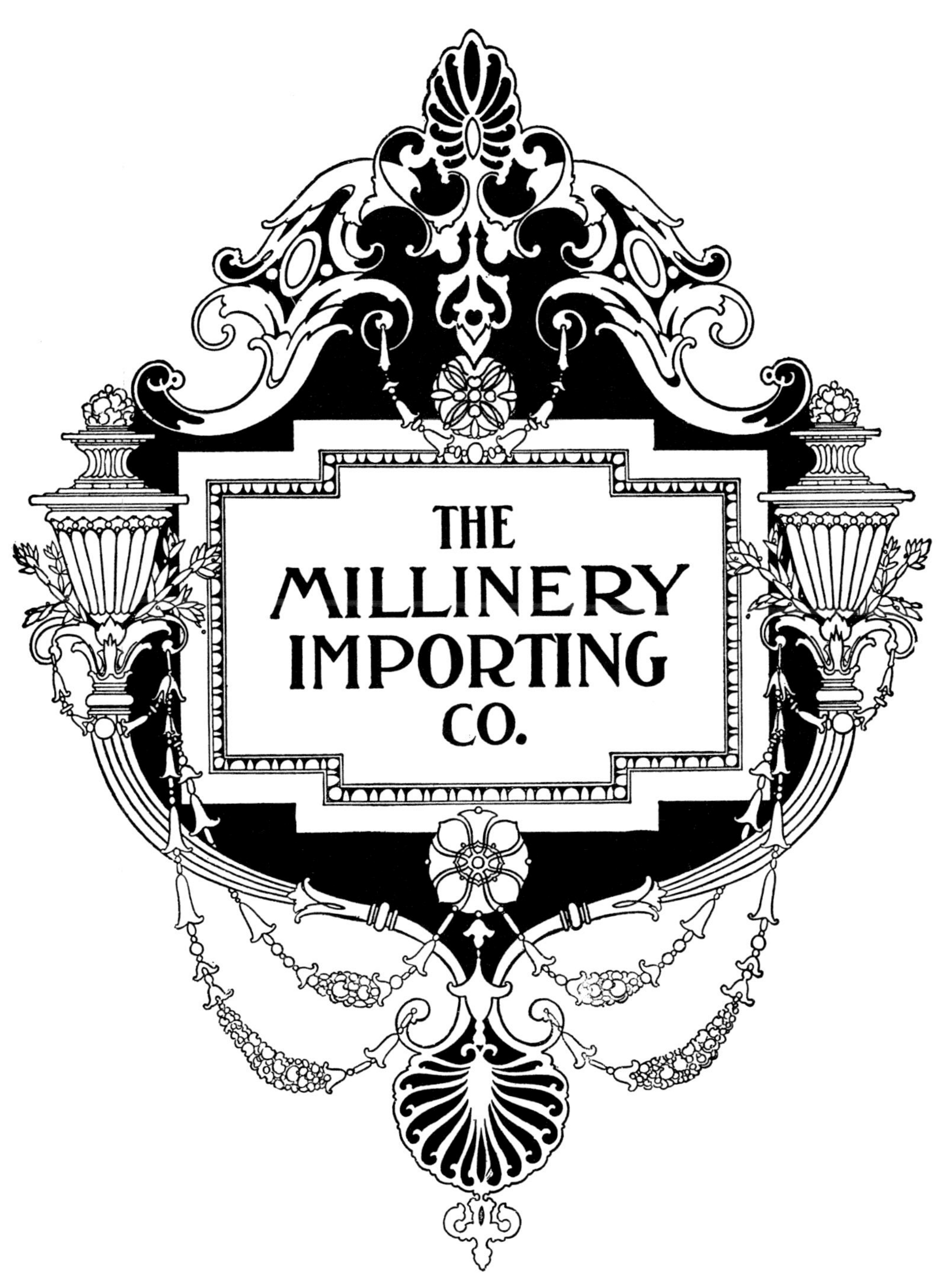
THE
MILLINERY
IMPORTING
CO.

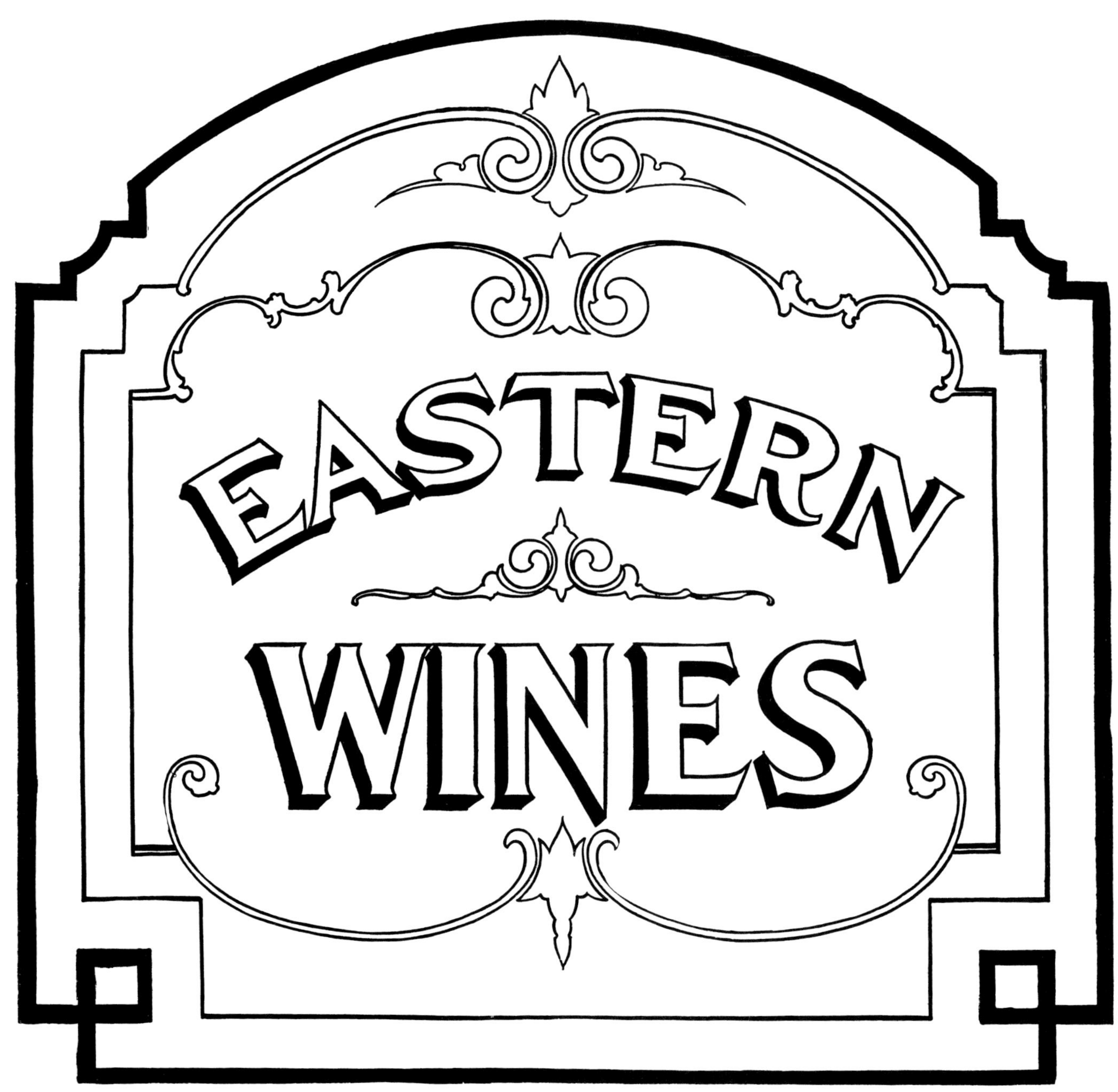
EASTERN
WINES

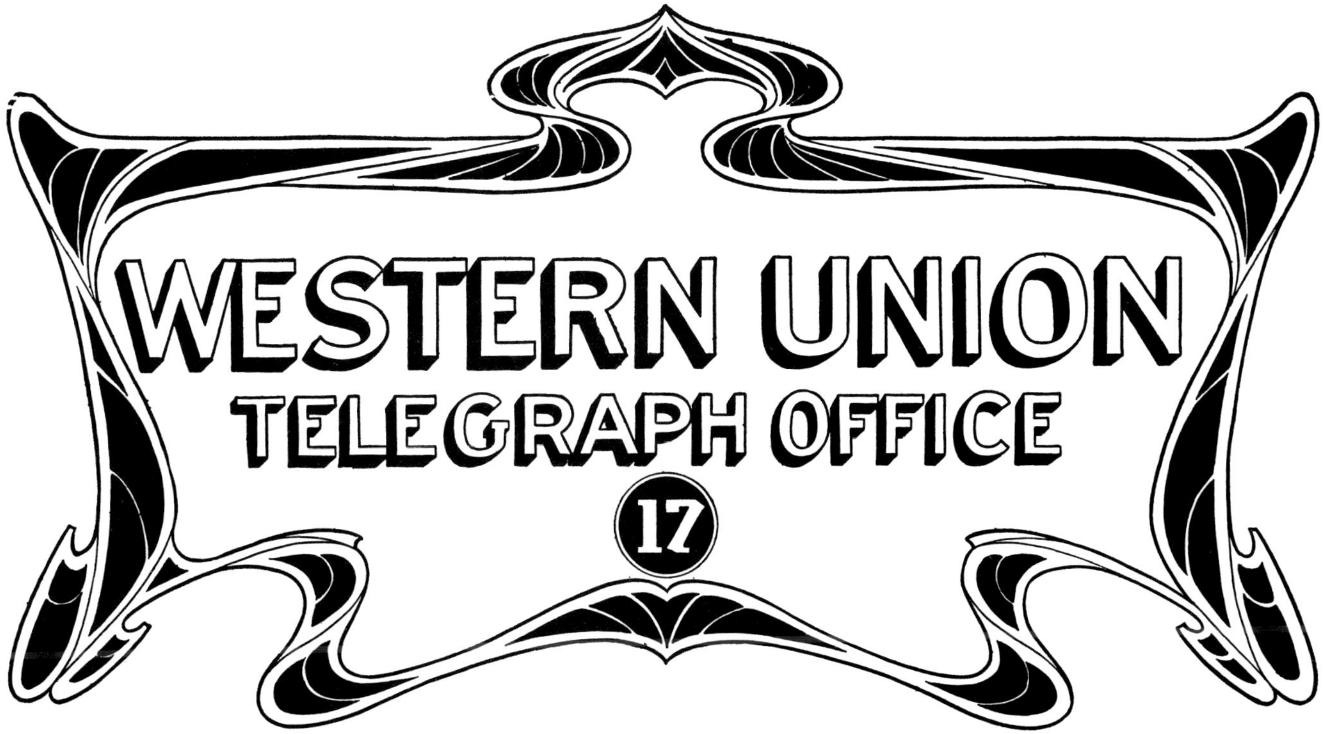

WESTERN UNION
TELEGRAPH OFFICE
17

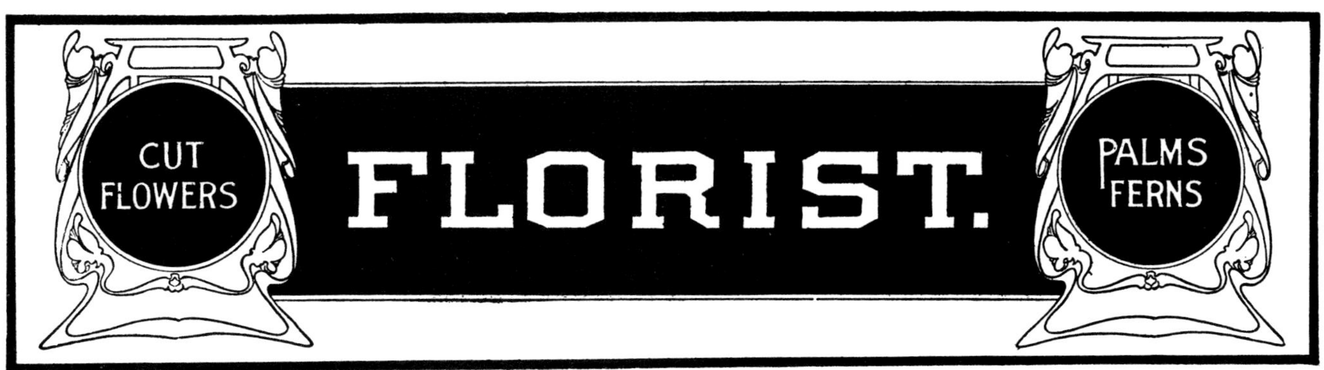

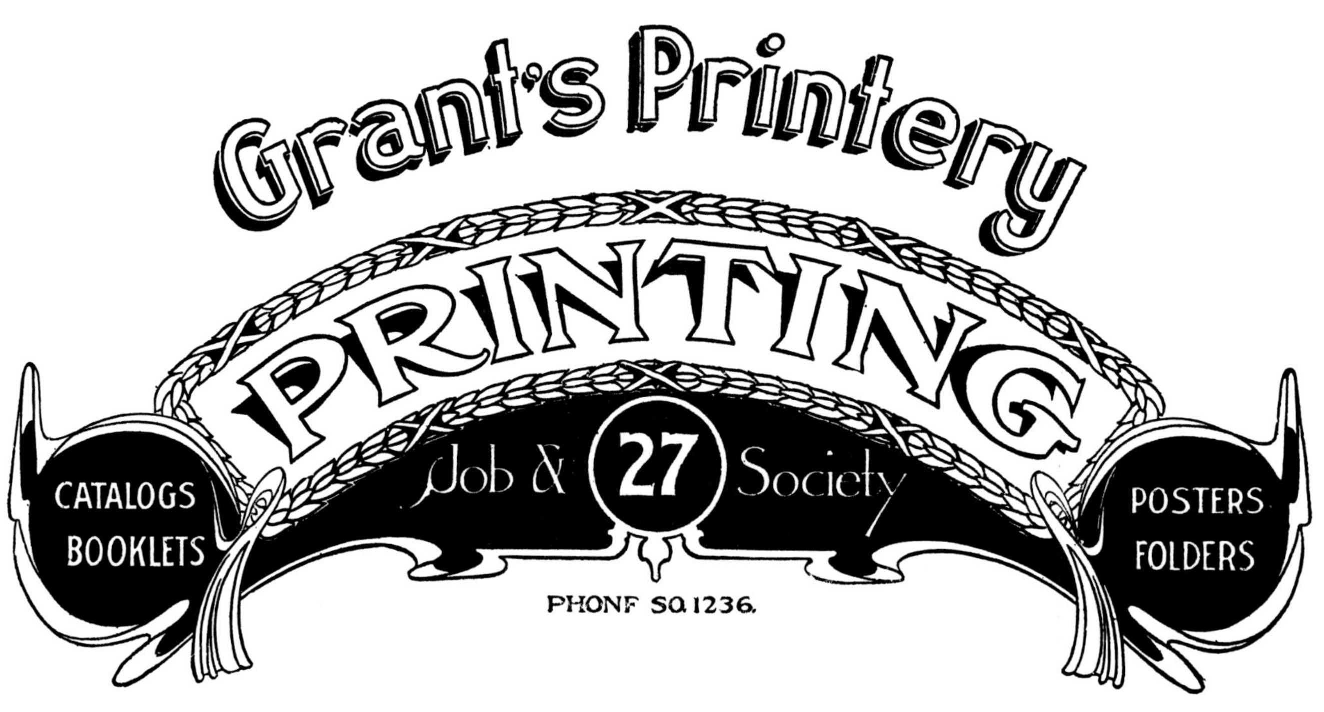
Grant's Printery
PRINTING
Job & 27 Society
CATALOGS
BOOKLETS
POSTERS
FOLDERS
PHONF SQ 1236.

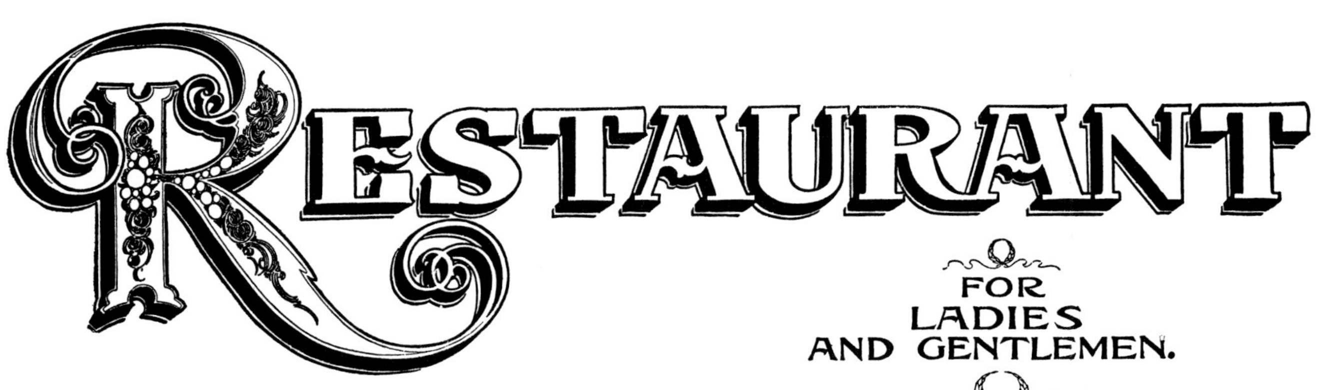
RESTAURANT
FOR
LADIES
AND GENTLEMEN.

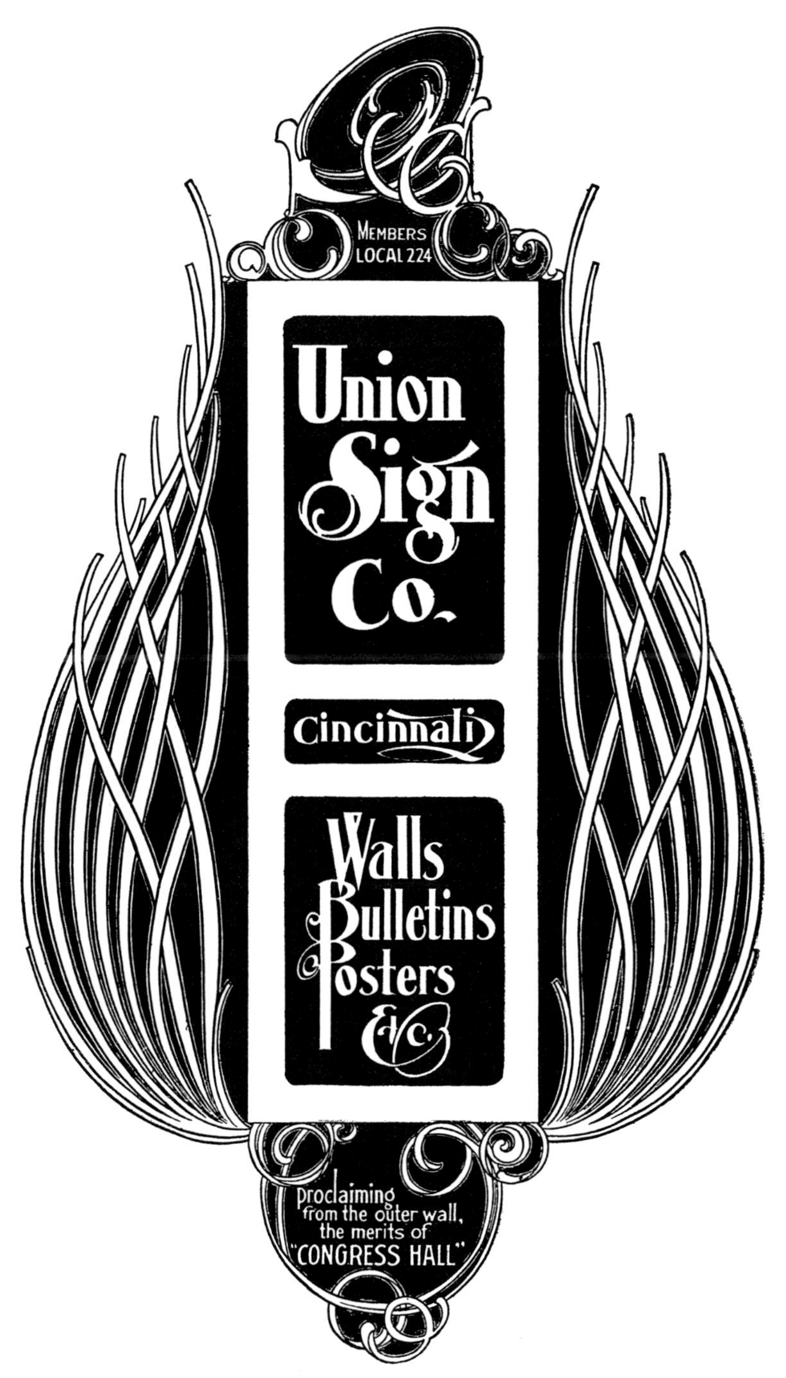
MEMBERS
LOCAL 224
Union
Sign
Co.
Cincinnati
Walls
Bulletins
Posters
&c.
proclaiming
from the outer wall,
the merits of
"CONGRESS HALL"

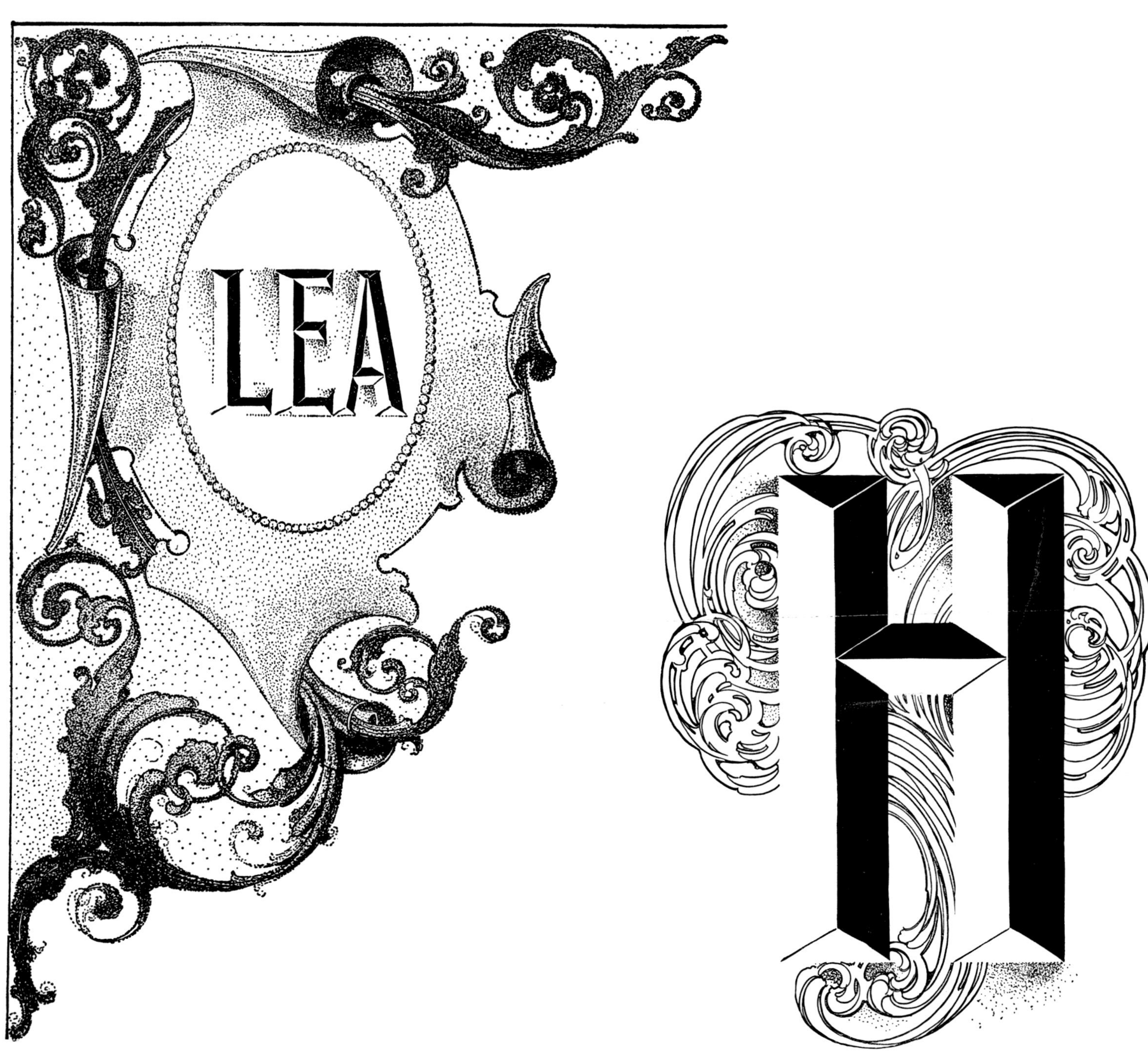
LEA

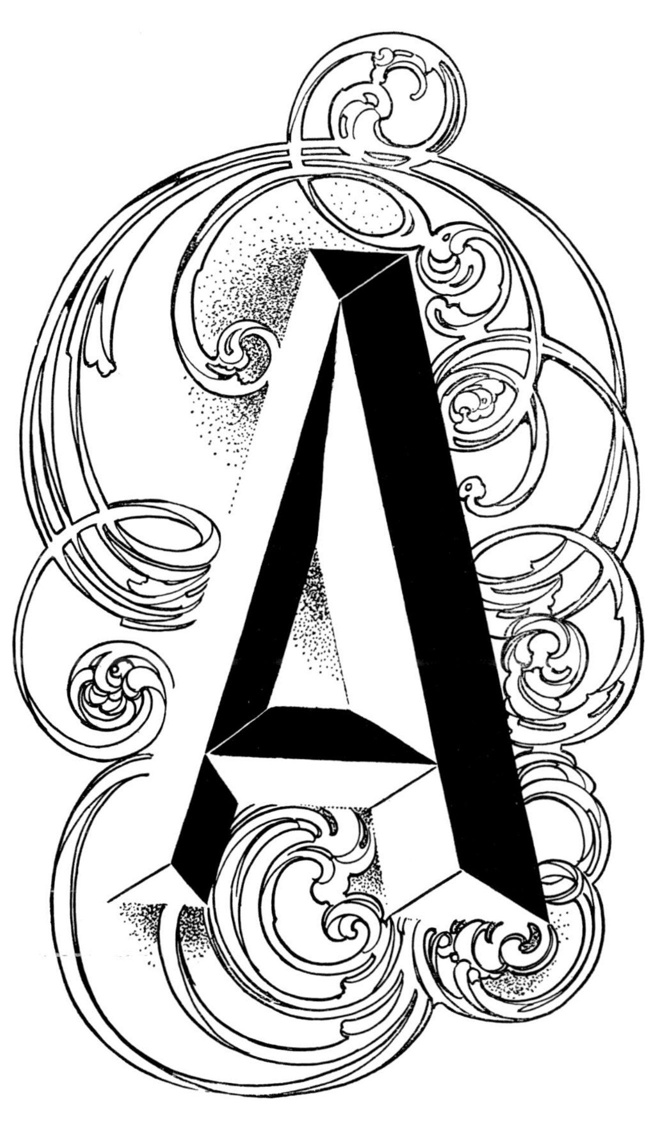

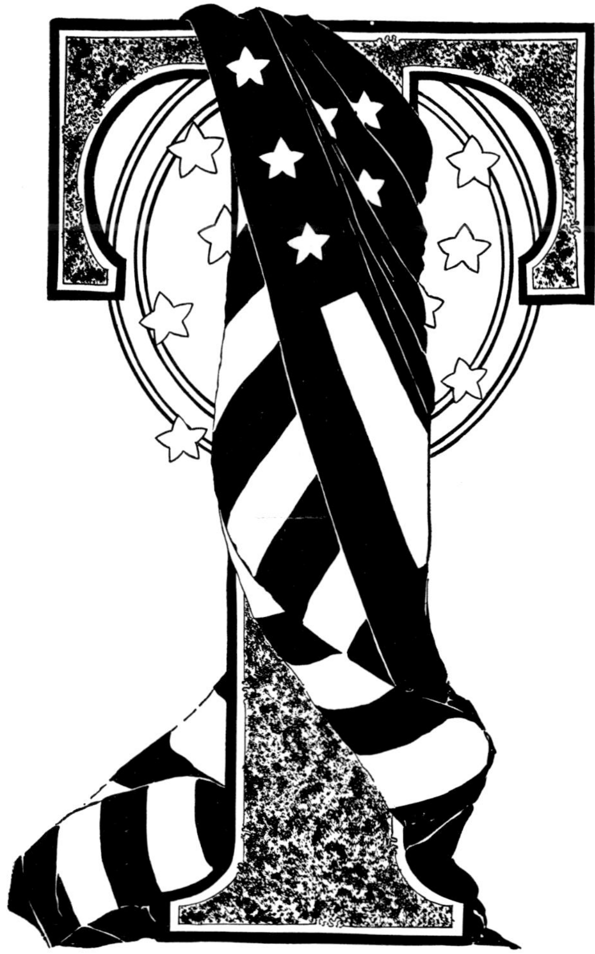

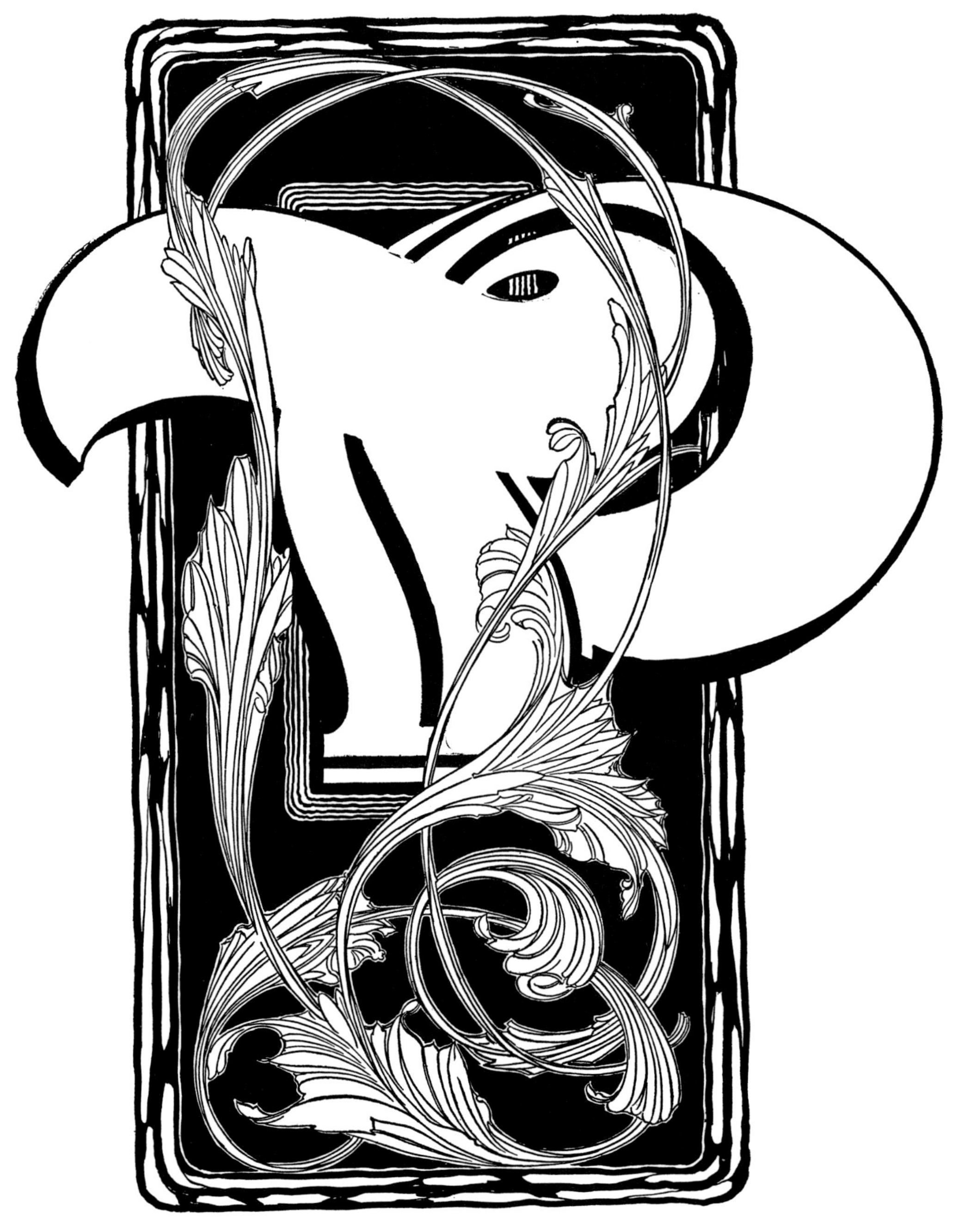

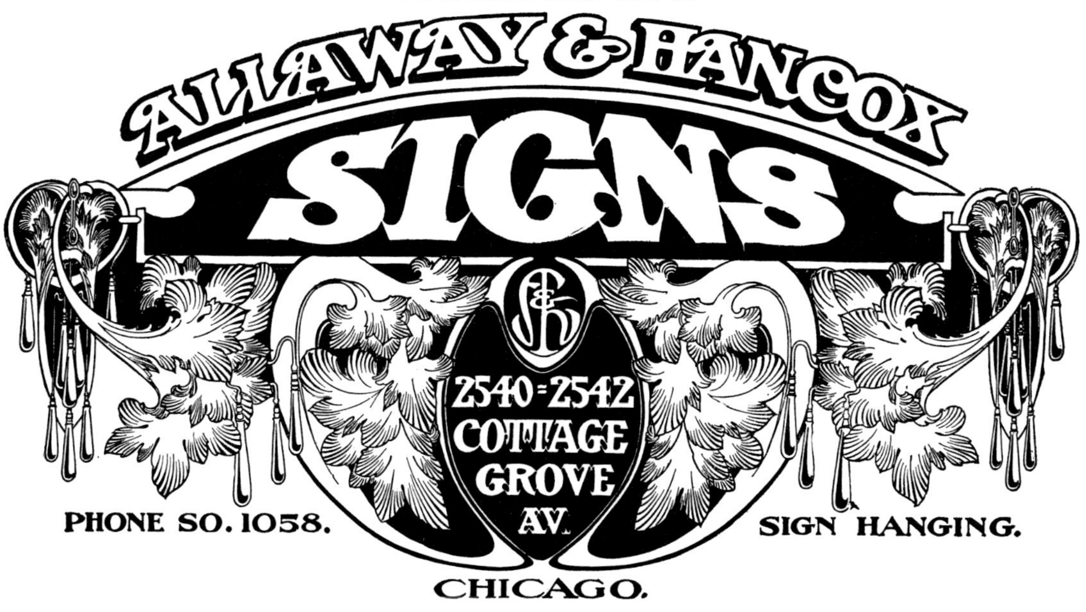
ESTABLISHED 1870.
ALLAWAY & HANCOX
SIGNS
2540-2542
COTTAGE
GROVE
AV.
PHONE SO. 1058.
SIGN HANGING.
CHICAGO.

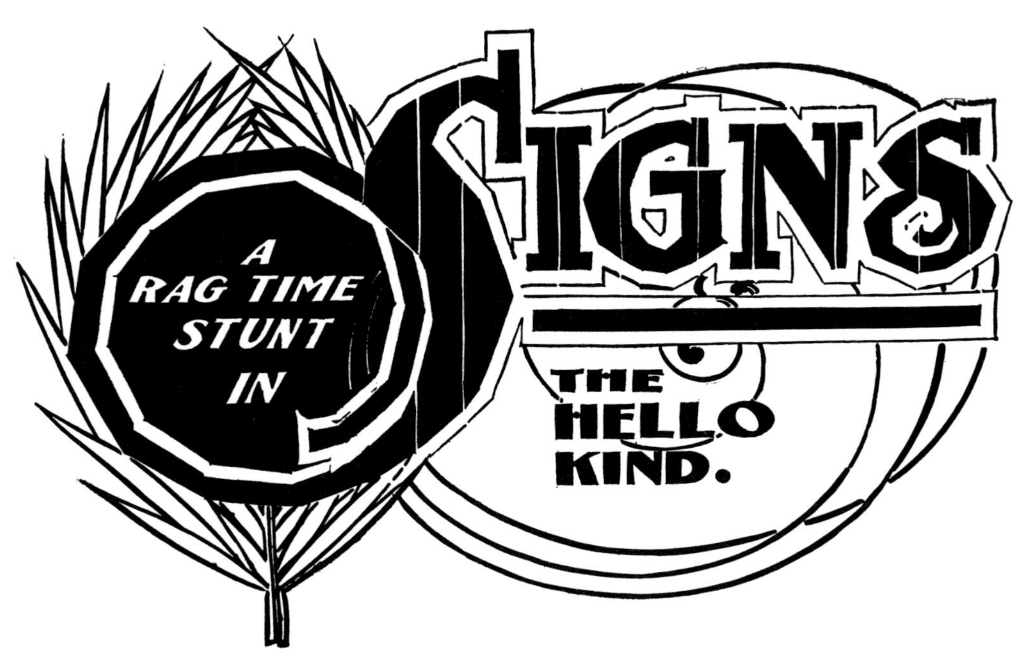
A
RAG TIME
STUNT
IN
SIGNS
THE
HELLO
KIND.

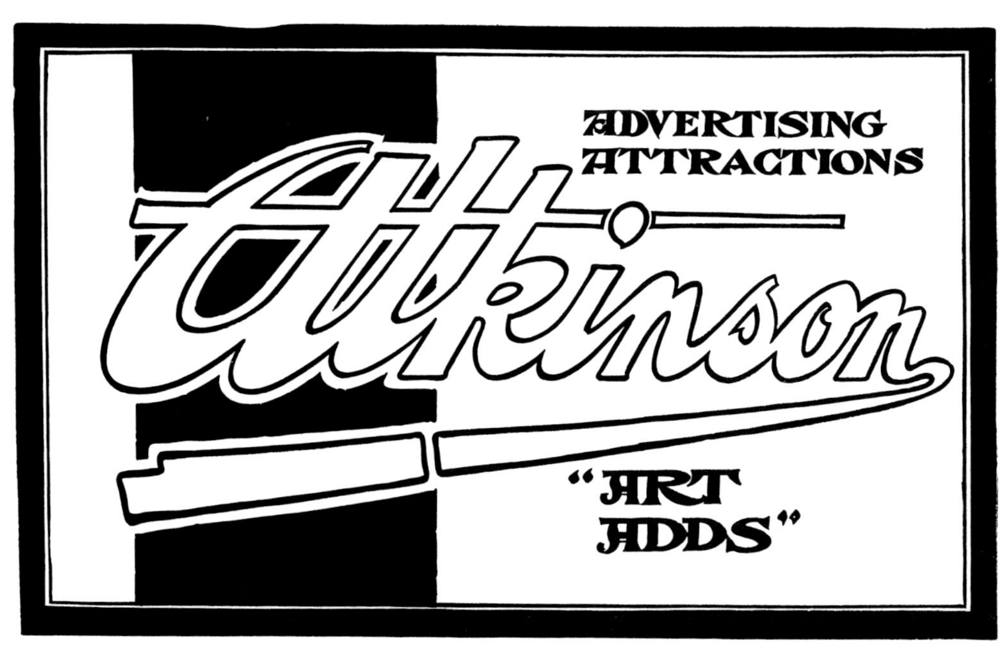
ADVERTISING
ATTRACTIONS
Atkinson
"ART
ADDS"

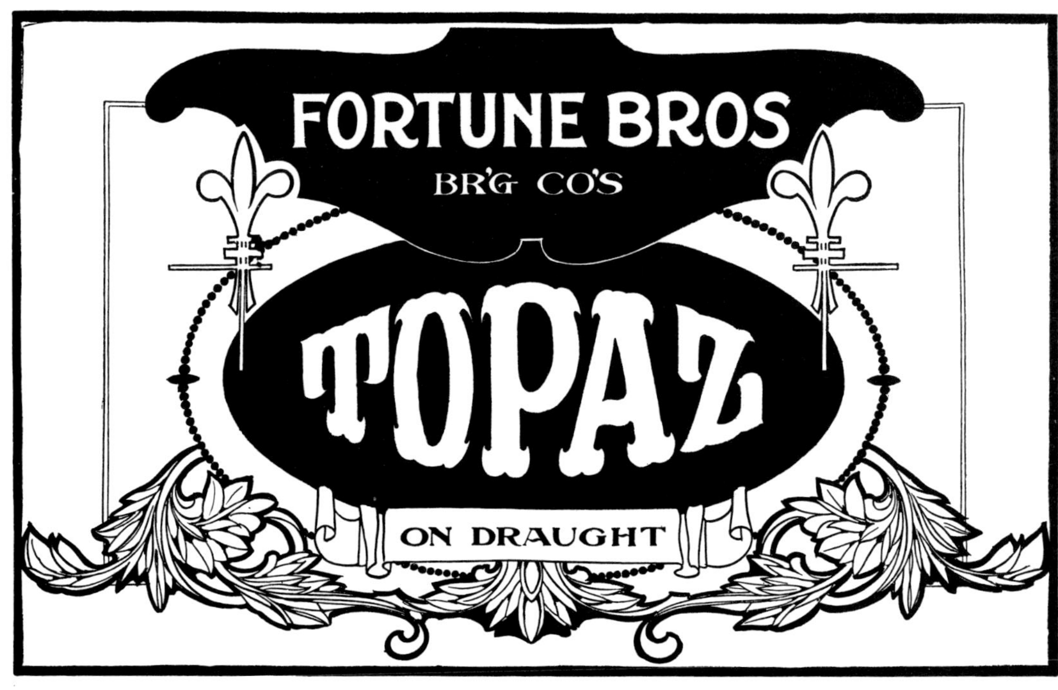
FORTUNE BROS
BR'G CO'S
TOPAZ
ON DRAUGHT

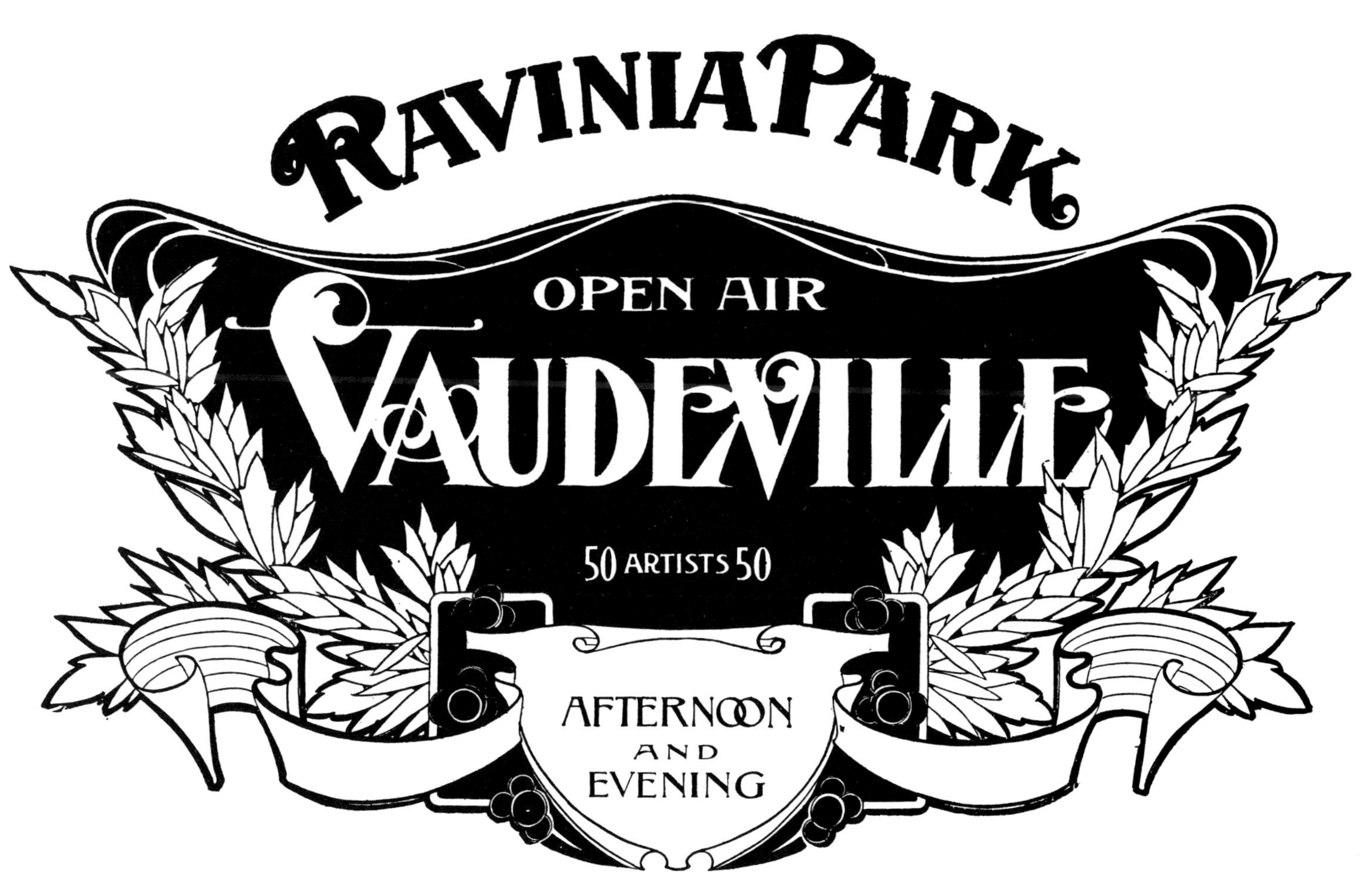
RAVINIA PARK
OPEN AIR
VAUDEVILLE
50 ARTISTS 50
AFTERNOON
AND
EVENING

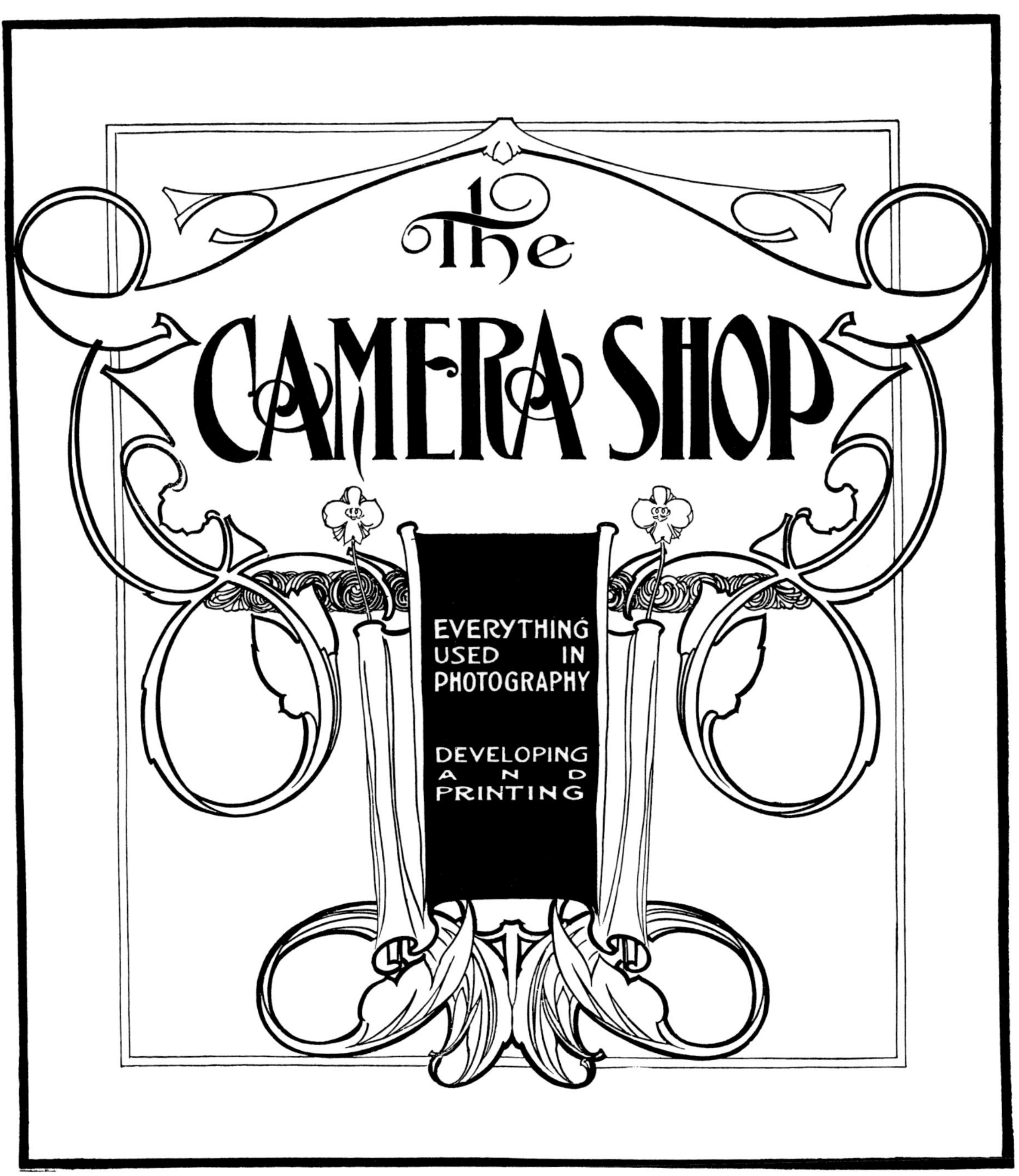
The
CAMERA SHOP
EVERYTHING
USED IN
PHOTOGRAPHY
DEVELOPING
AND
PRINTING

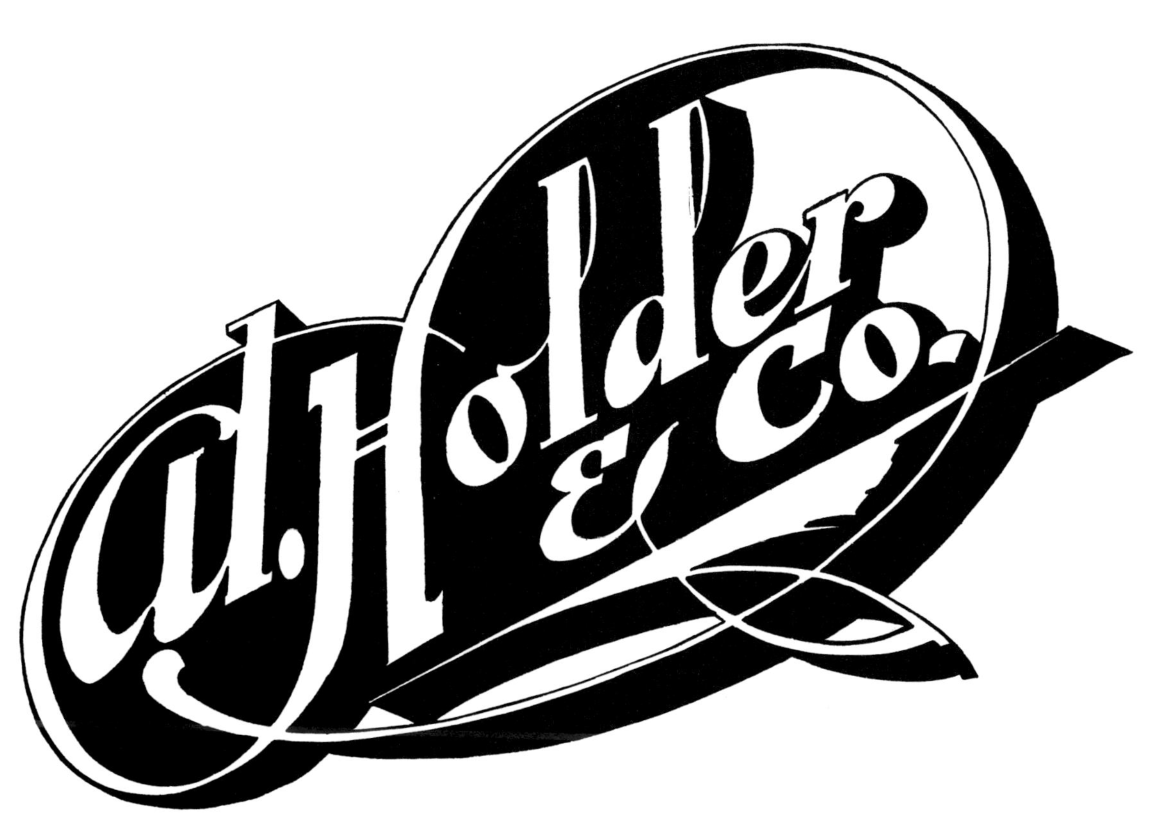
A. Holder & Co.

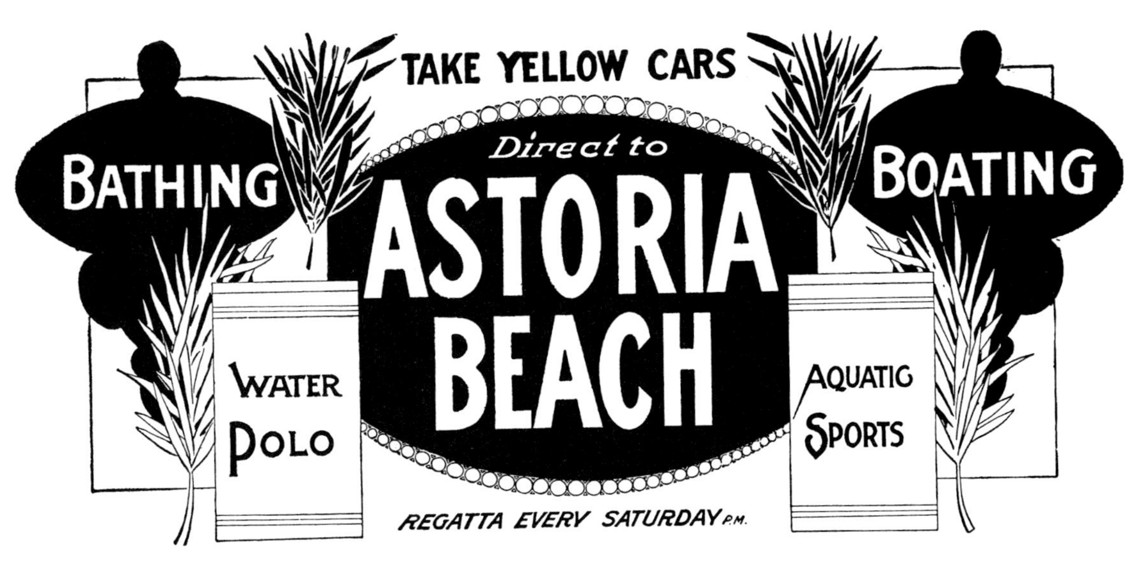
TAKE YELLOW CARS
Direct to
ASTORIA
BEACH
BATHING
BOATING
WATER
POLO
AQUATIC
SPORTS
REGATTA EVERY SATURDAY P.M.

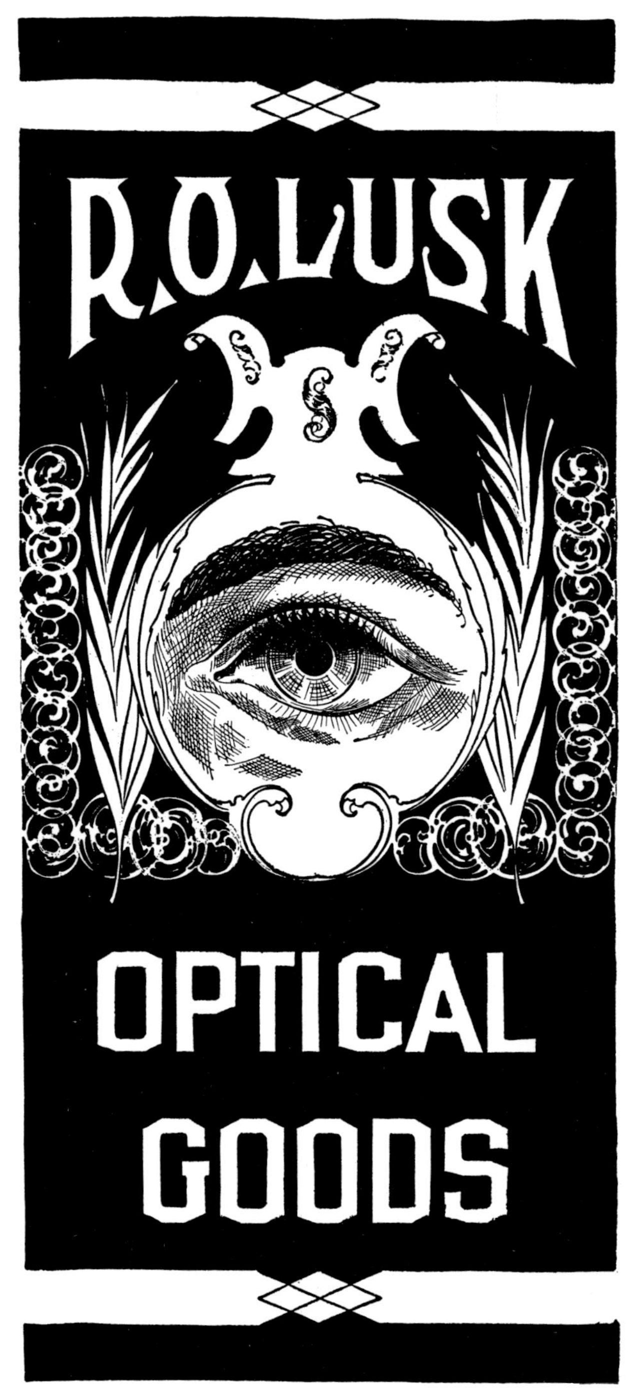
R.O. LUSK
OPTICAL
GOODS

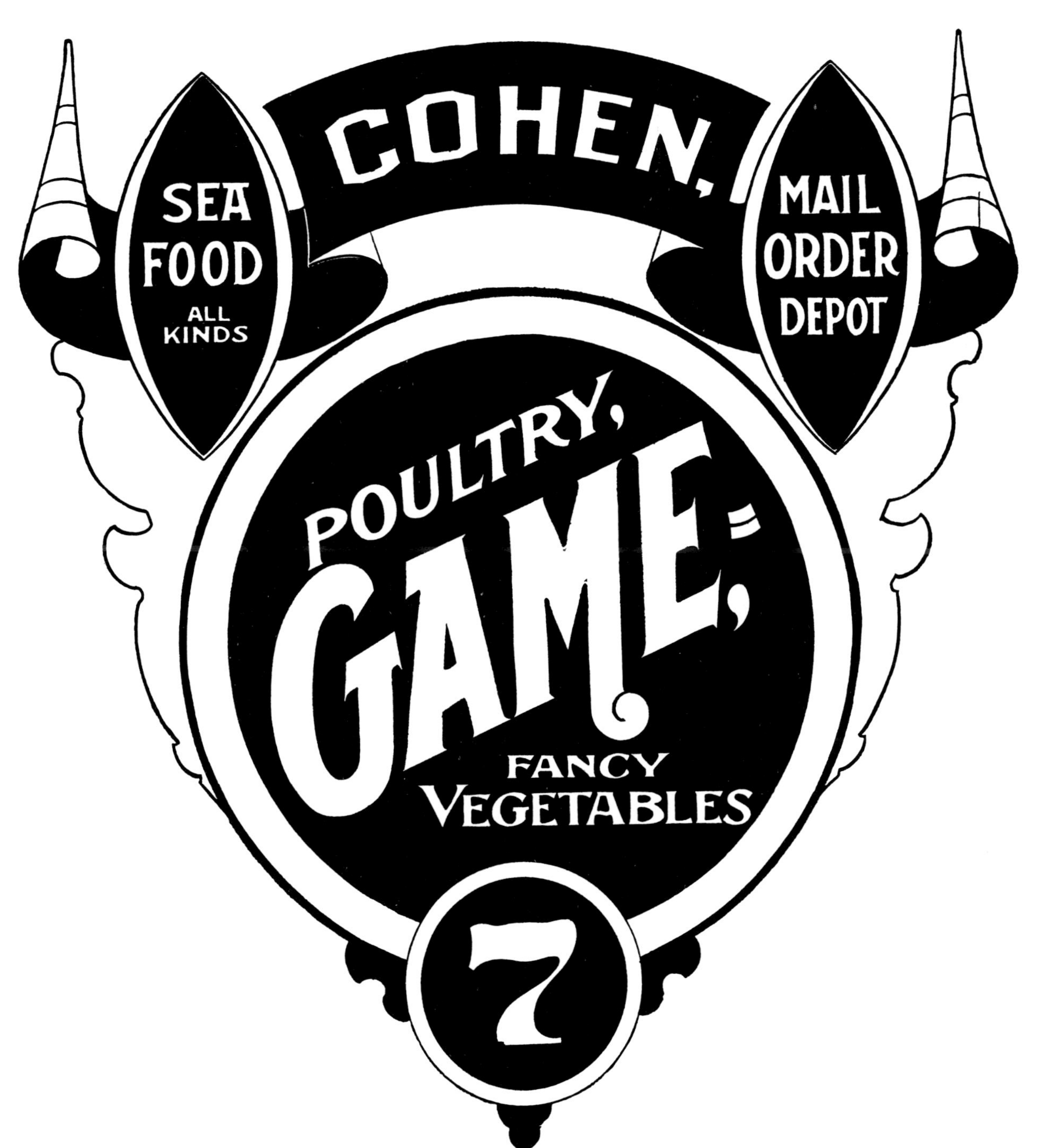
COHEN,
SEA
FOOD
ALL
KINDS
MAIL
ORDER
DEPOT
POULTRY,
GAME,
FANCY
VEGETABLES
7

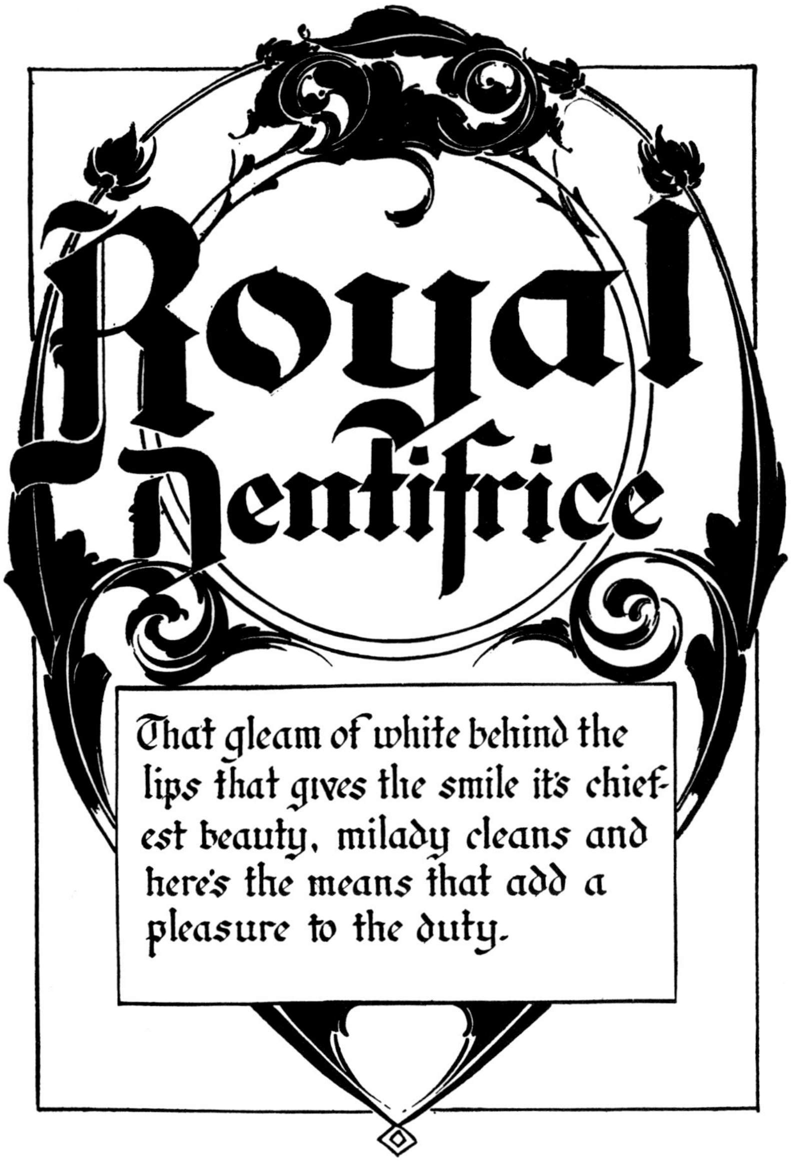

Royal Dentifrice

That gleam of white behind the lips that gives the smile it's chiefest beauty, milady cleans and here's the means that add a pleasure to the duty.

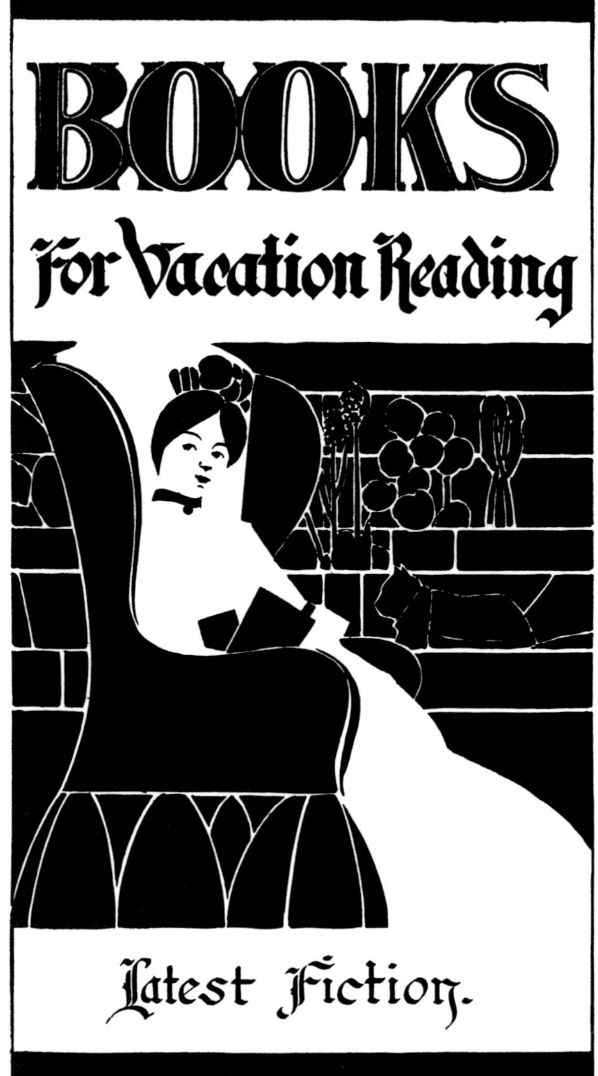

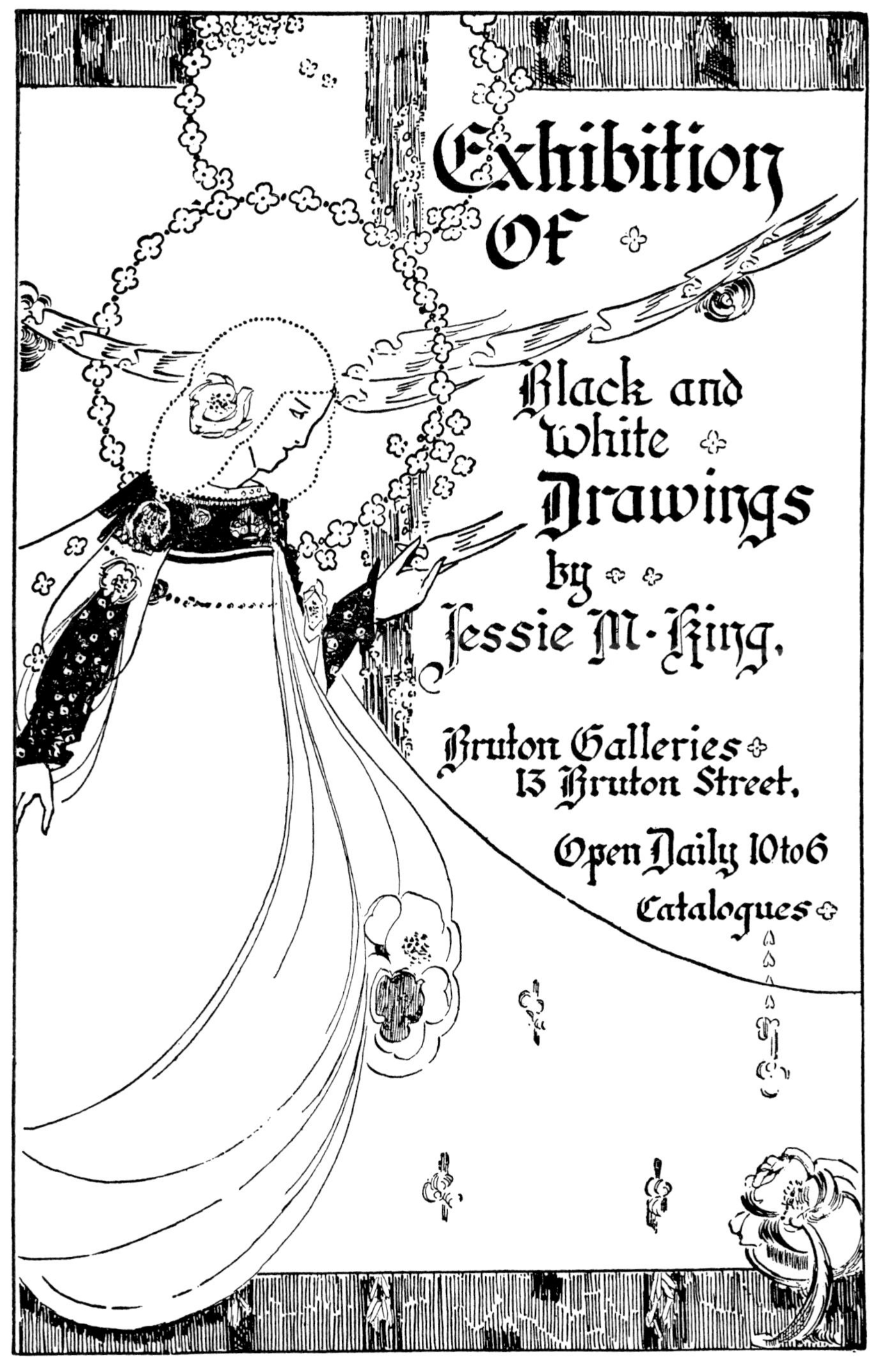
Exhibition
Of
Black and
White
Drawings
by
Jessie M. King.
Bruton Galleries
13 Bruton Street.
Open Daily 10 to 6
Catalogues

Antique Roman

ABCDEFGHIJ
KLMNOPQRST
UVWXYZ&
ÆŒ
abcdefghijklmnopqrst
uvwxyz 123456789

FRENCH ROMAN

A		a
CD	1	dcb
BEF	234	efg
GHIJK	5	hijlmnok
LMNOPQR	6	prstq
STUV	7	uv
WXY	89	w

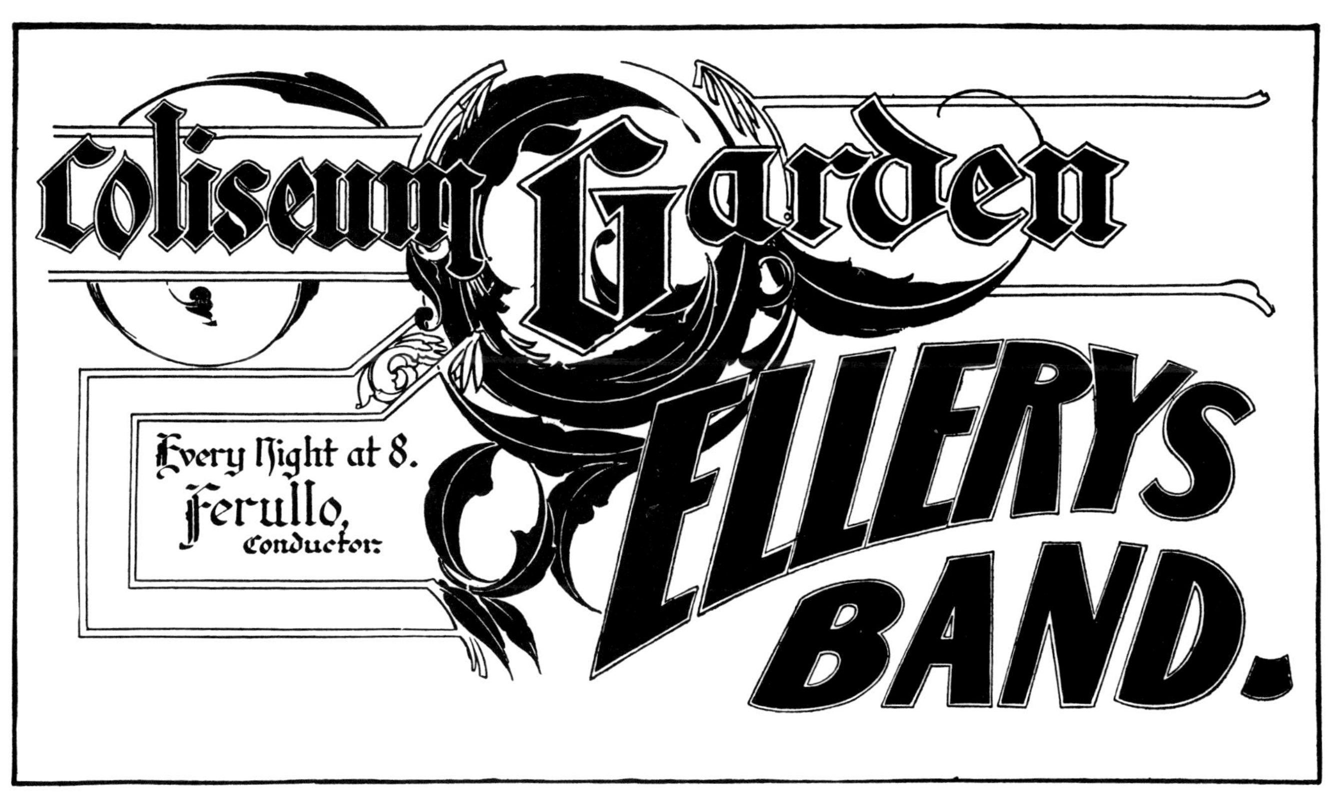
Coliseum Garden
Every Night at 8.
Ferullo,
Conductor.
ELLERYS
BAND.

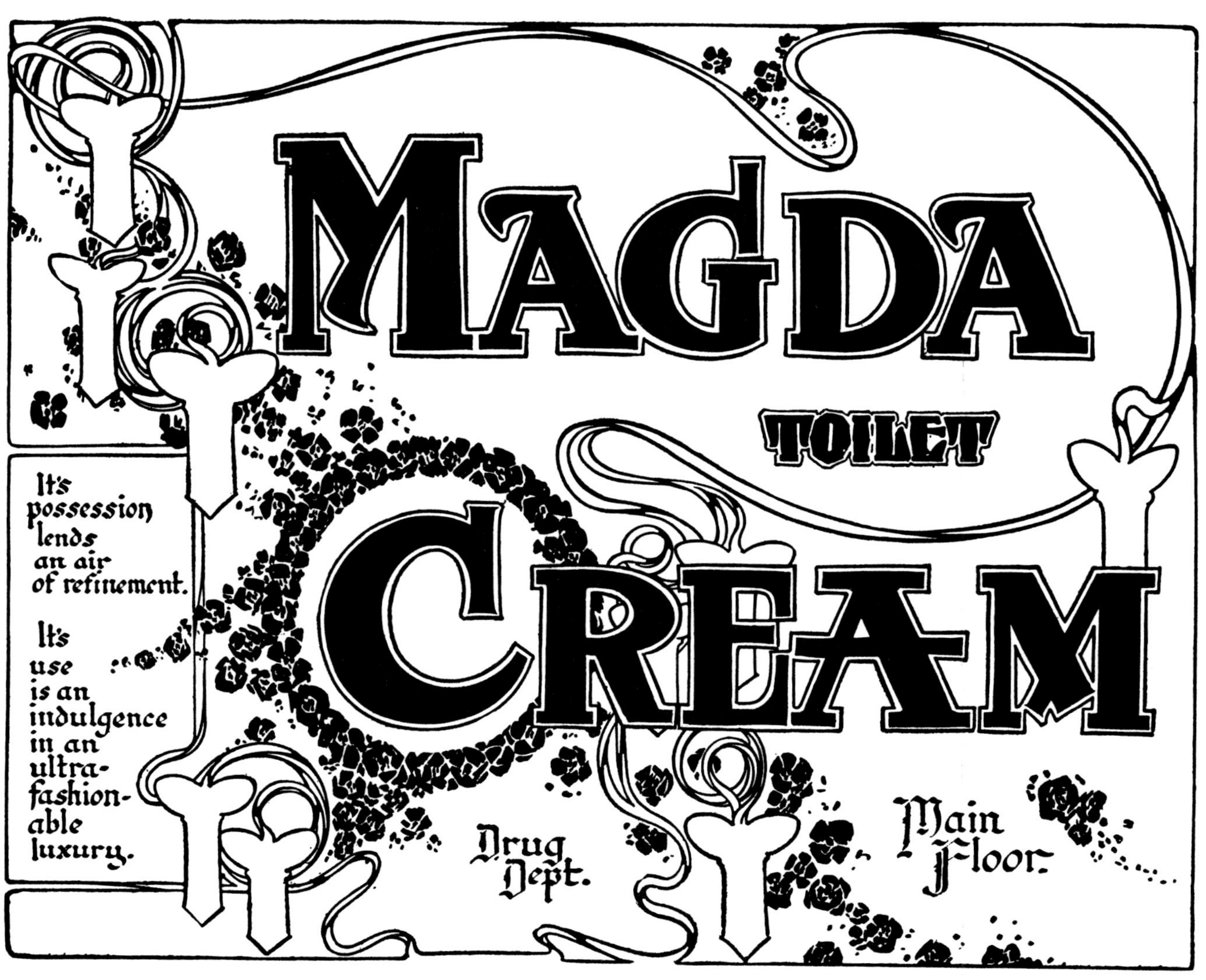
MAGDA
TOILET
CREAM
It's possession lends an air of refinement.
It's use is an indulgence in an ultra-fashionable luxury.
Drug Dept.
Main Floor.

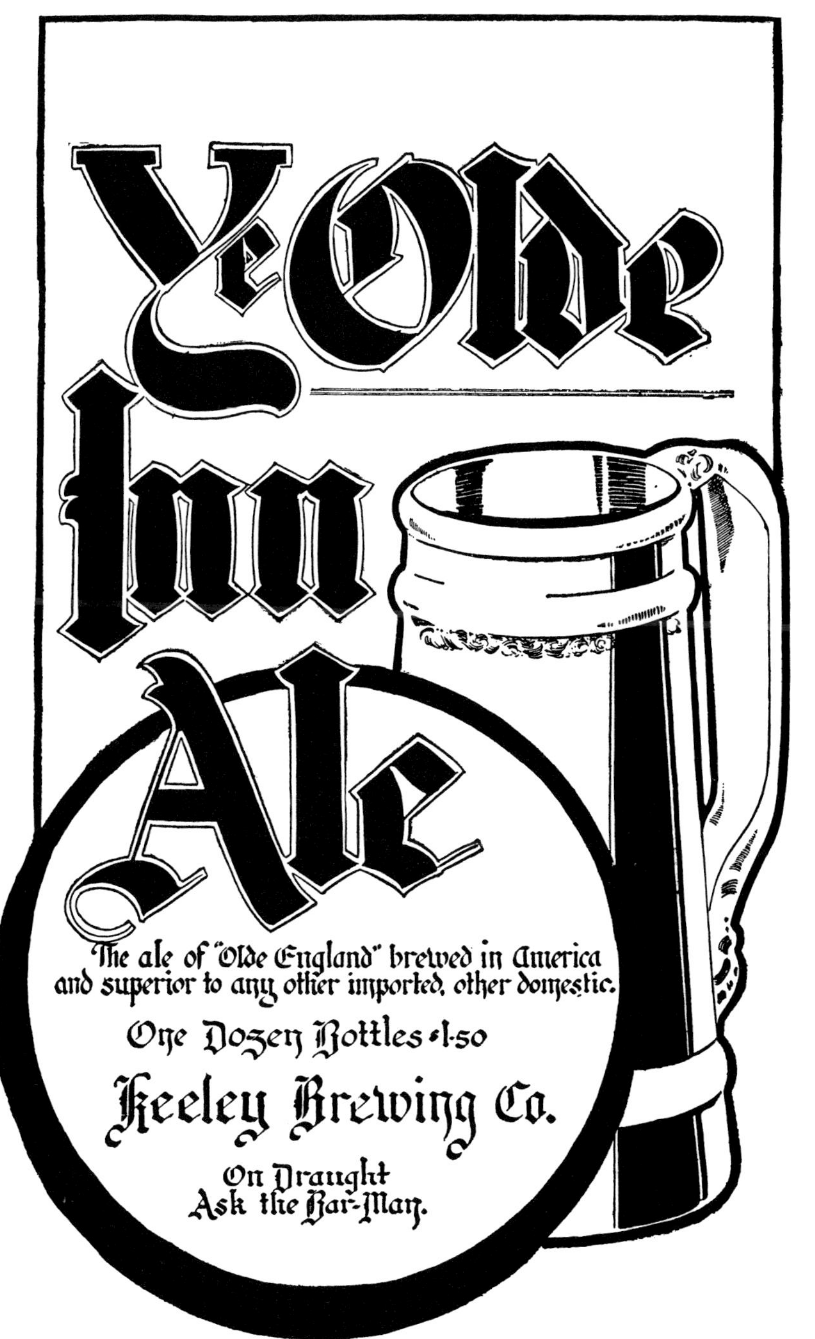
Ye Olde
Inn
Ale
The ale of "Olde England" brewed in America
and superior to any other imported, other domestic.
One Dozen Bottles $1.50
Keeley Brewing Co.
On Draught
Ask the Bar-Man.

ATKINSON TUSCAN ROMAN (Light)

A B C D E F G
H I J K L M O P
Q R S T U V W
X Y Z
&

FRENCH ROMAN (LIGHT)

A
BC
DEF
GHIJK
LMNOPQR
STUV
WXY
Z
&

4123
956
78
0

a
dcb
efg
hijlmnok
pstq
uv
w
xy
z

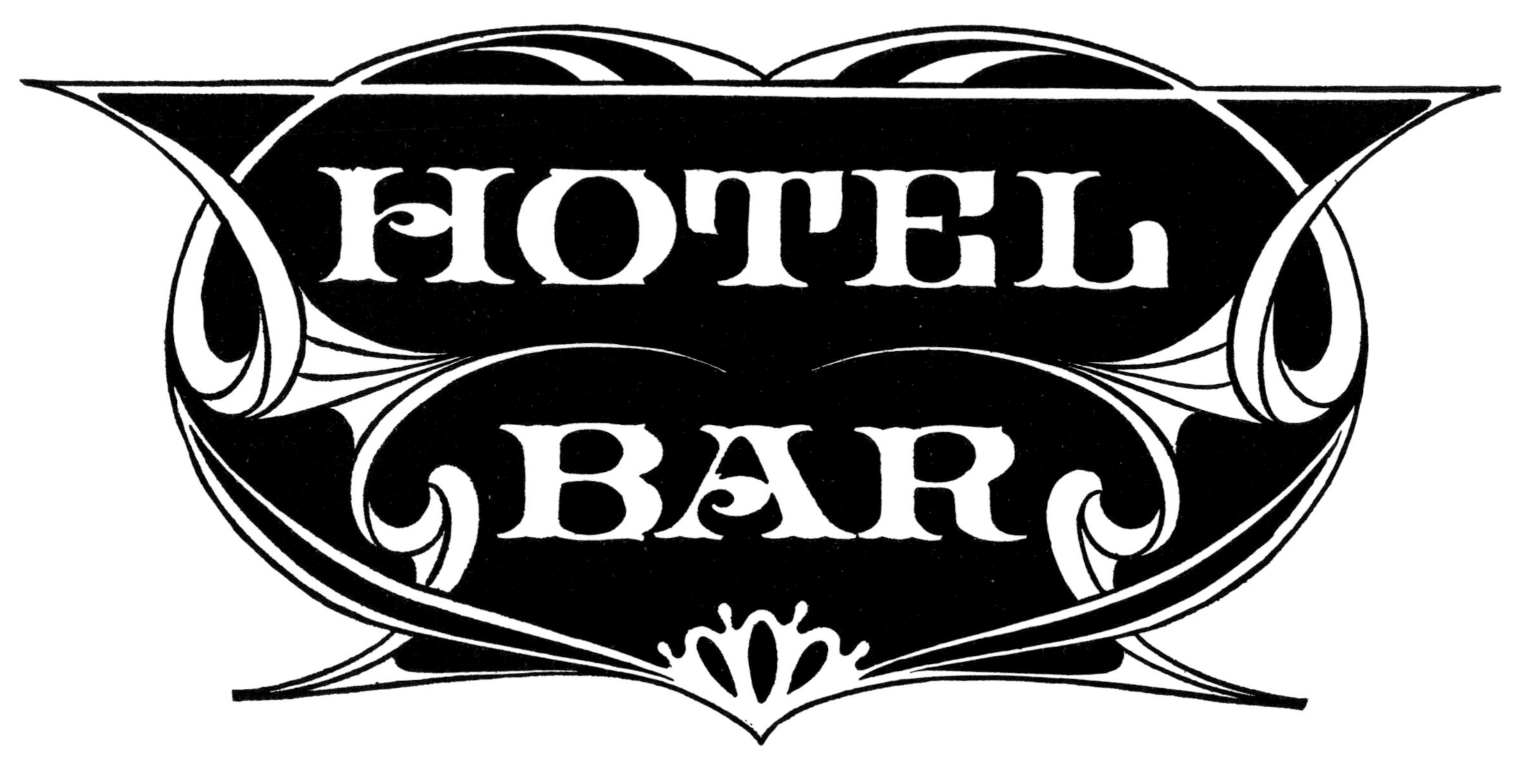

Extreme French

ABCDFGHIJKLMNOPQ
RSTUVWXYZ&E
a 12 34 567 89 wyxz
abcdefgghijklmnoopqrsstuv

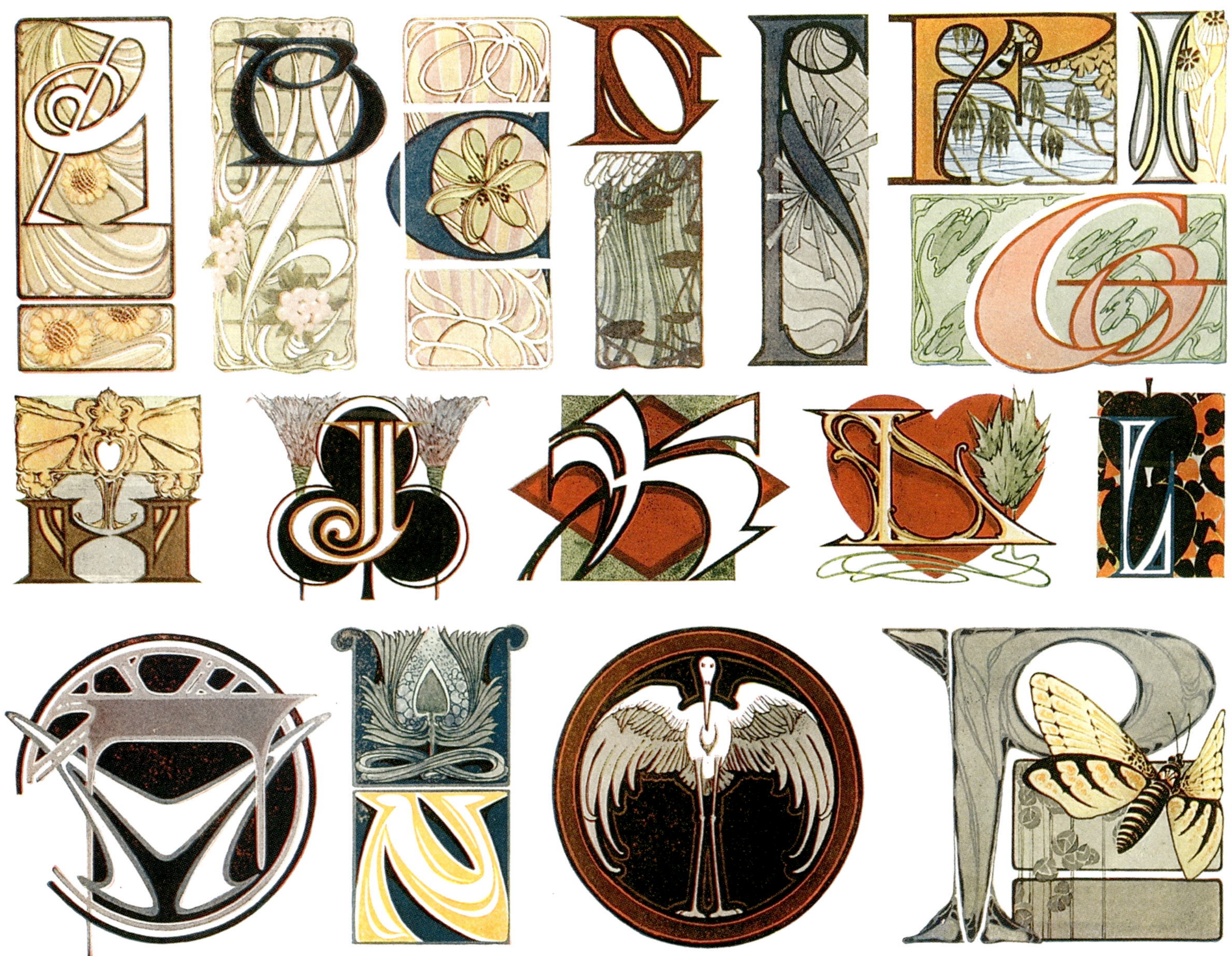

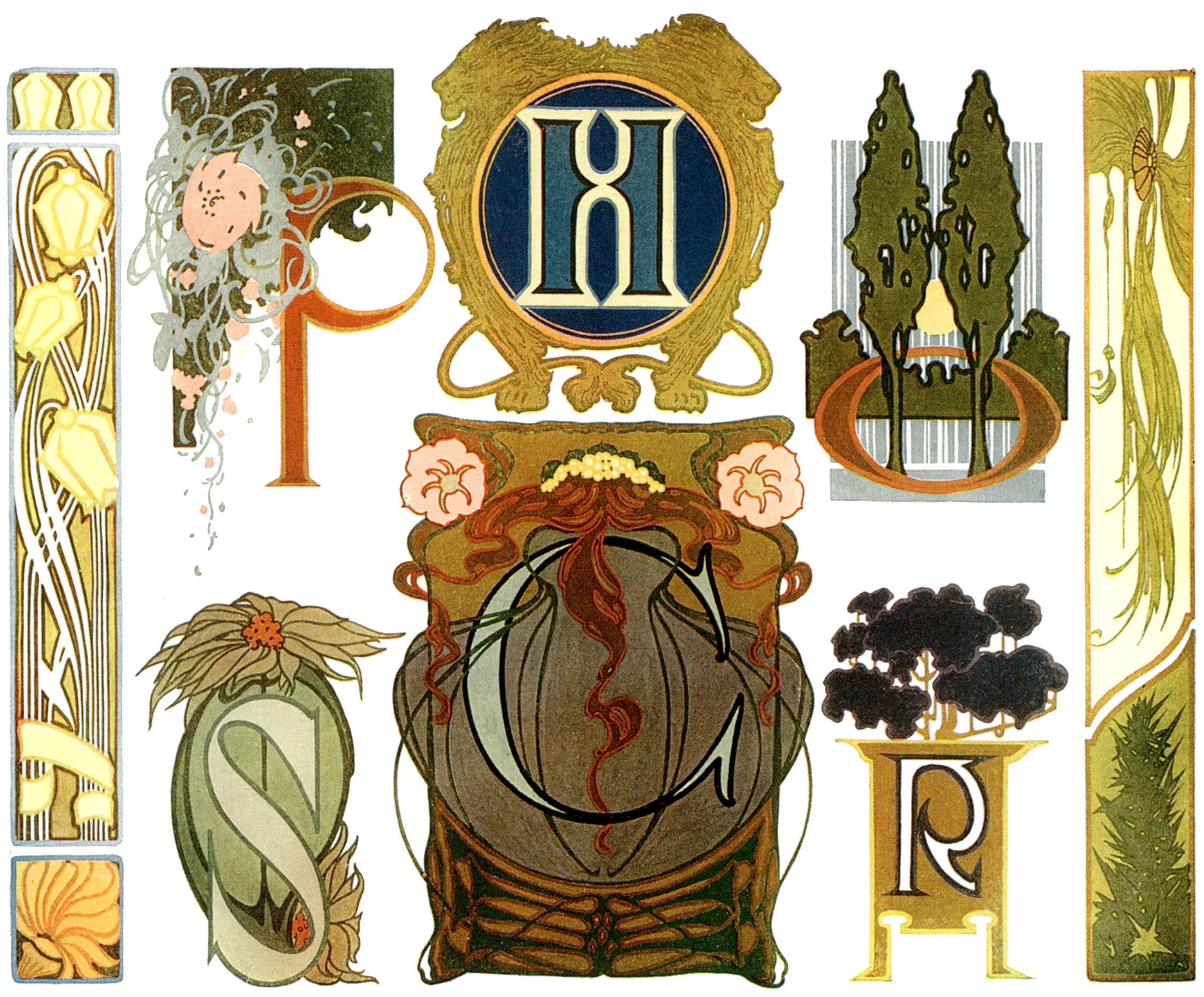

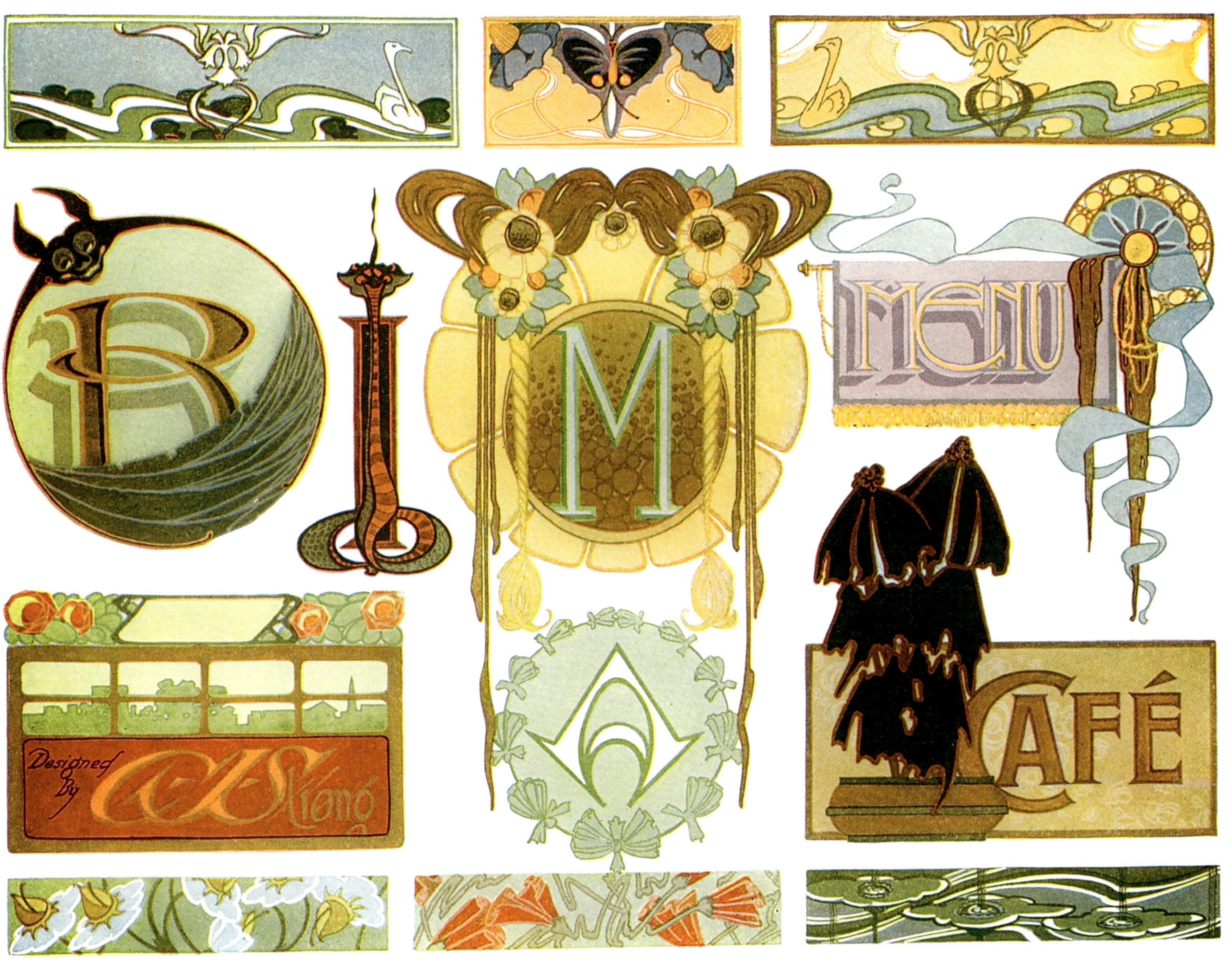
MENU
CAFÉ
Designed By

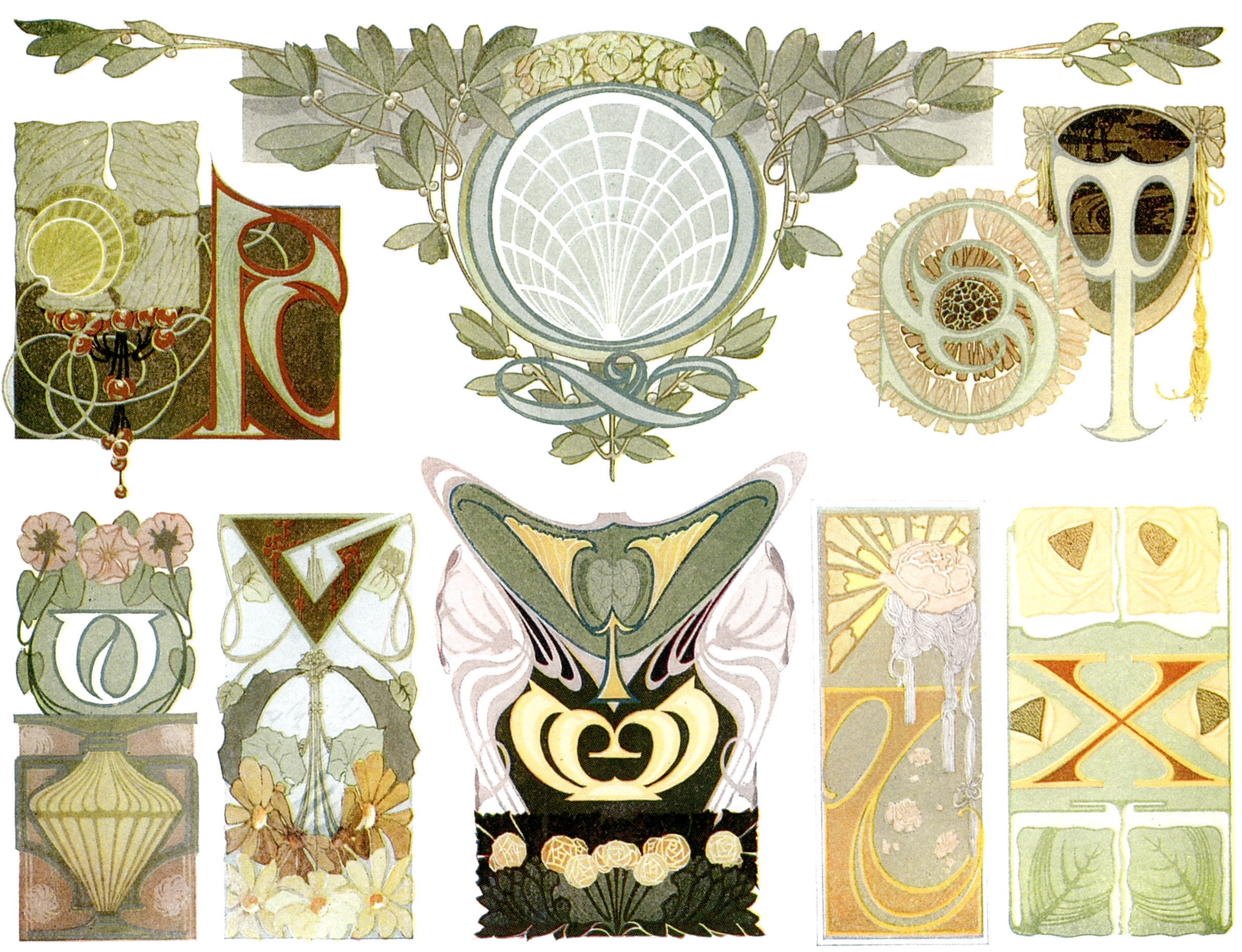

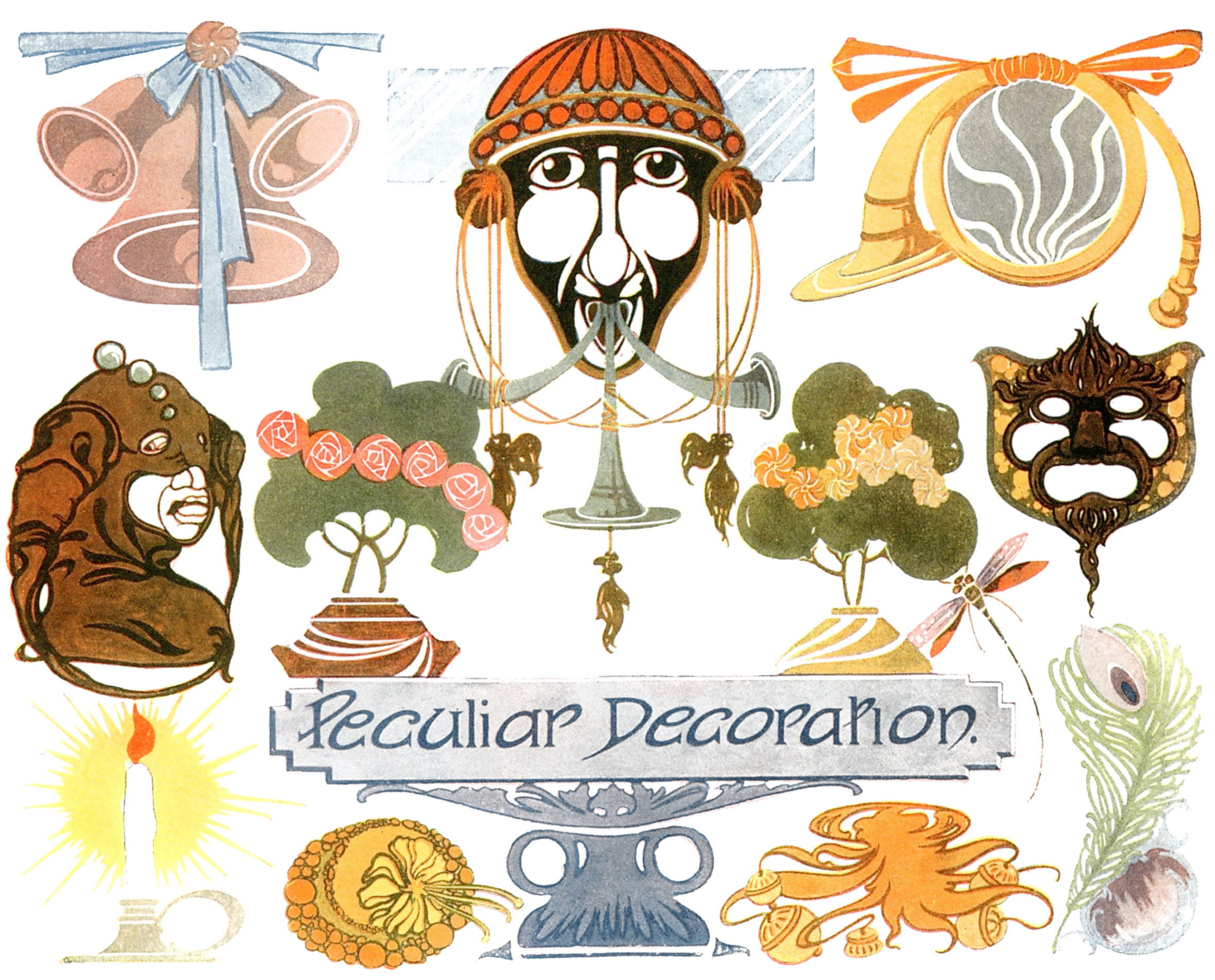
Peculiar Decoration.

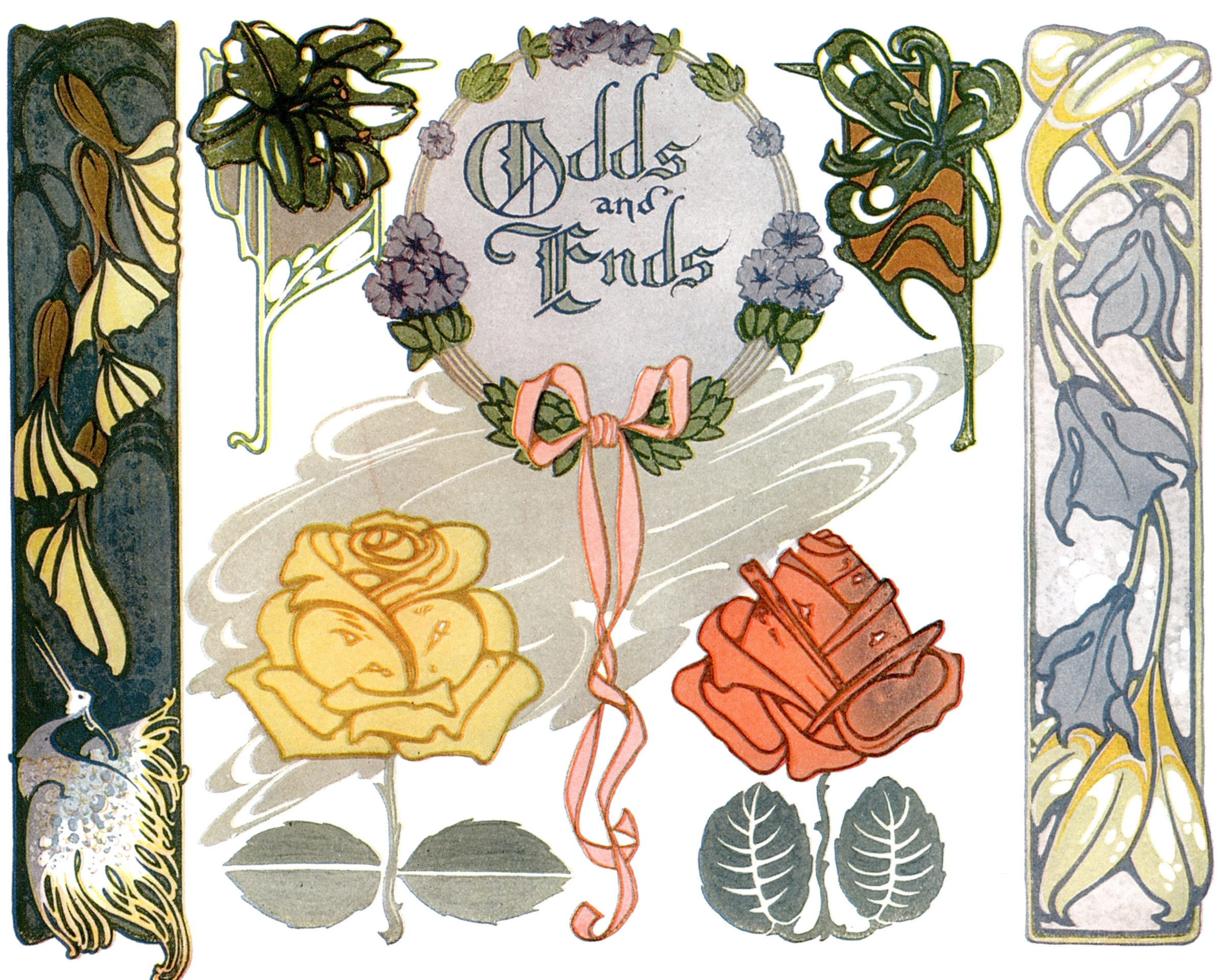
Odds and Ends

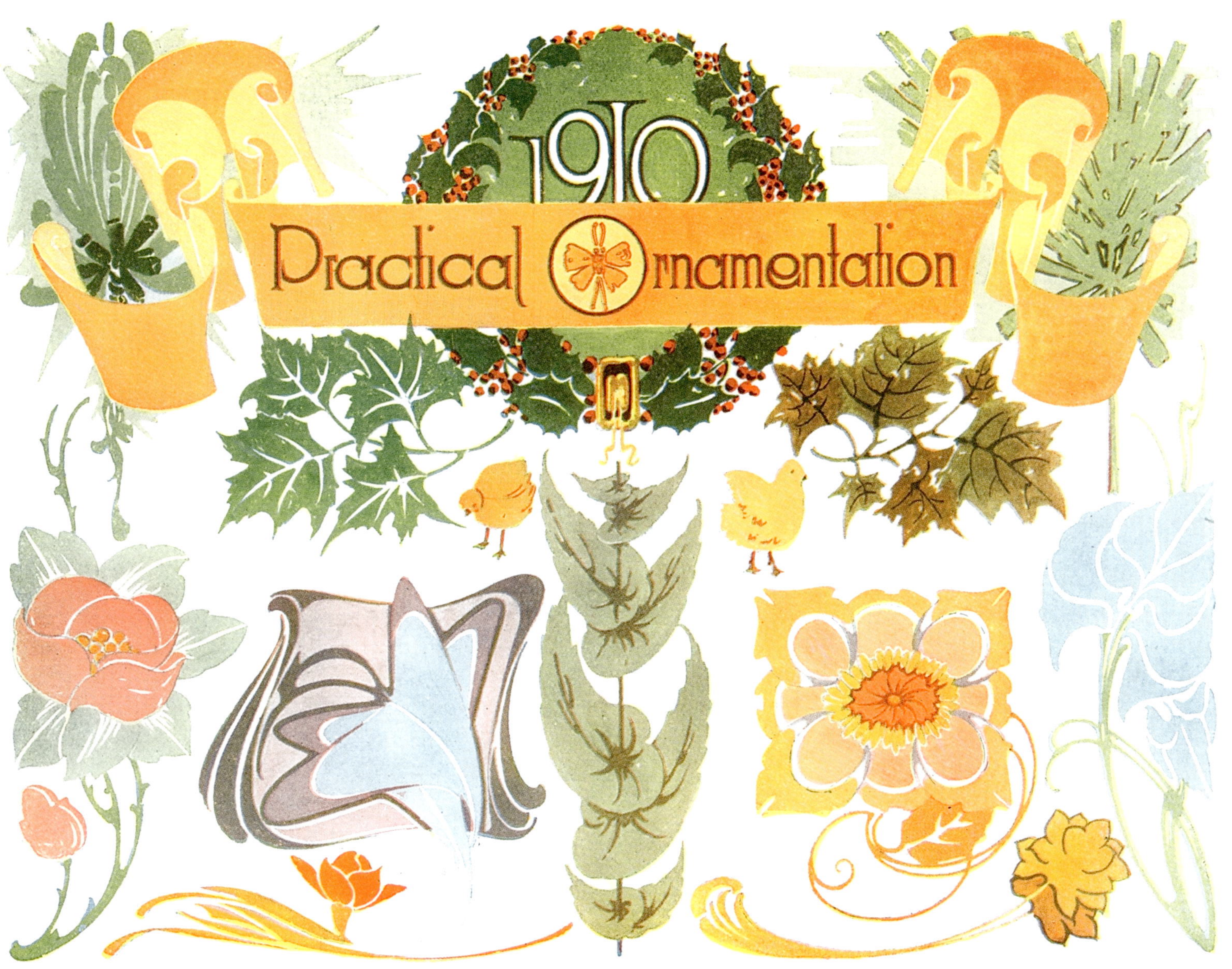
1910
Practical Ornamentation

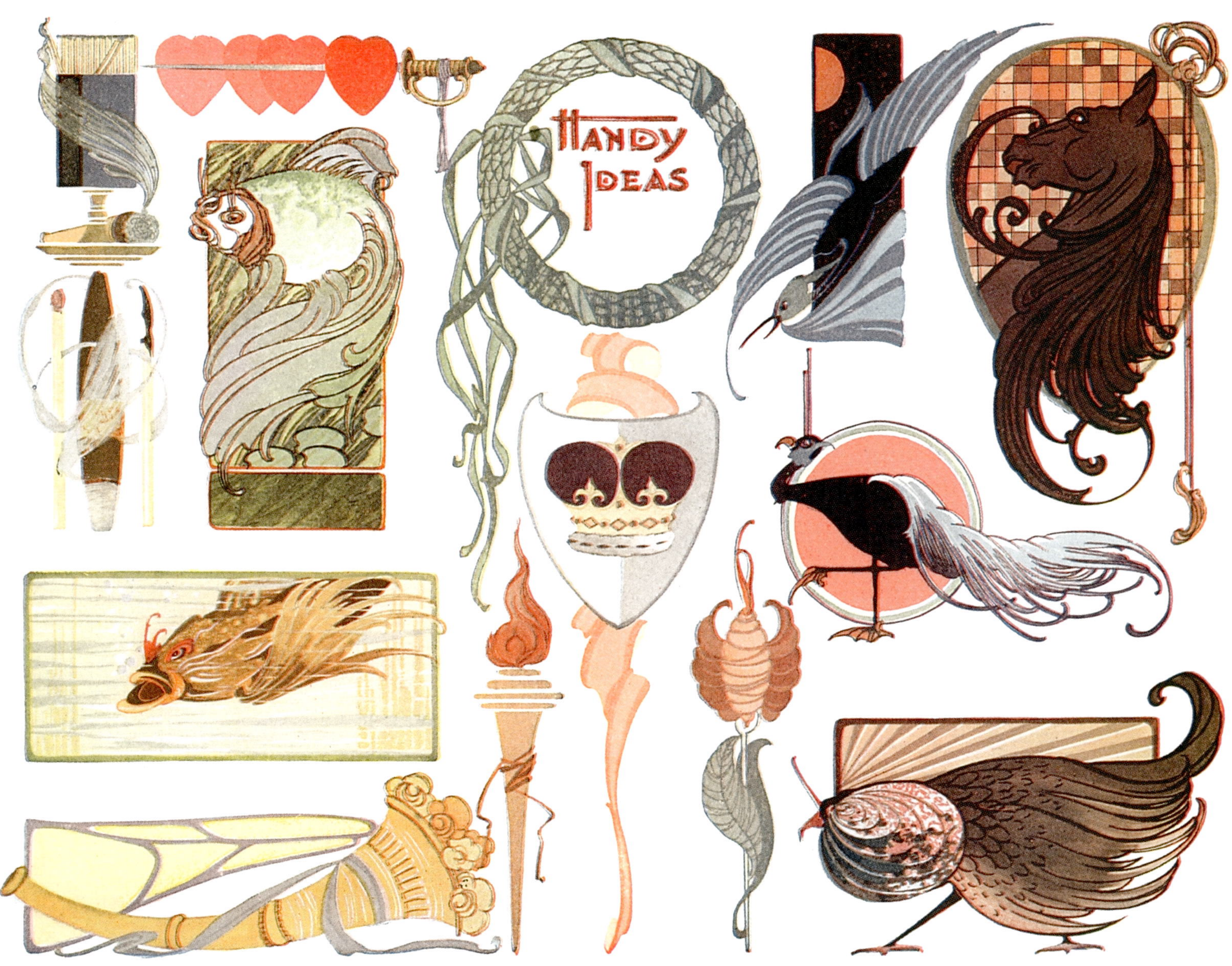
HANDY IDEAS

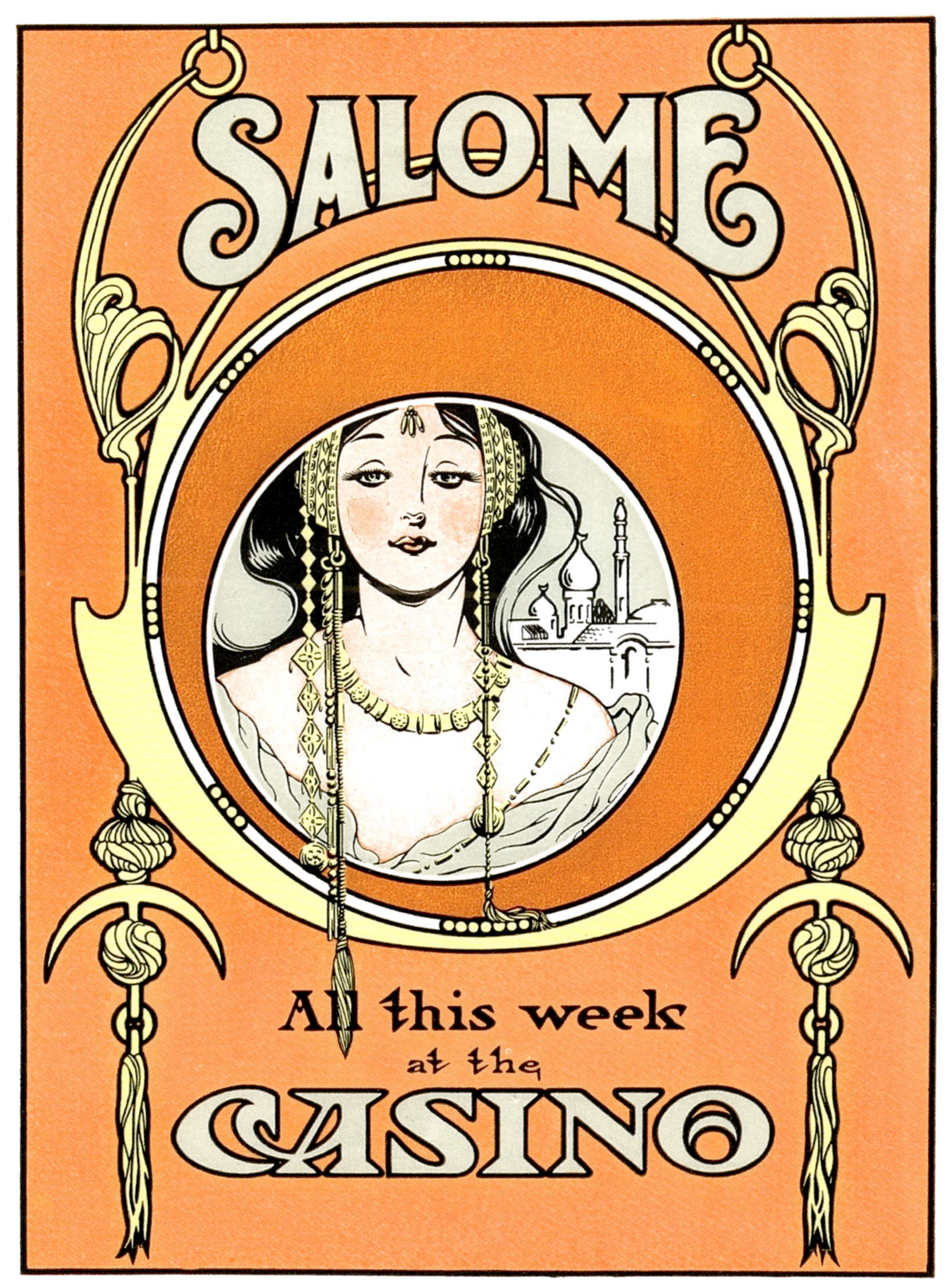
SALOME
All this week
at the
CASINO

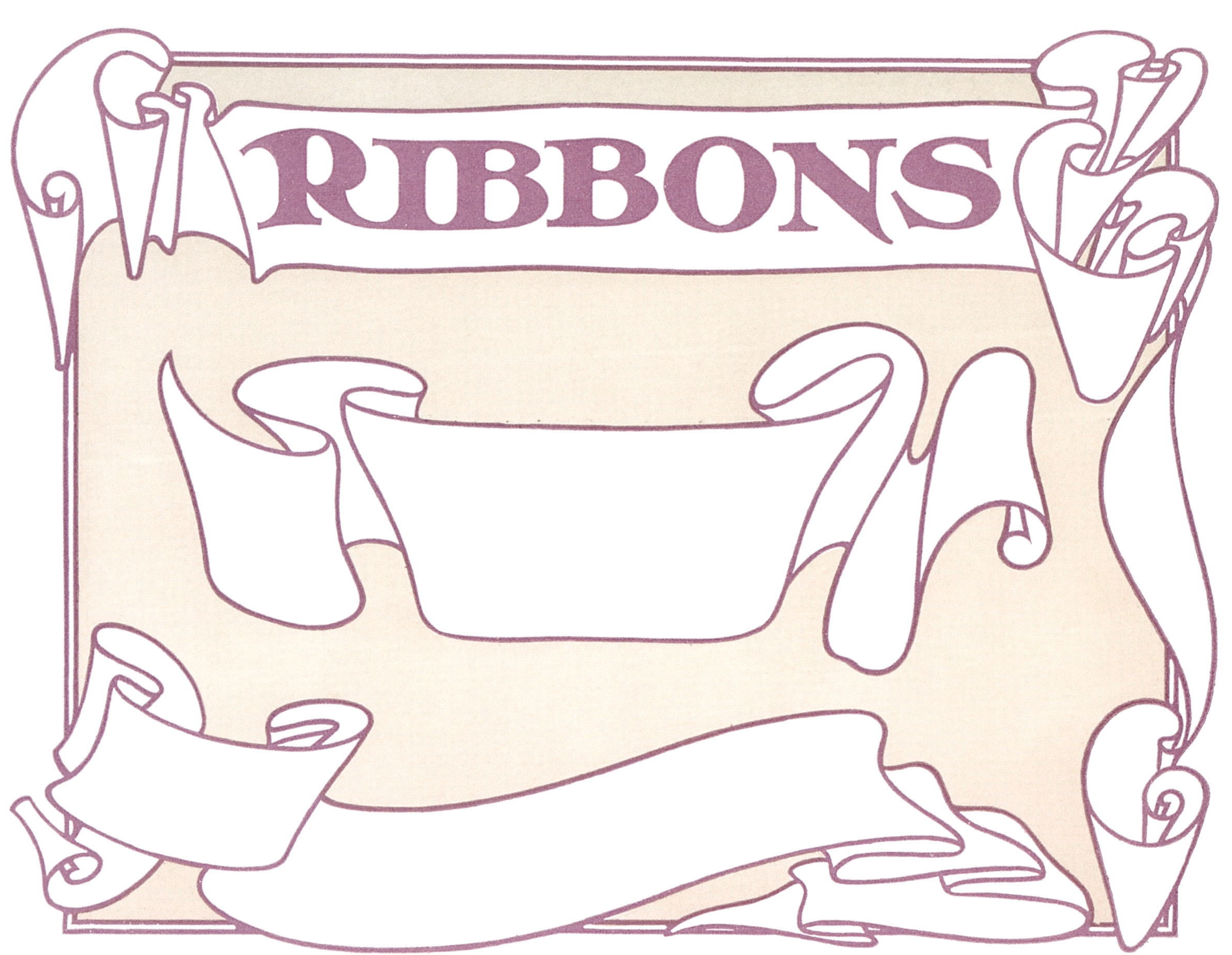
RIBBONS

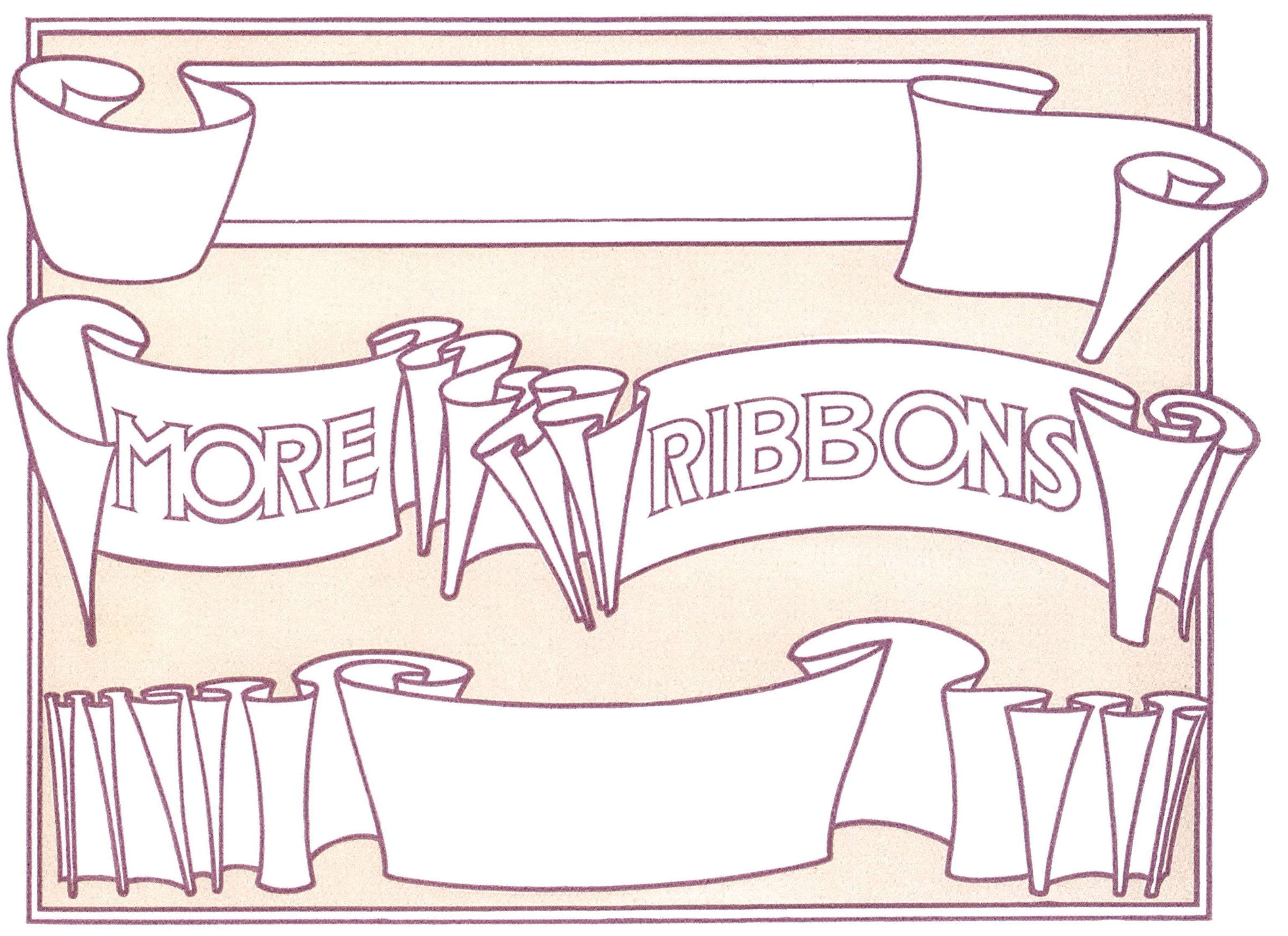
MORE
RIBBONS

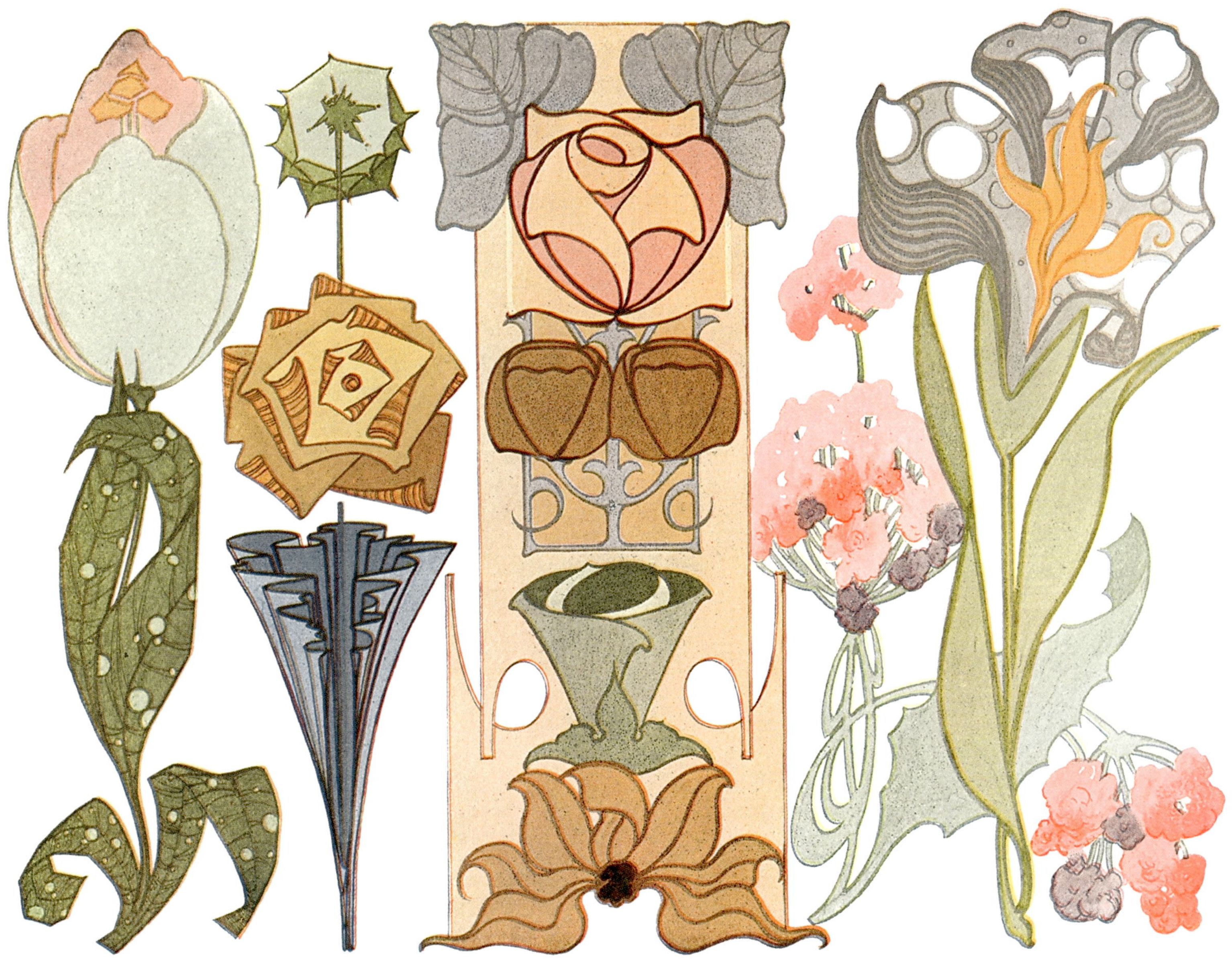

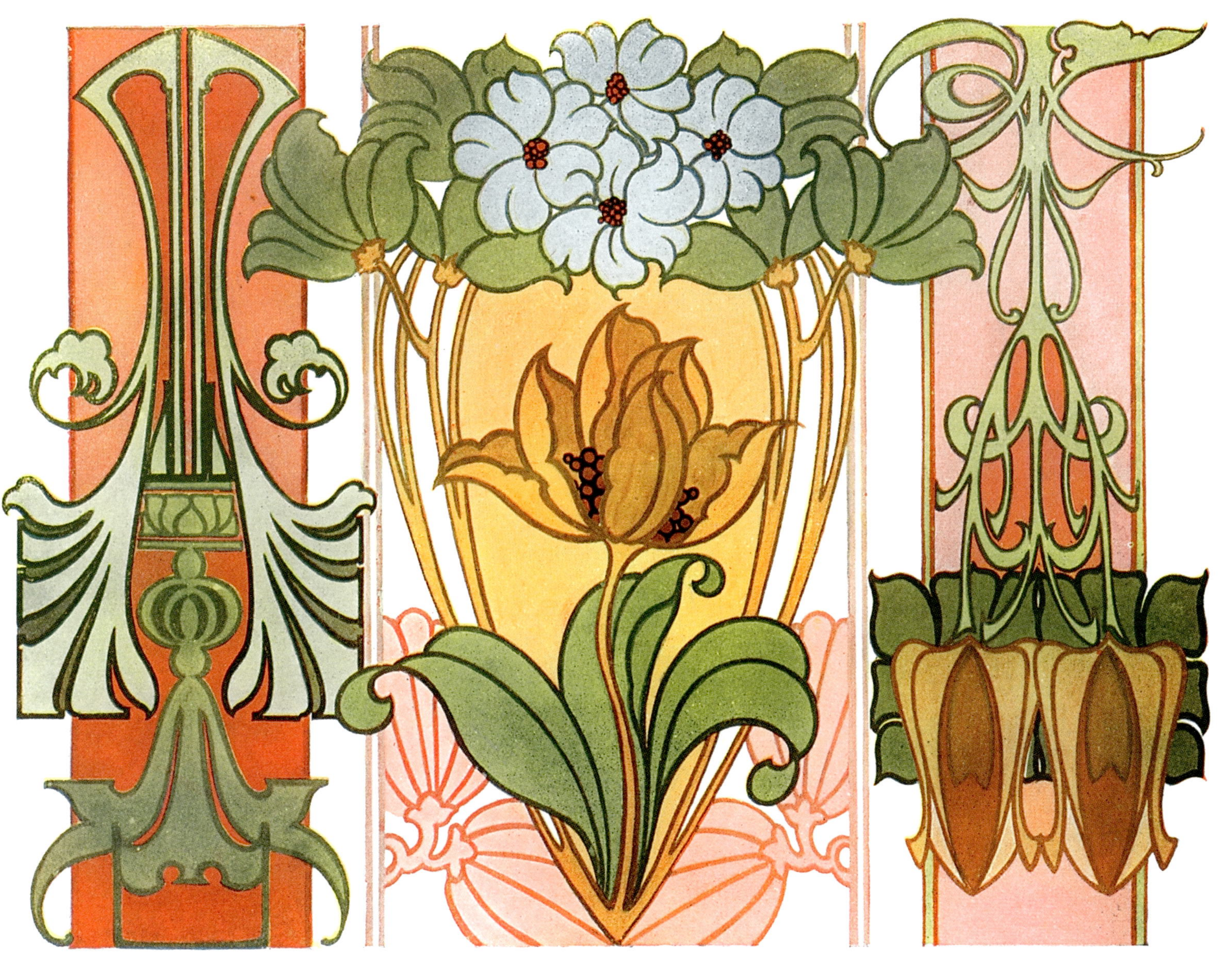

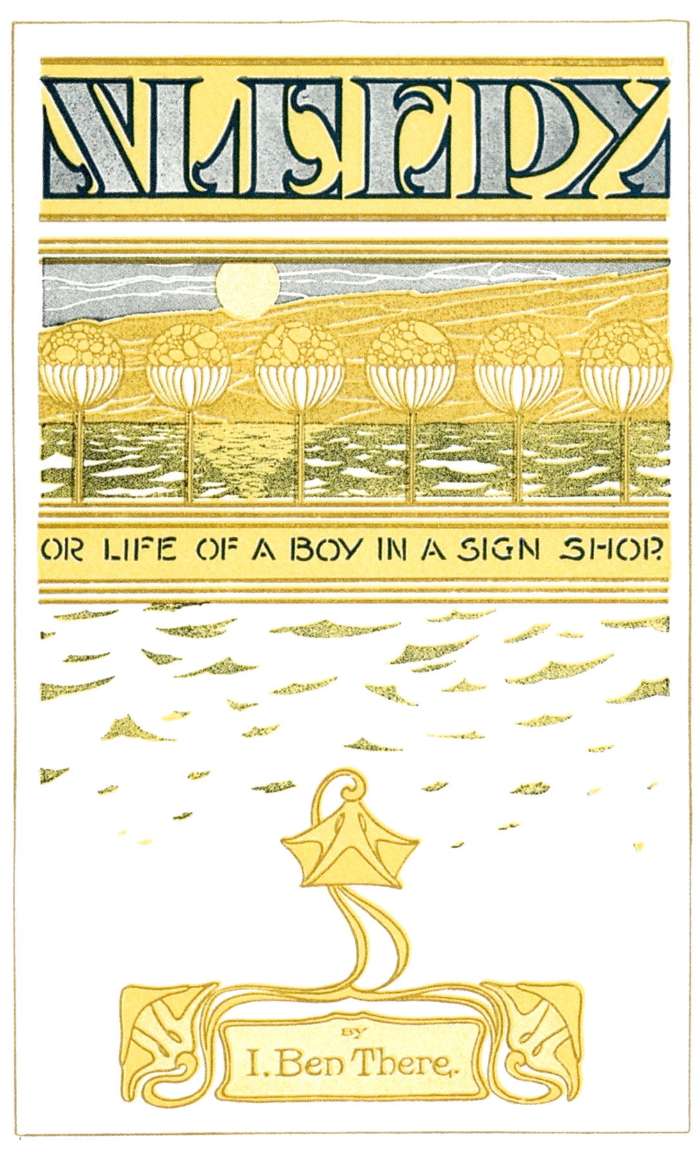
SLEEPY
OR LIFE OF A BOY IN A SIGN SHOP
BY
I. Ben There.

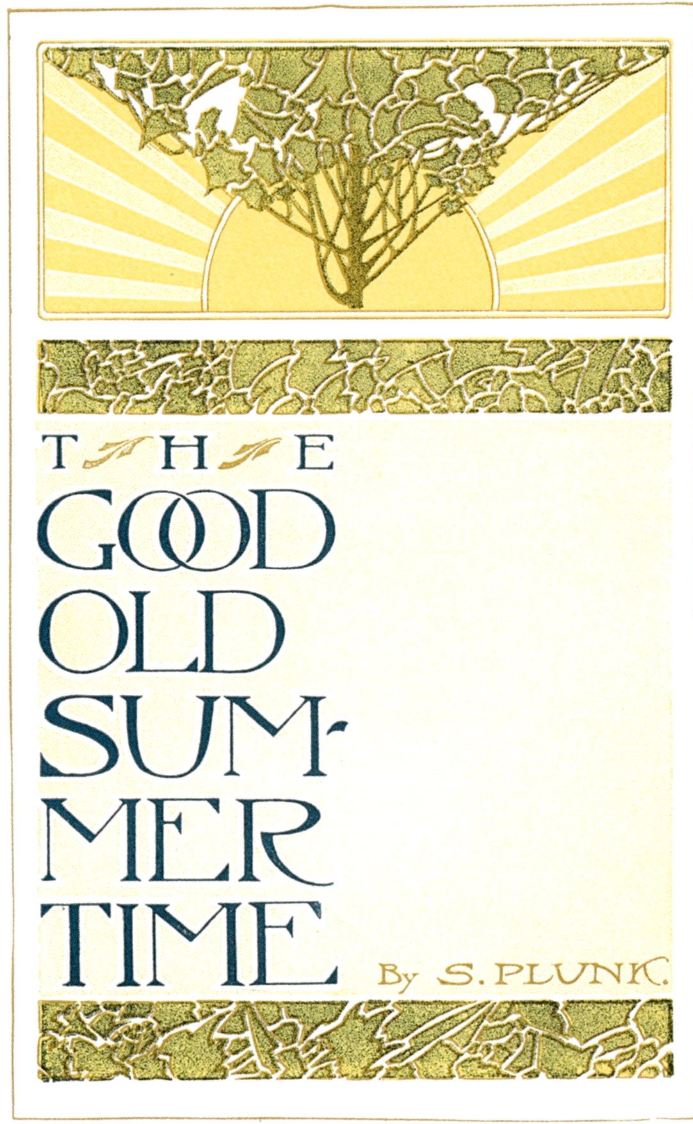
THE
GOOD
OLD
SUM-
MER
TIME
By S. PLUNK.

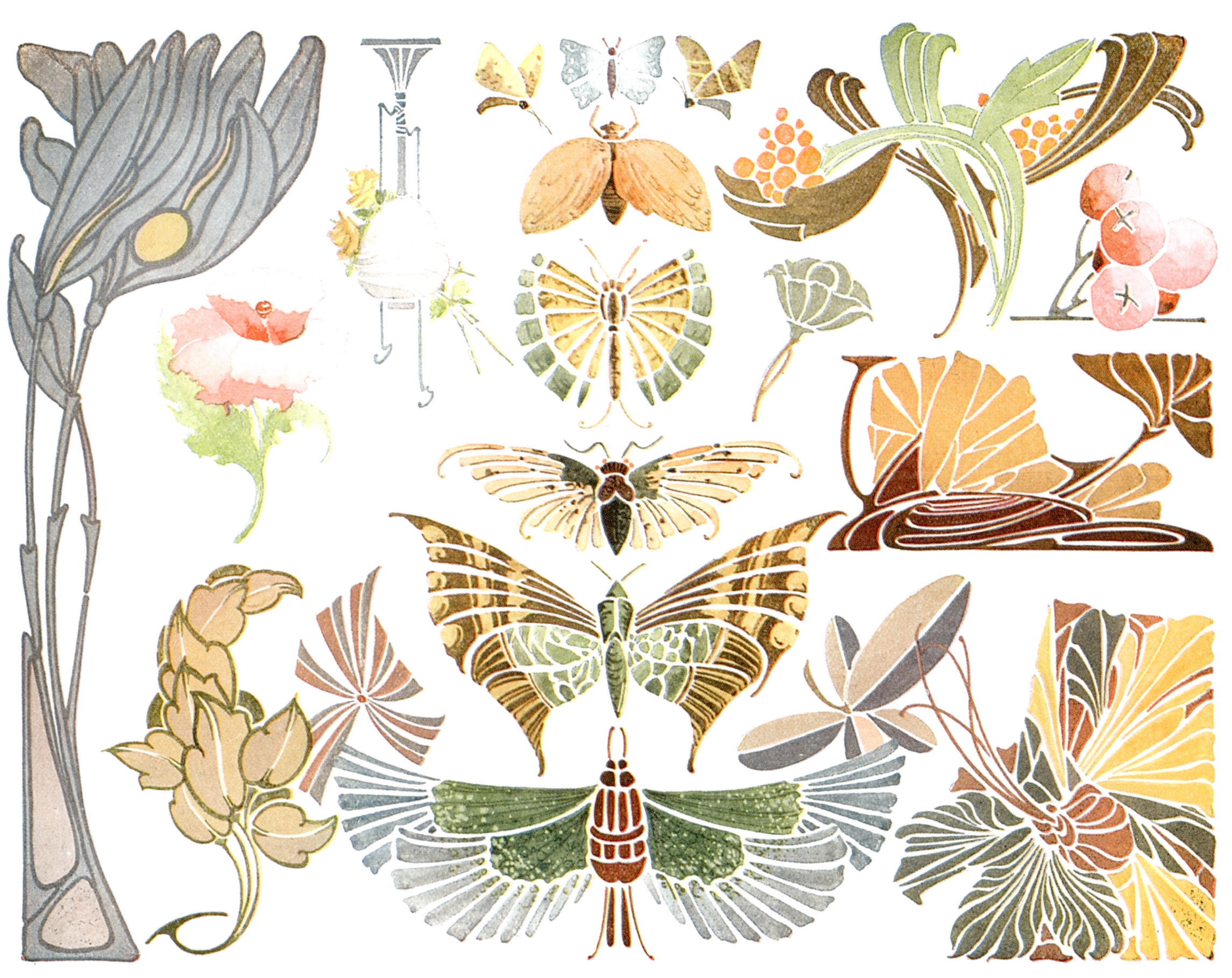

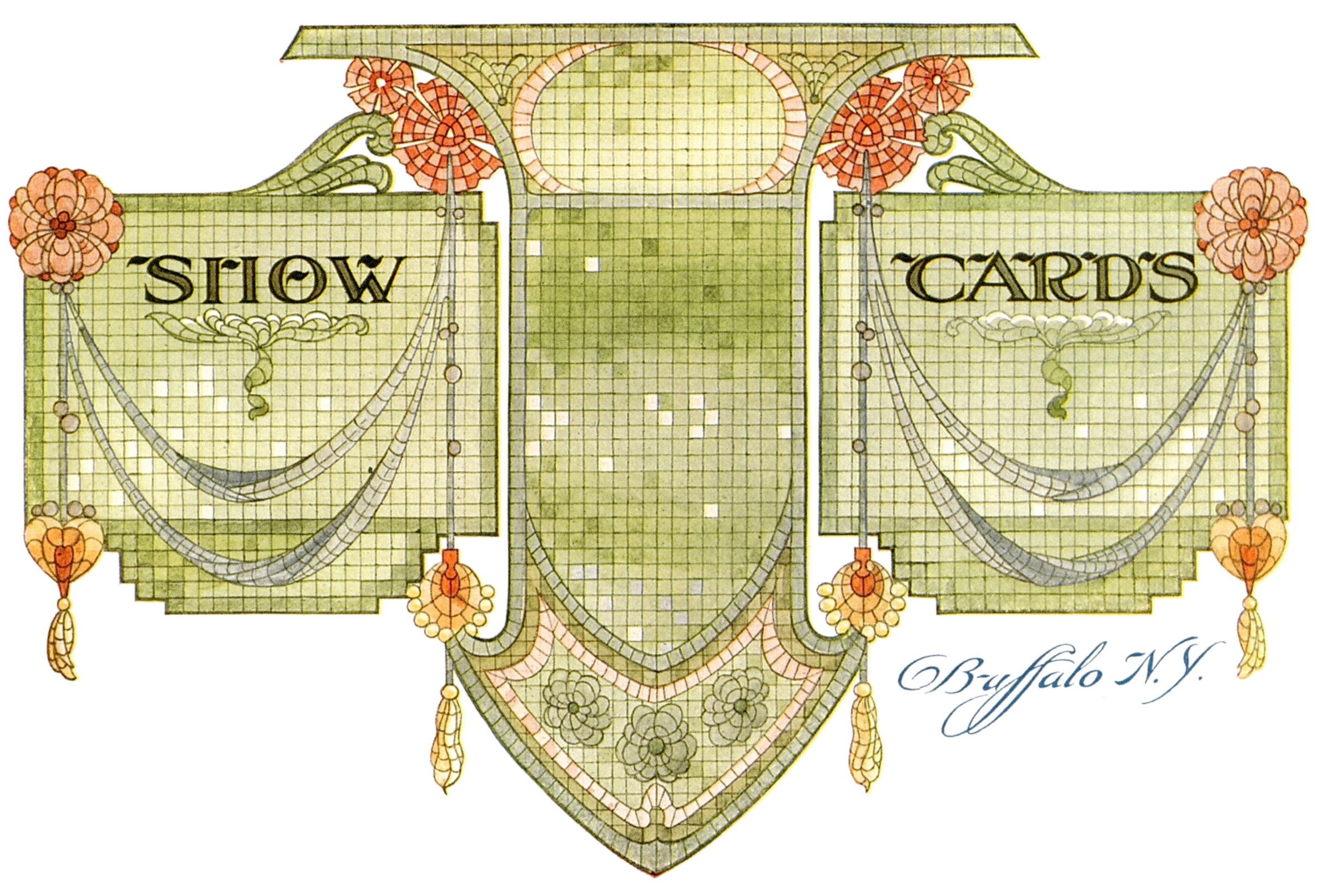
SHOW
CARDS
Buffalo N.Y.

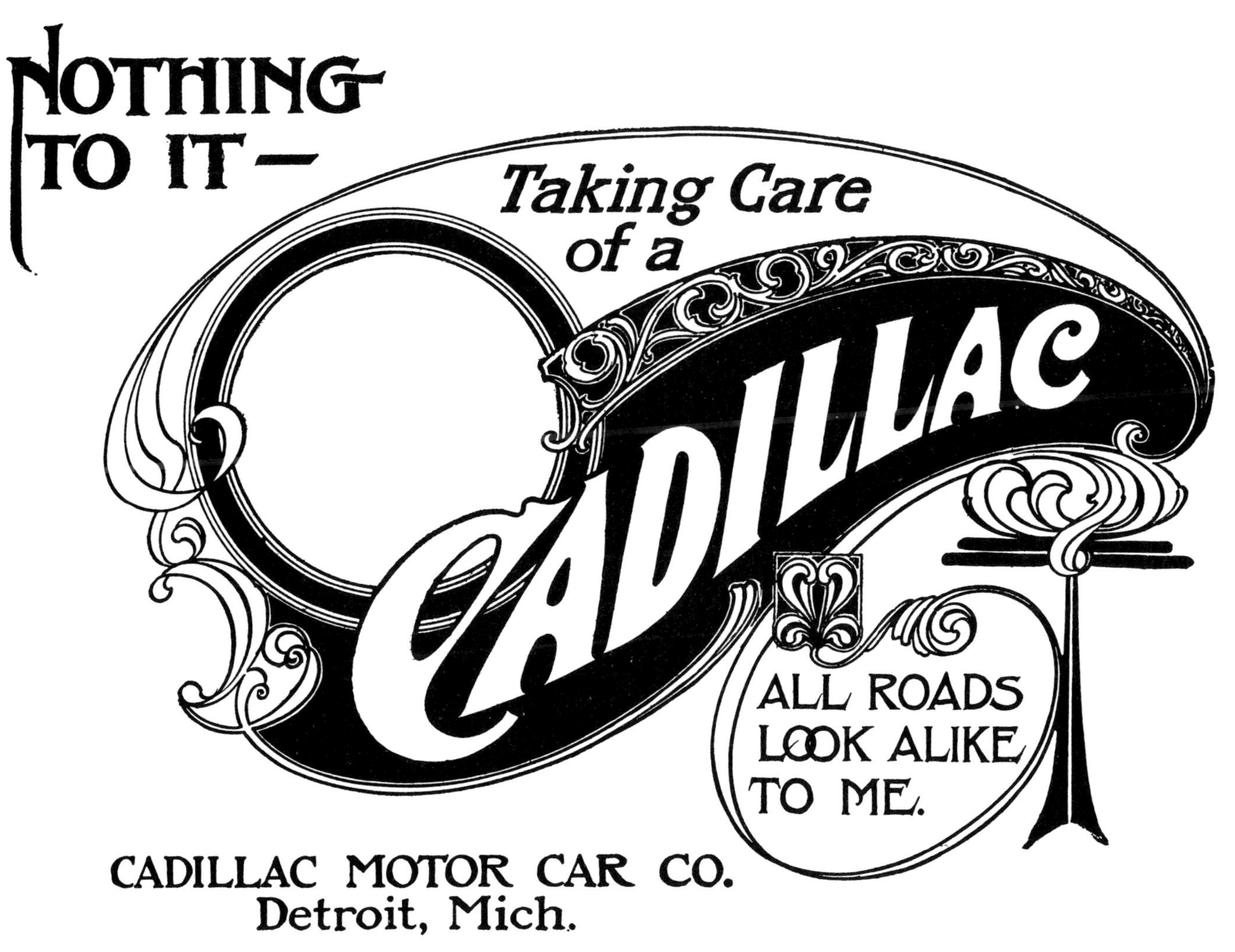
NOTHING
TO IT—
Taking Care
of a
CADILLAC
ALL ROADS
LOOK ALIKE
TO ME.
CADILLAC MOTOR CAR CO.
Detroit, Mich.

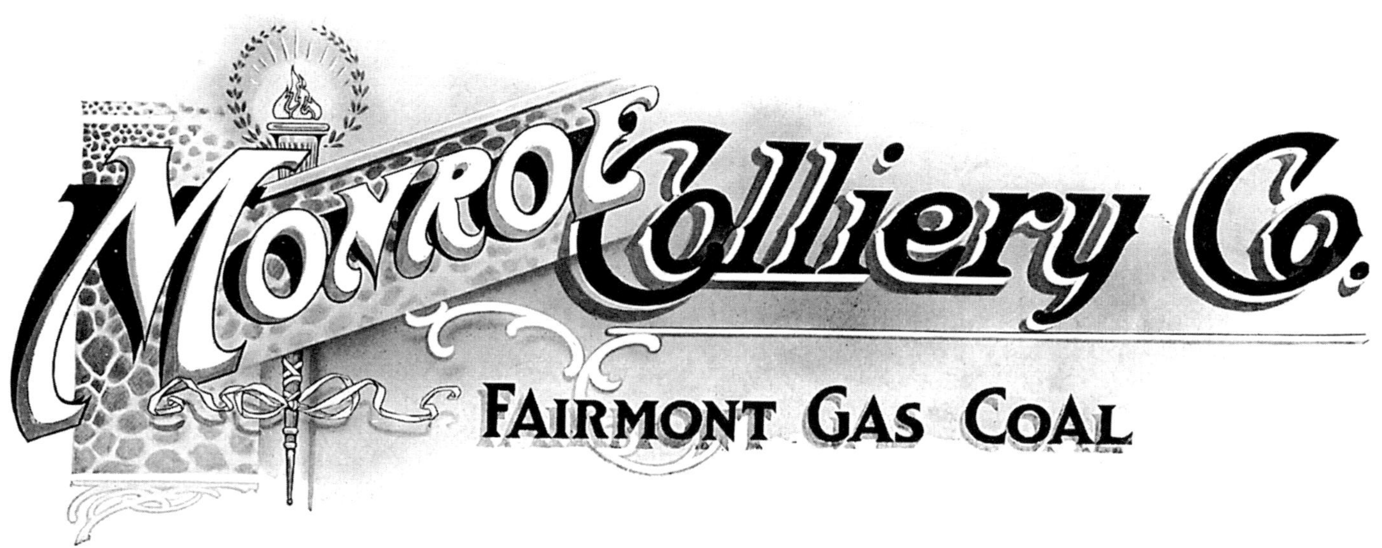
Monroe Colliery Co.
FAIRMONT GAS COAL

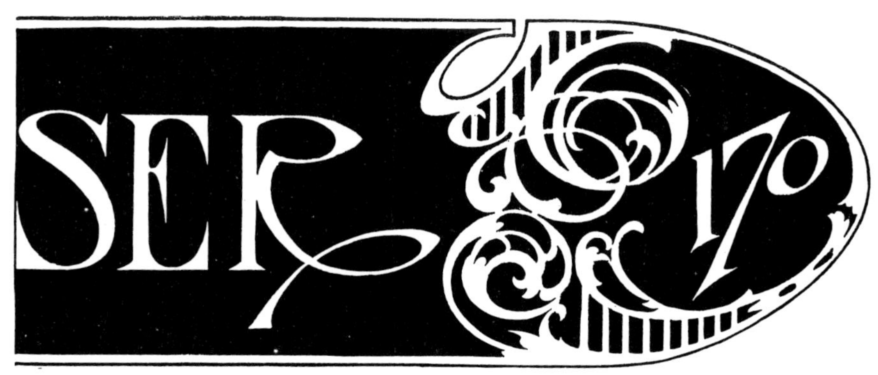
SEP 17

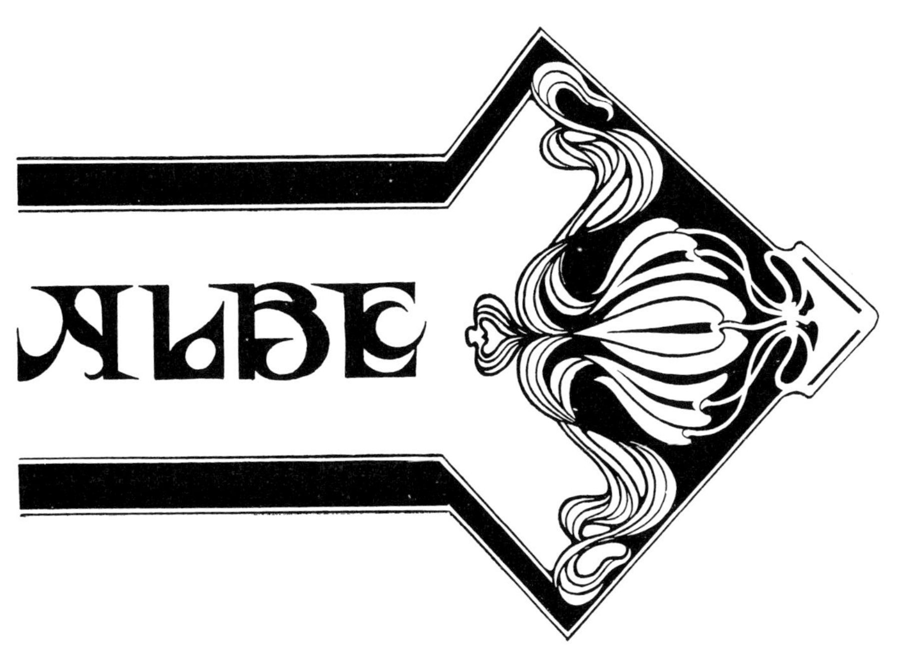

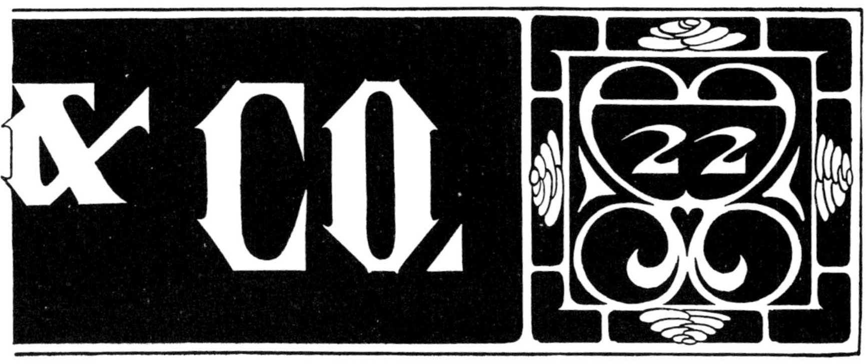
& CO.
22

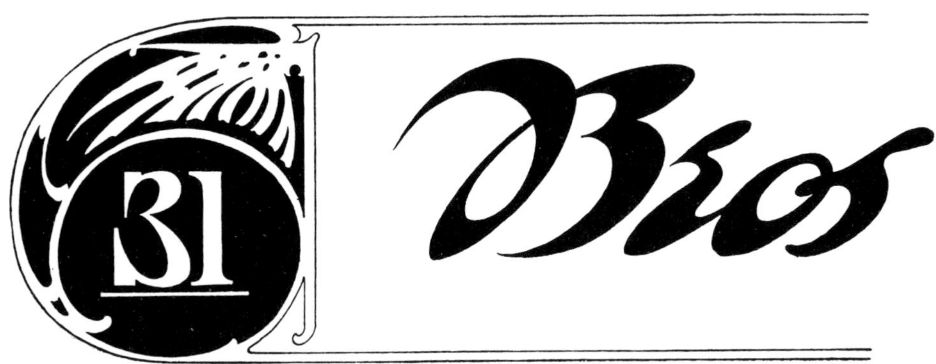
Bros

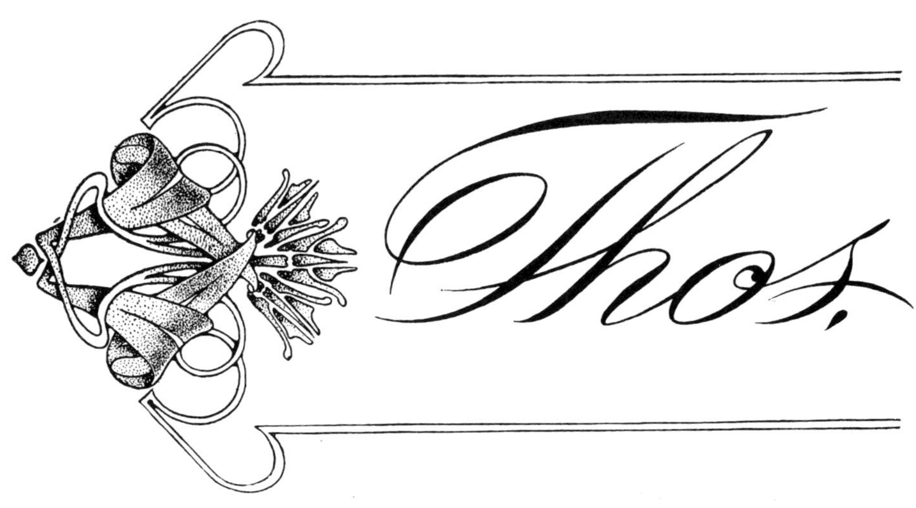
Thos.

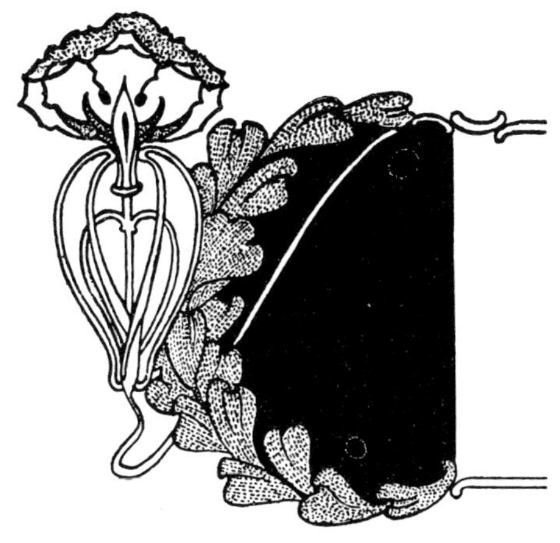

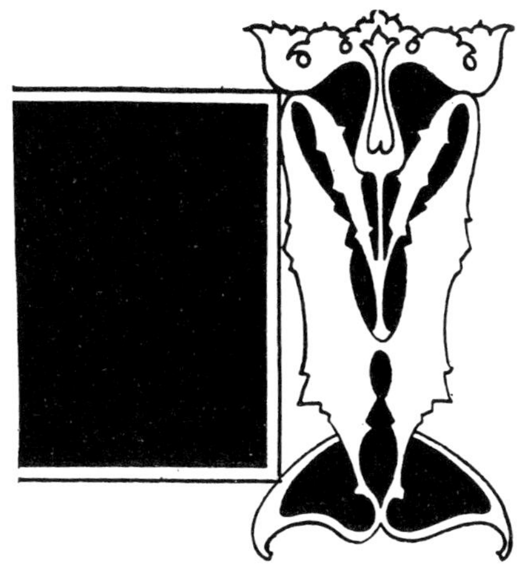

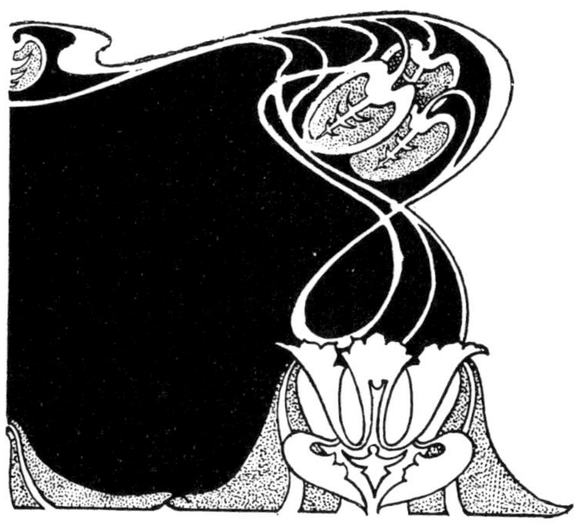

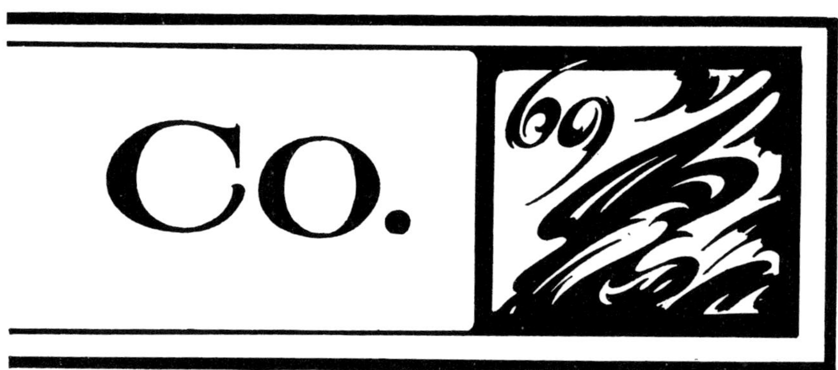
Co.

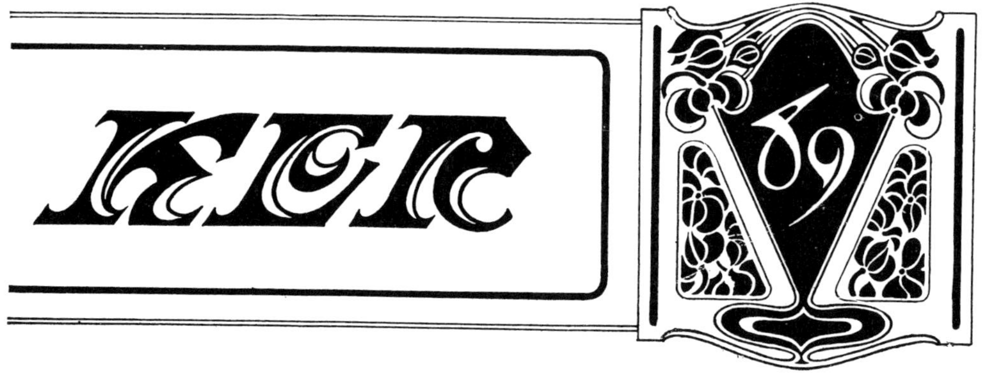

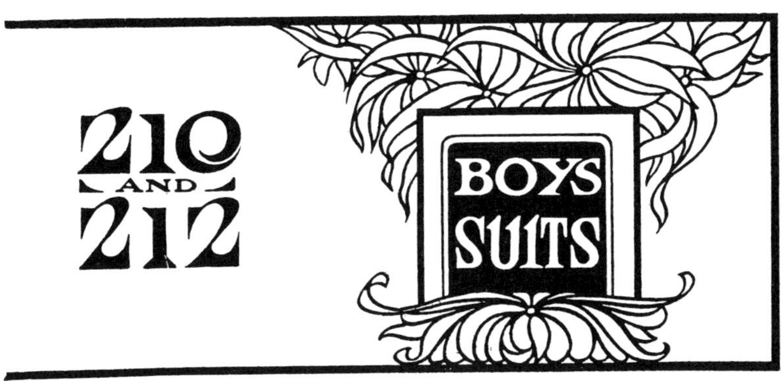
210
AND
212
BOYS
SUITS

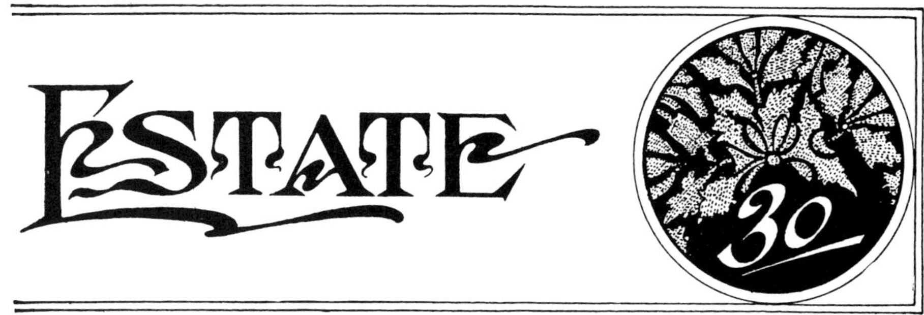
ESTATE
30

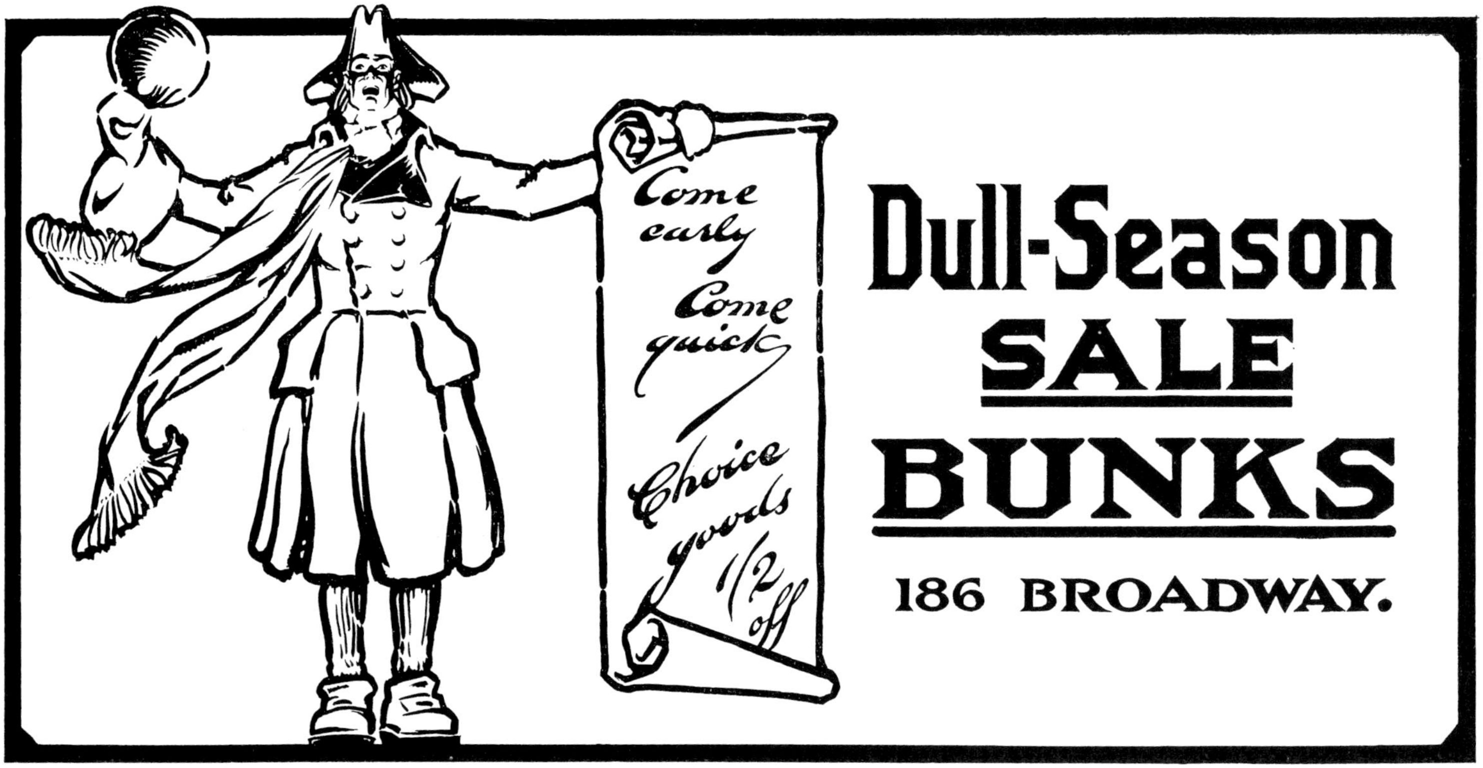

Come early

Come quick

Choice goods 1/2 off

Dull-Season
SALE
BUNKS

186 BROADWAY.

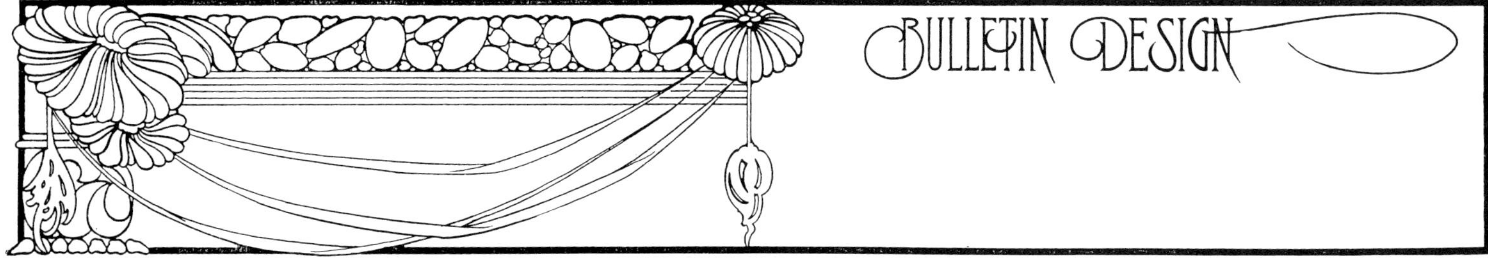

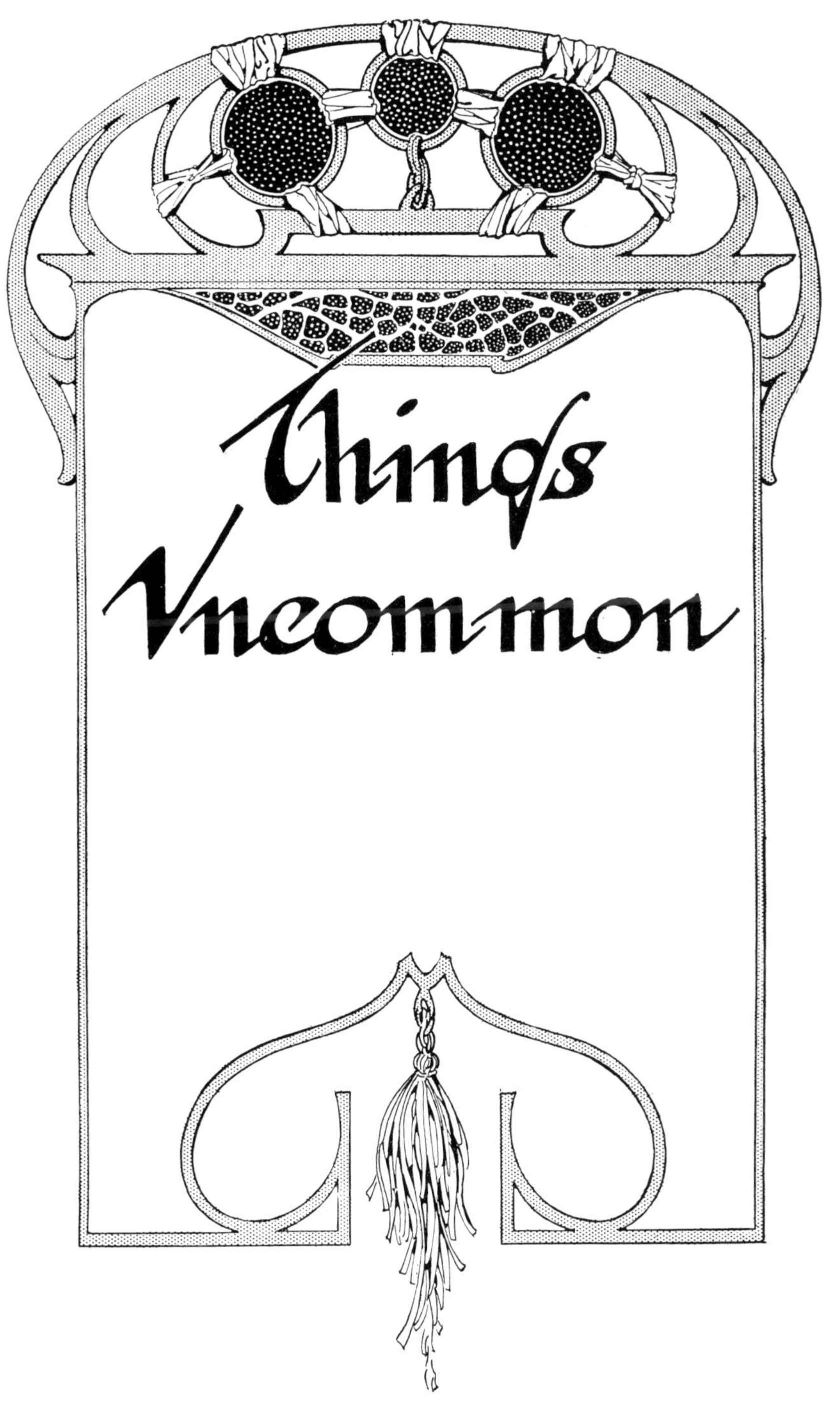
Things
Uncommon

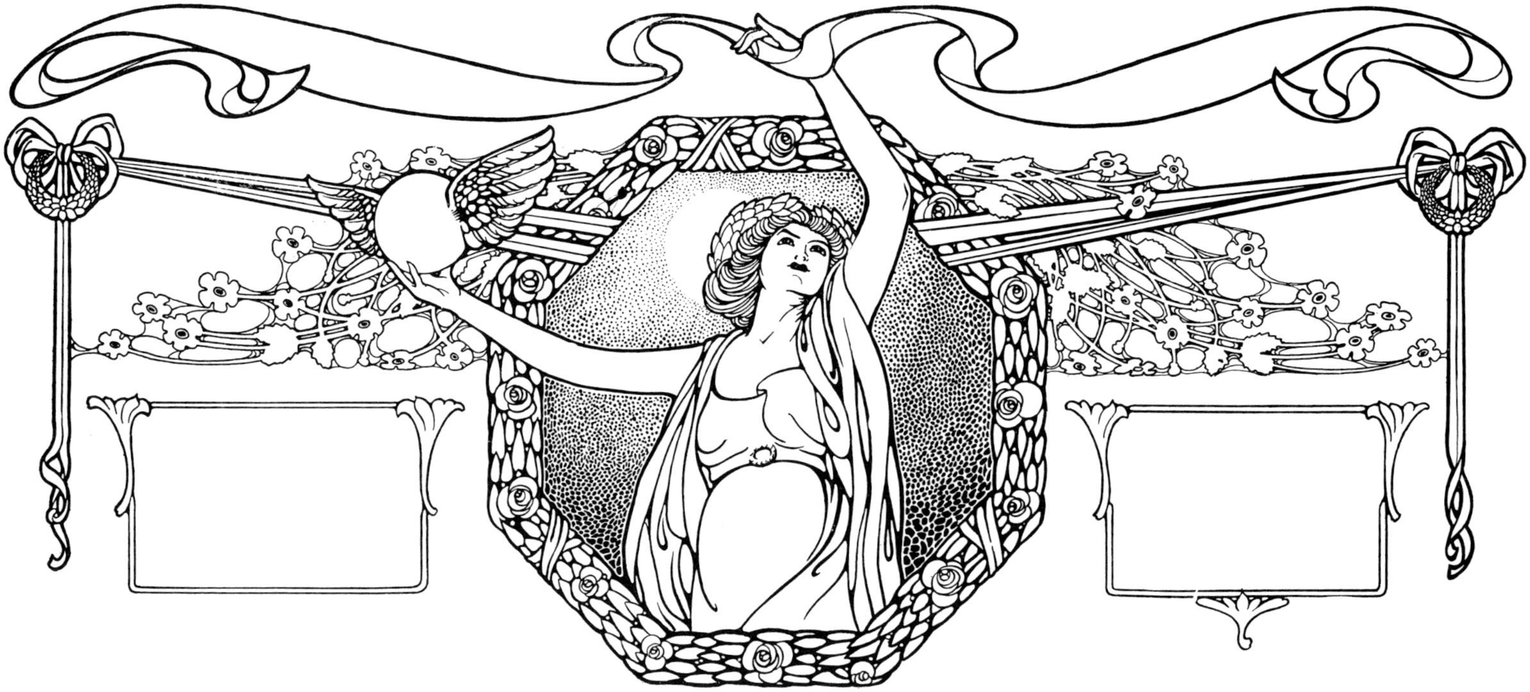

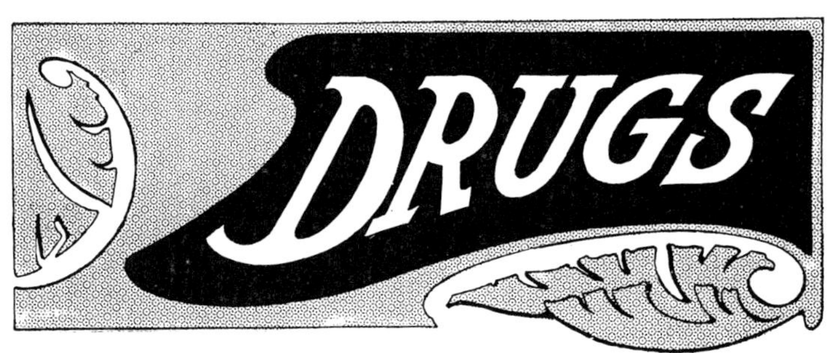
DRUGS

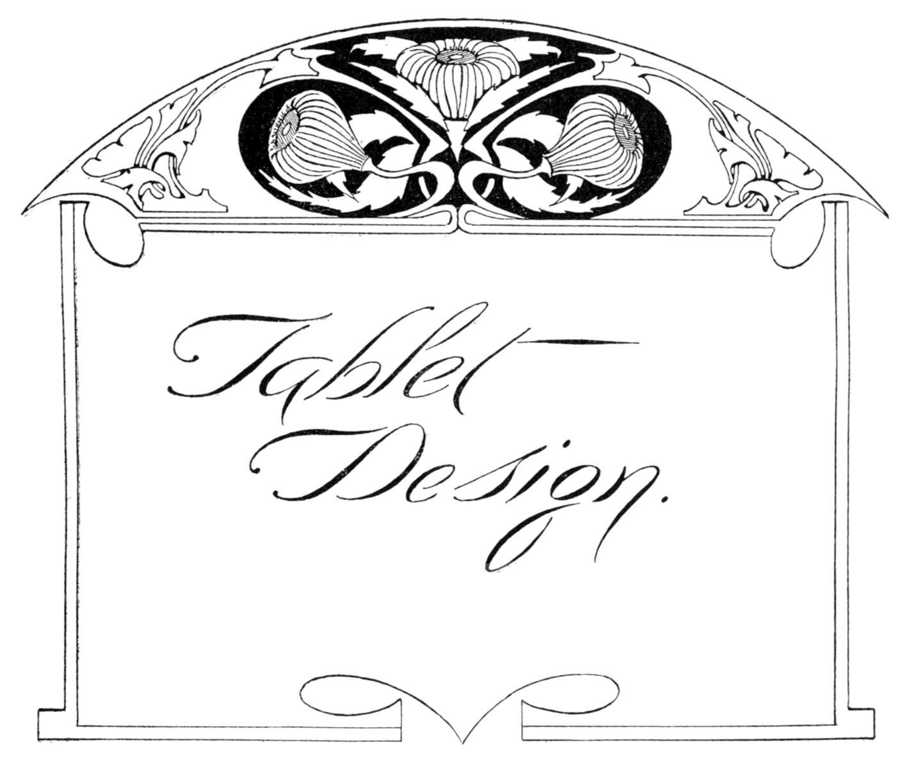
Tablet Design.

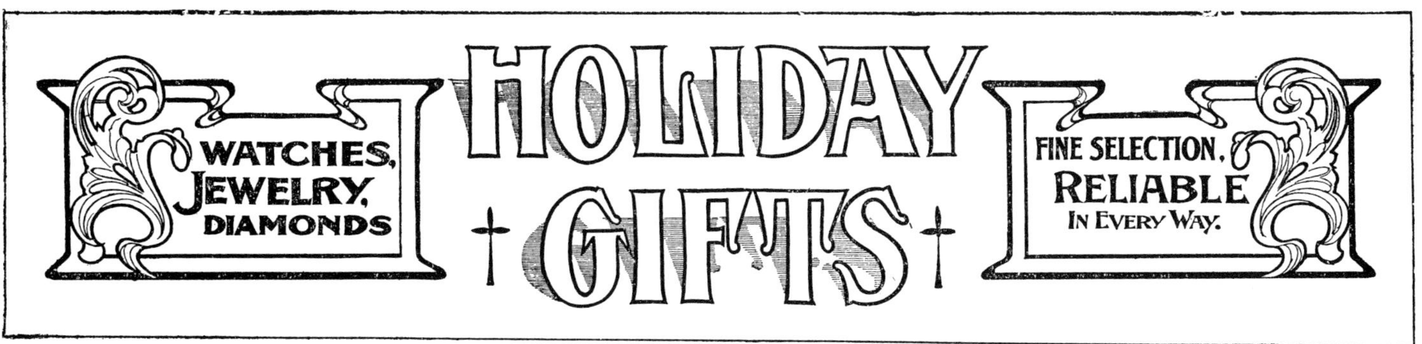
WATCHES,
JEWELRY,
DIAMONDS
HOLIDAY
GIFTS
FINE SELECTION,
RELIABLE
IN EVERY WAY.

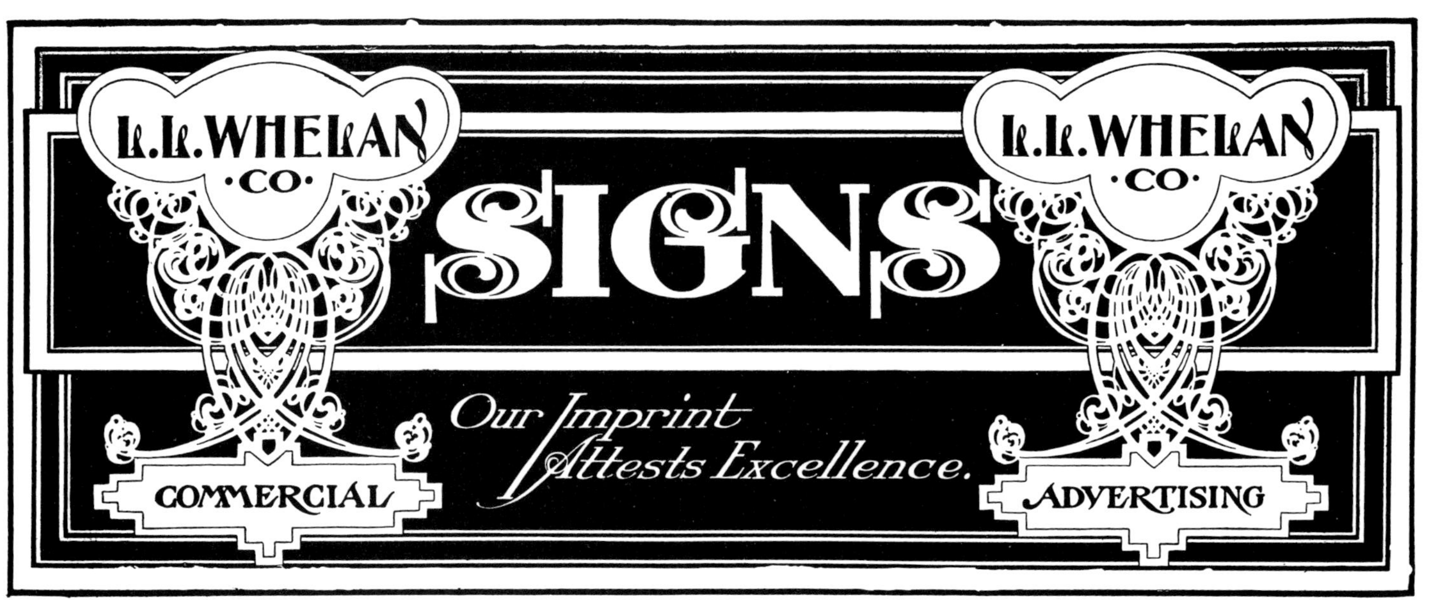
L.L. WHELAN
·CO·
SIGNS
L.L. WHELAN
·CO·
Our Imprint
Attests Excellence.
COMMERCIAL
ADVERTISING

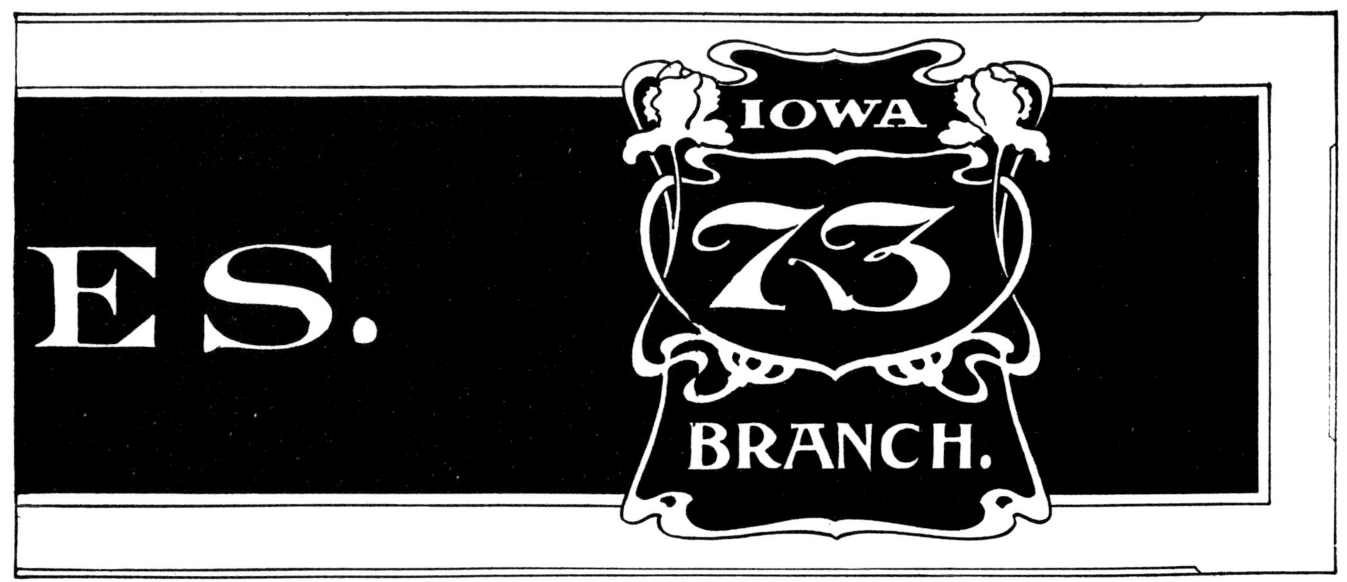
ES.
IOWA
73
BRANCH.

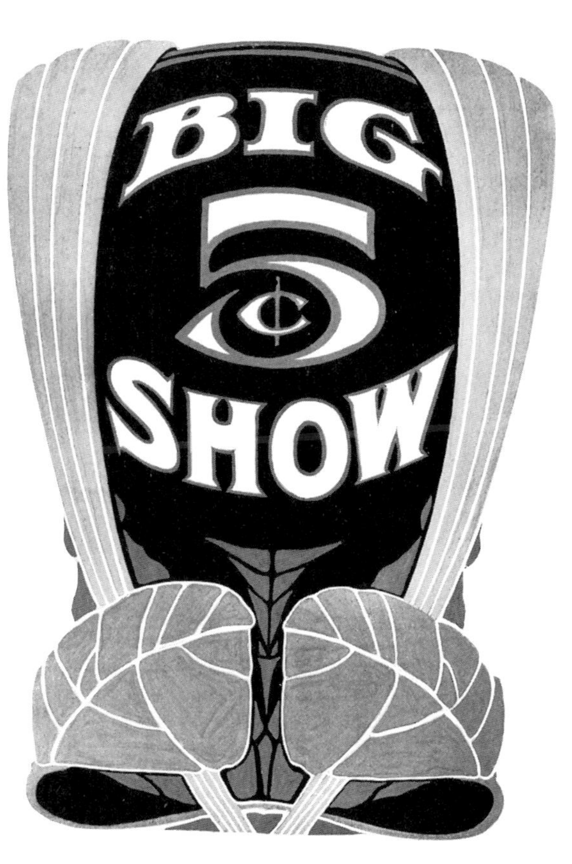
BIG
5
¢
SHOW

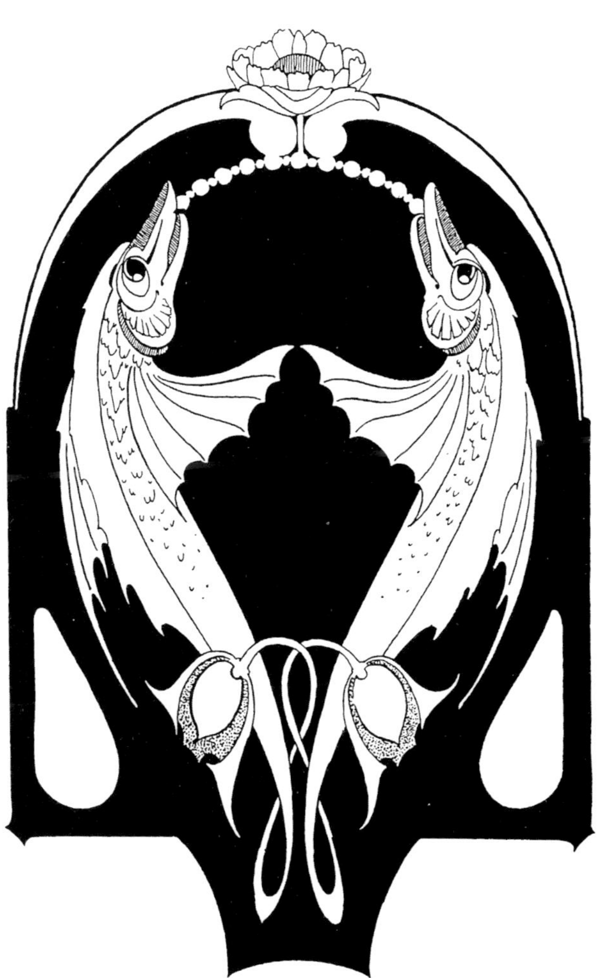

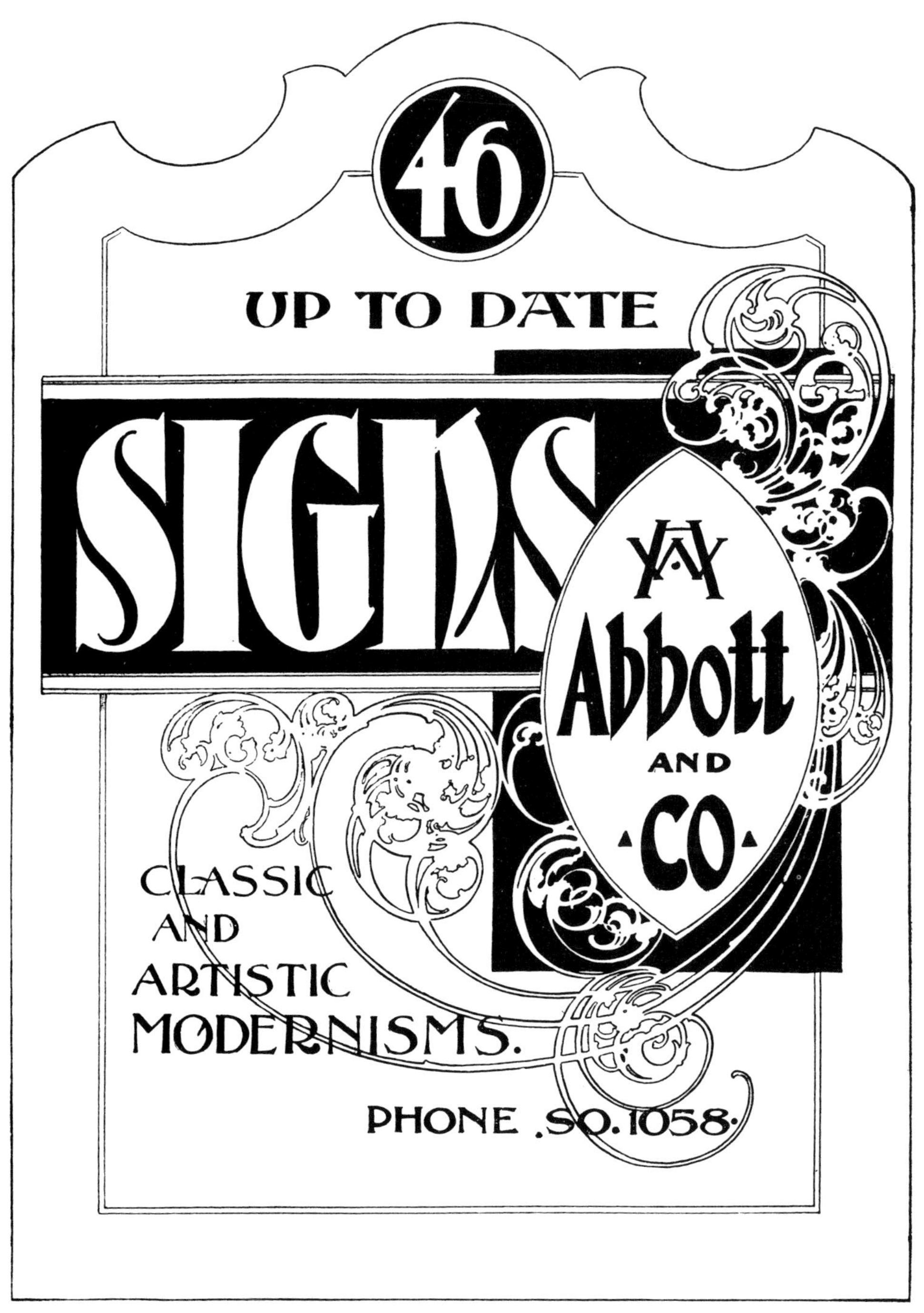
46
UP TO DATE
SIGNS
Abbott
AND
CO
CLASSIC
AND
ARTISTIC
MODERNISMS.
PHONE .SO.1058.

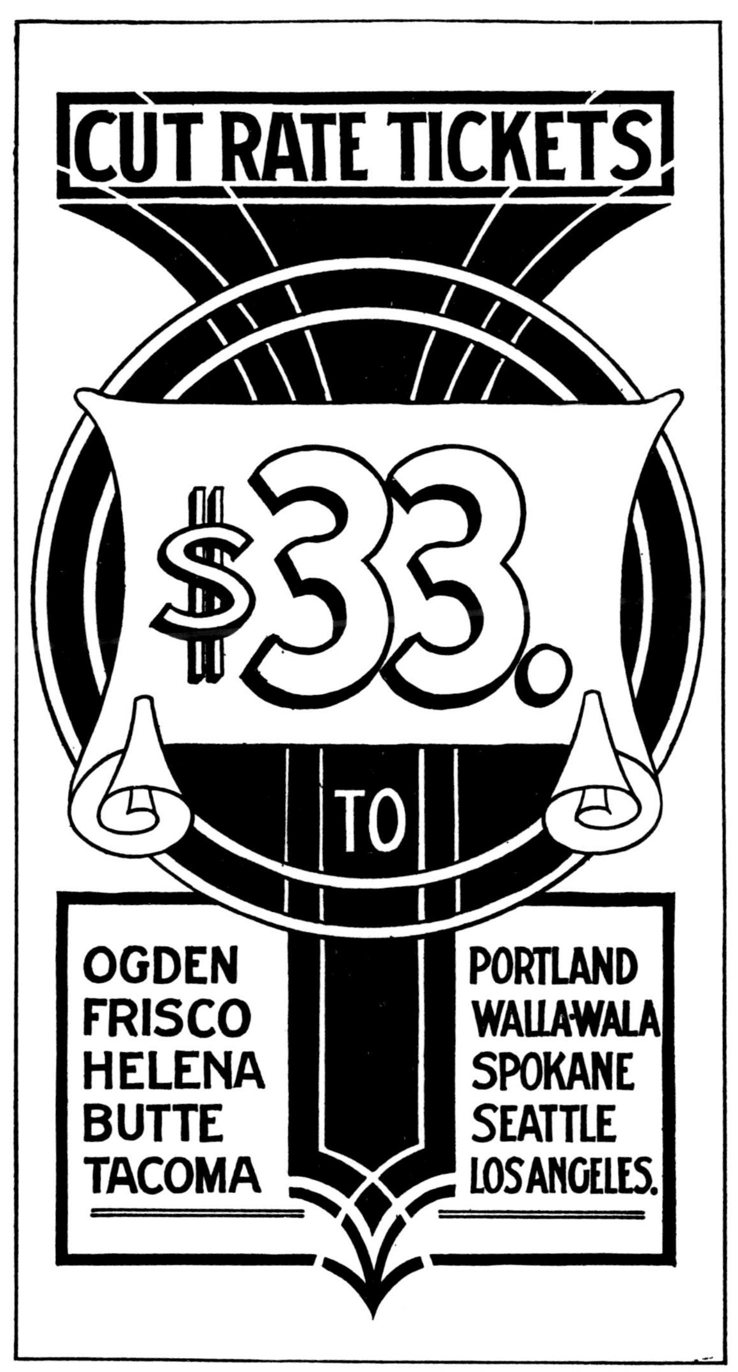
CUT RATE TICKETS
$33.
TO
OGDEN
FRISCO
HELENA
BUTTE
TACOMA
PORTLAND
WALLA-WALA
SPOKANE
SEATTLE
LOS ANGELES.

Eccentric French

ABCCDEFFGJHIKLM
NQPRSTUVWXYZ&
acbdefghijkmnoprstuvwxyz
ESSE SS &&& L EE L
SE E E L L E NAMES

Heavy Sign Script

ABCDEFGHIJKLMNOQ
PRSUVWXYZ

Show Card French

ABCDEFGHIJKLMN
OPQRSTUVWXY
Z&
abcdefghijklmnopqr
aadf xystuvwz g s w
1 3245678 9 3

After

You have used

Sanitol

Your teeth will
gleam like Ivory
and your breath
will have the
delicate fragrance
of the rose.

The Sanitol Co.

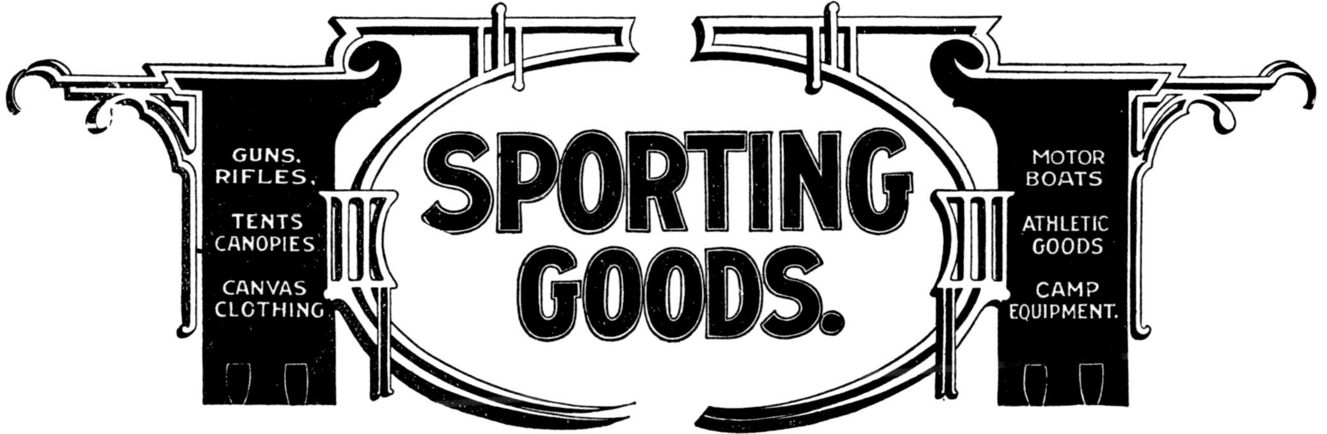
THE EBNER CO.
GUNS. RIFLES.
TENTS CANOPIES
CANVAS CLOTHING
SPORTING GOODS.
MOTOR BOATS
ATHLETIC GOODS
CAMP EQUIPMENT.

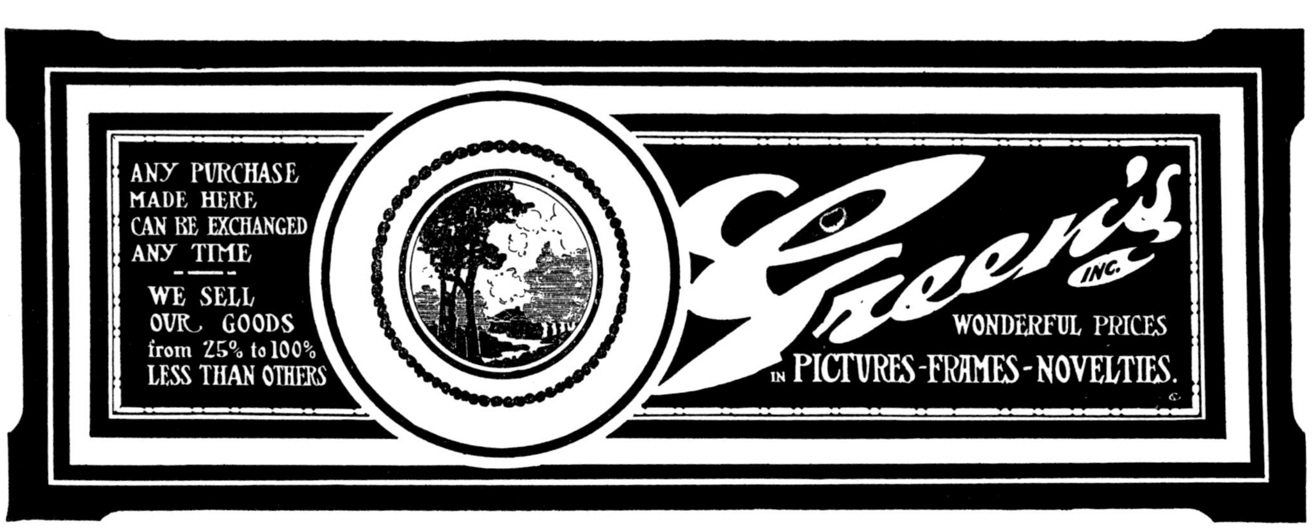
ANY PURCHASE MADE HERE CAN BE EXCHANGED ANY TIME
WE SELL OUR GOODS from 25% to 100% LESS THAN OTHERS
Green's INC.
WONDERFUL PRICES
IN PICTURES-FRAMES-NOVELTIES.

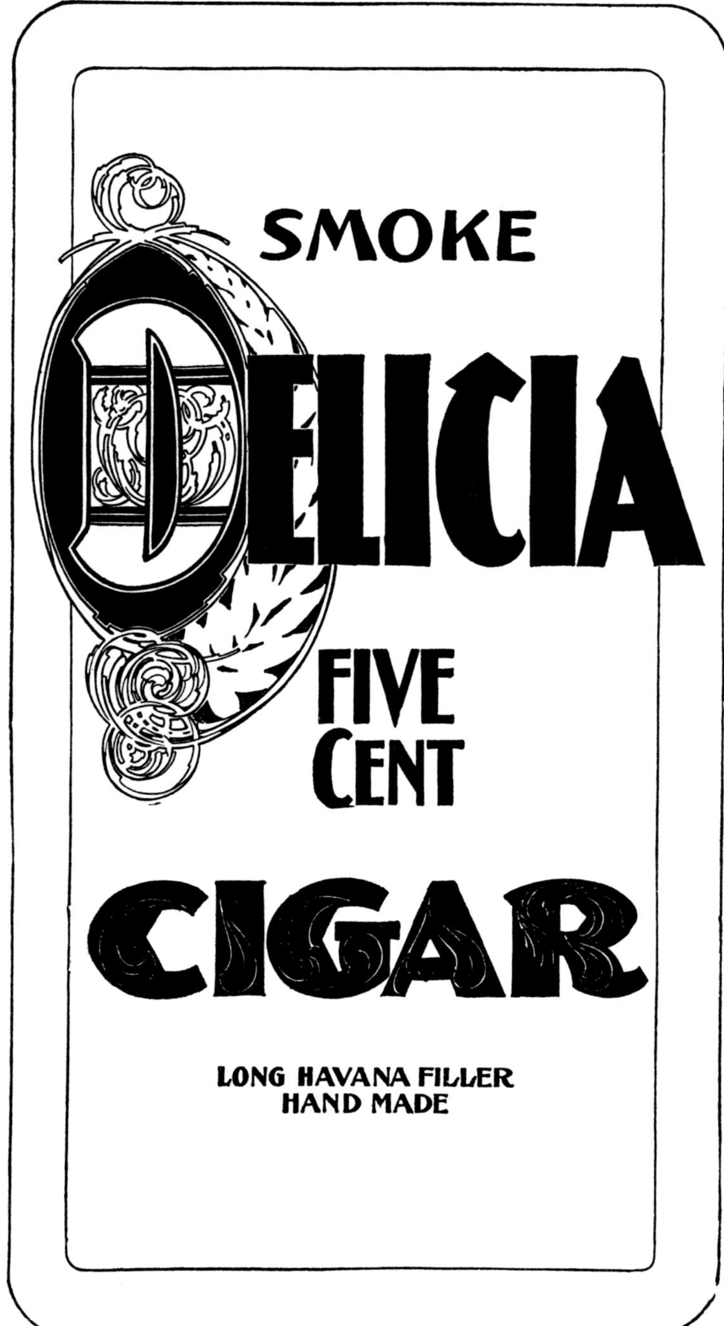
SMOKE
DELICIA
FIVE
CENT
CIGAR
LONG HAVANA FILLER
HAND MADE

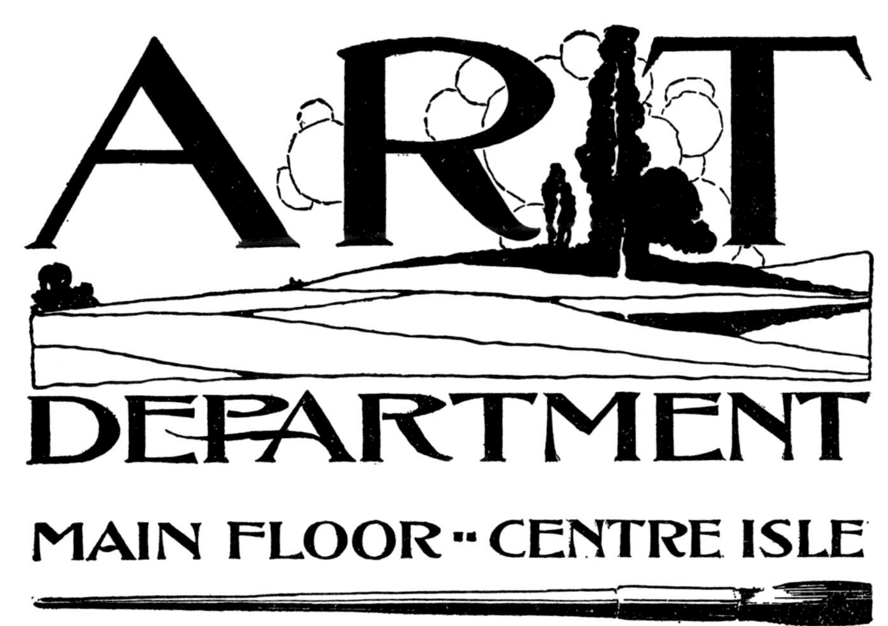
ART
DEPARTMENT
MAIN FLOOR — CENTRE ISLE

ABCDEFG
NOPQRST
12345678Z
efghijklmnopr

CHICAGO TUSCAN

HIJKLM
UVWXY
908&abcd
stuvwxyz

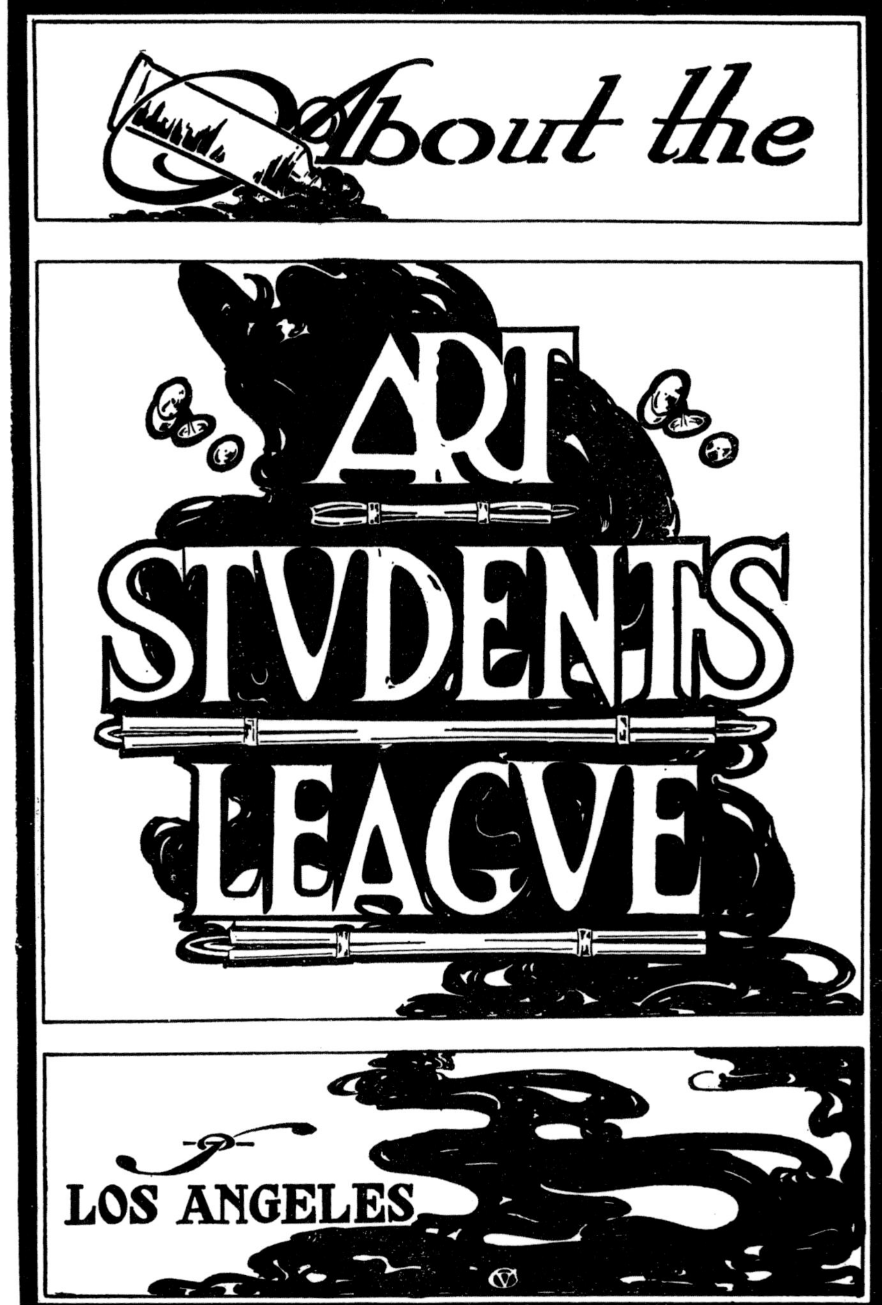
About the
ART
STVDENTS
LEAGVE
LOS ANGELES
MCMVI
VAL COSTELLO

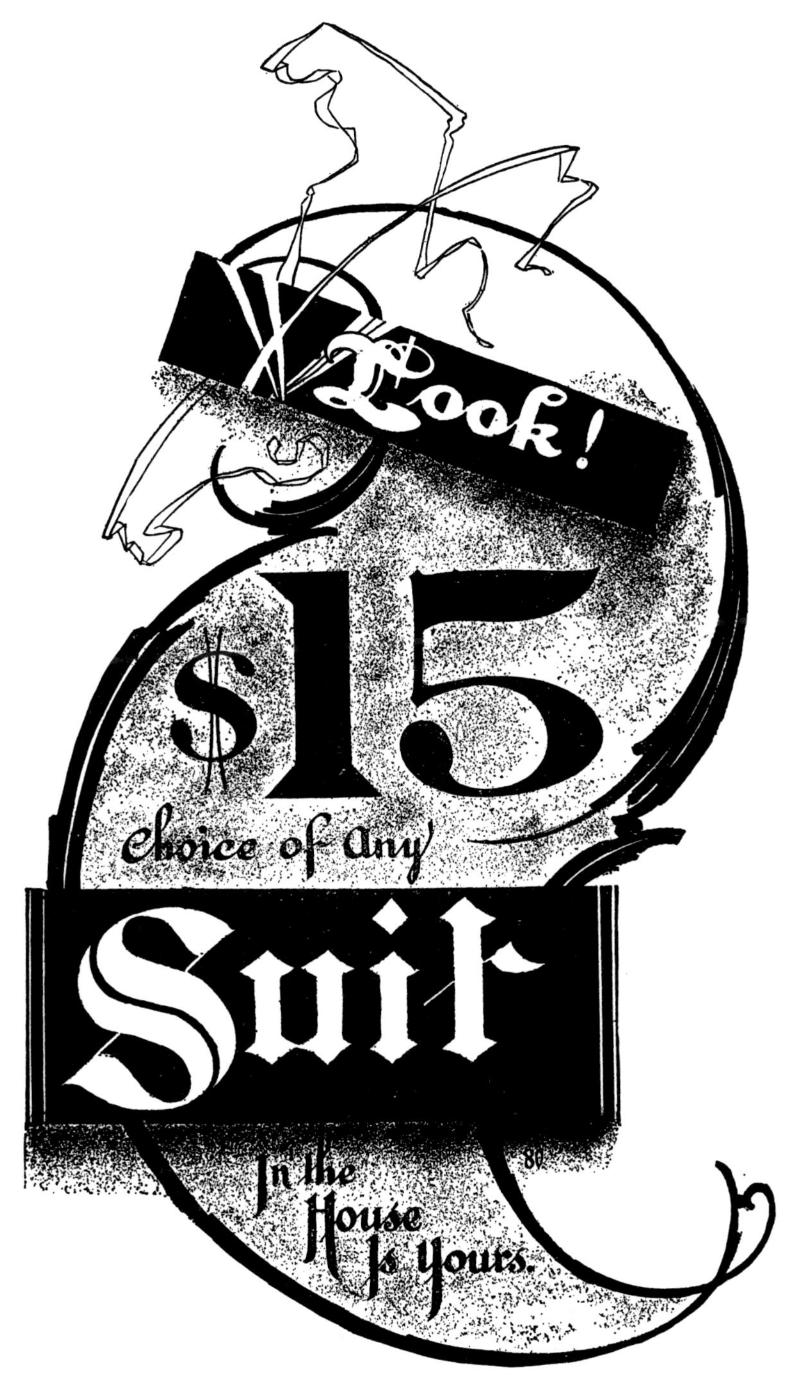
Look!
$15
choice of any
Suit
In the House Is Yours.

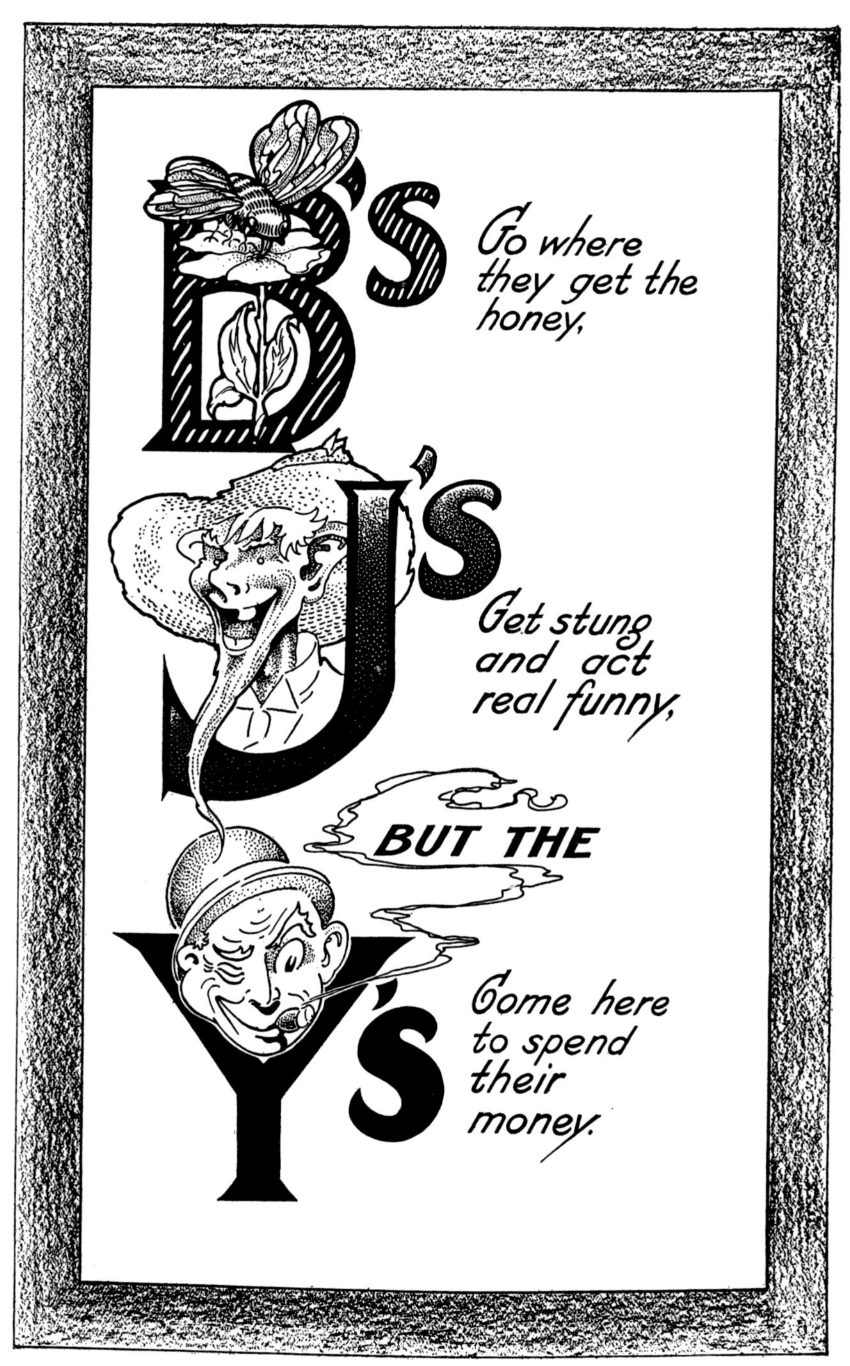
B's
Go where they get the honey,
J's
Get stung and act real funny,
BUT THE
Y's
Come here to spend their money.

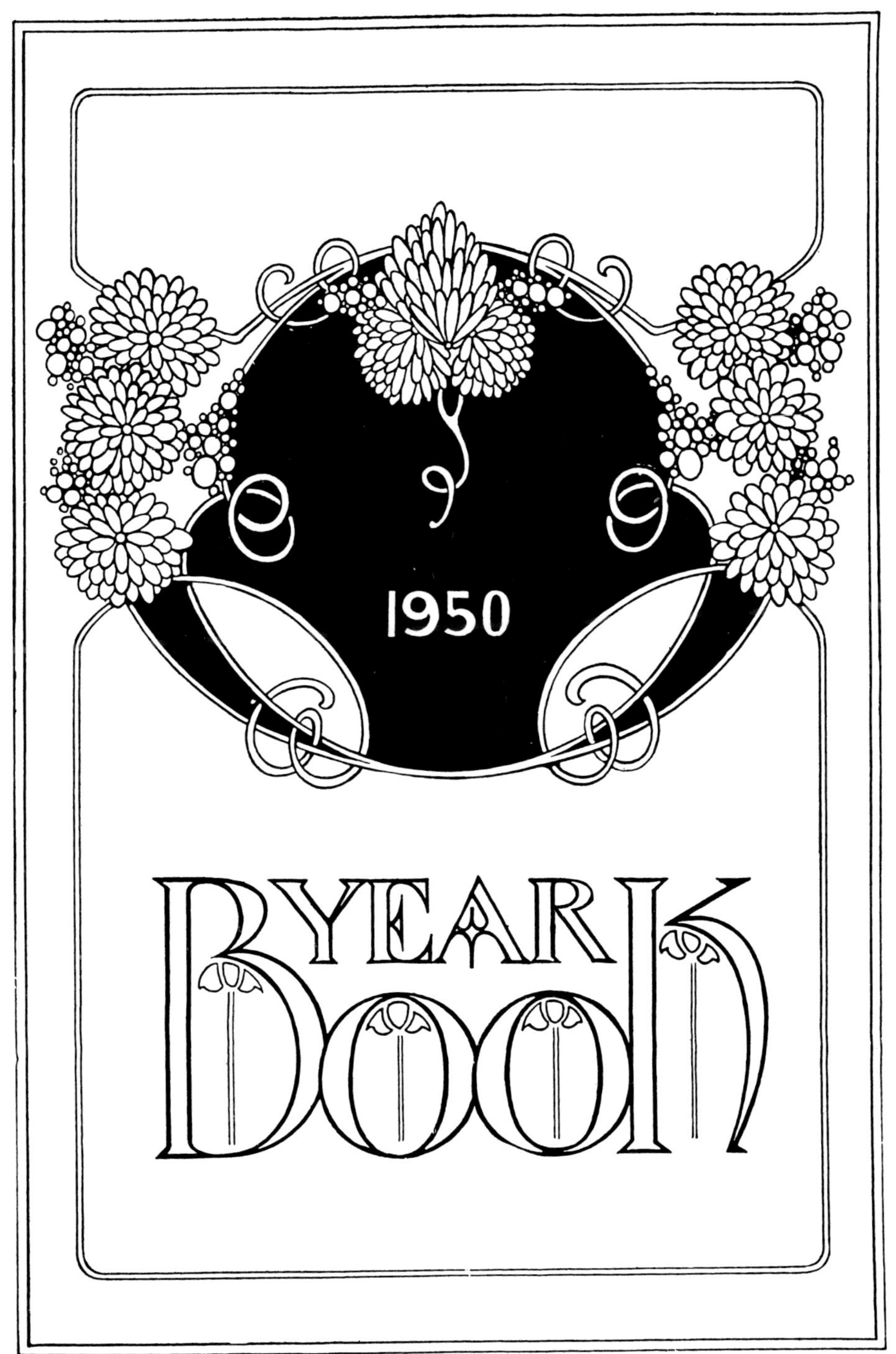
1950
YEAR
BOOK

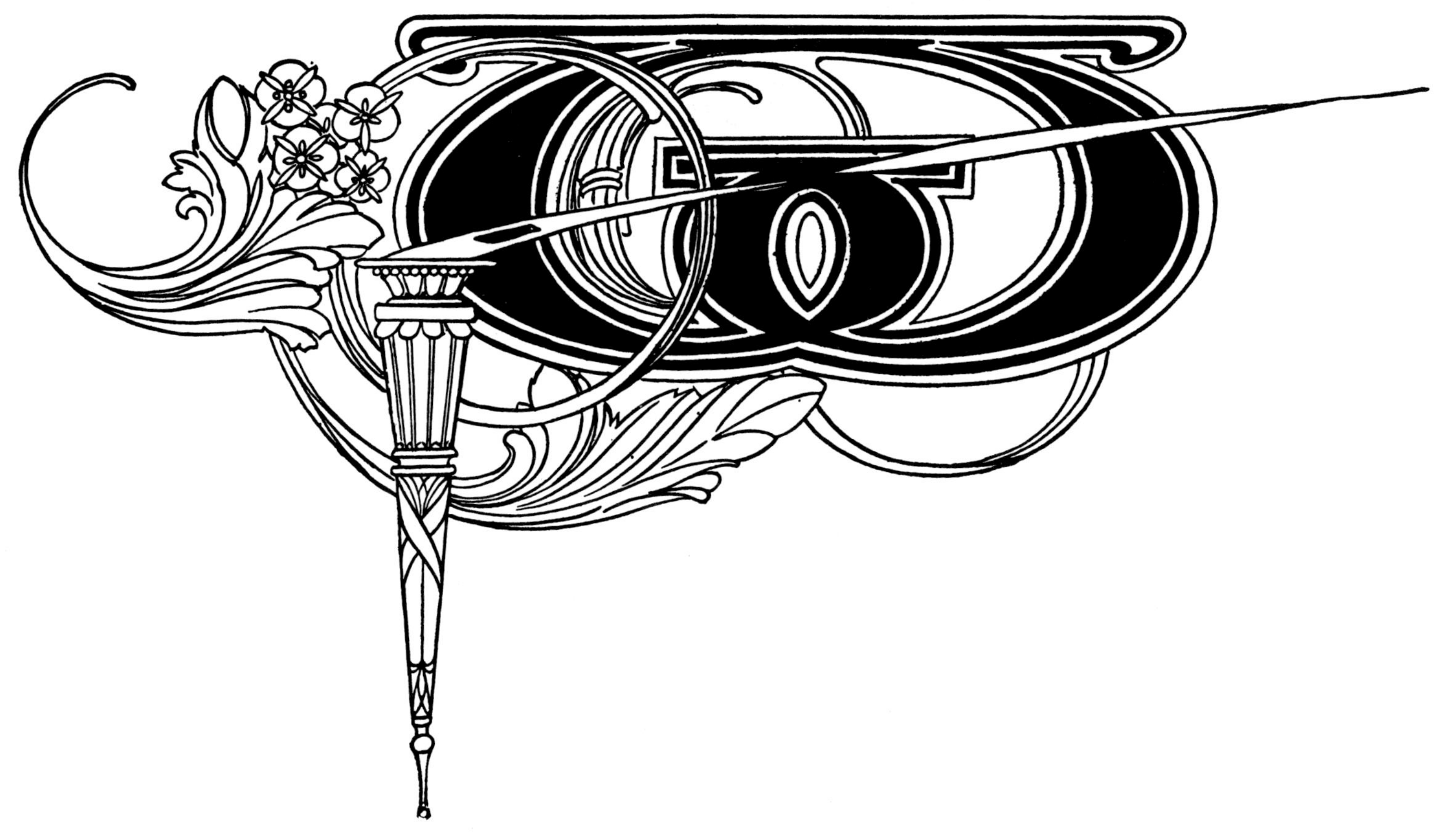

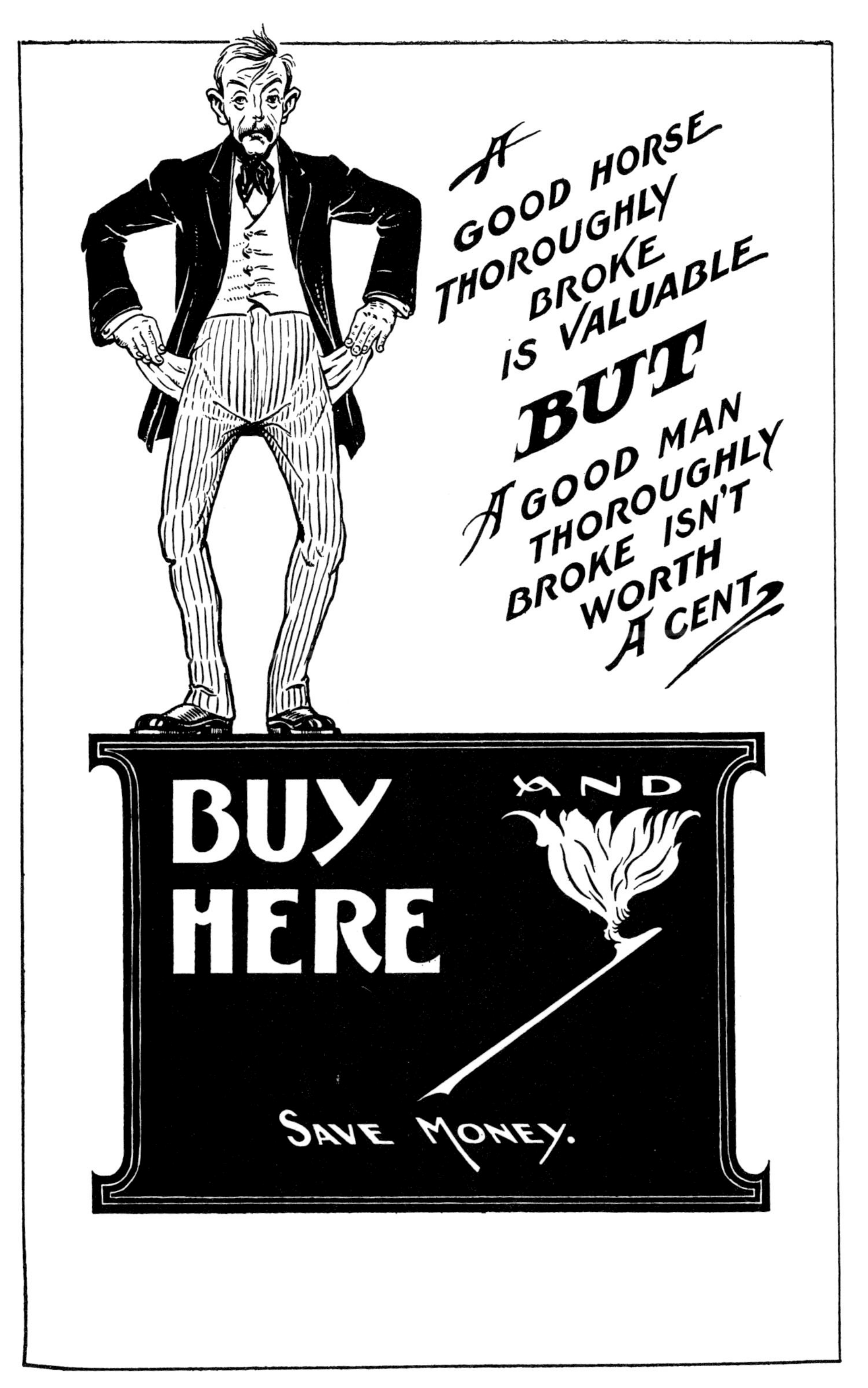
A GOOD HORSE THOROUGHLY BROKE IS VALUABLE
BUT
A GOOD MAN THOROUGHLY BROKE ISN'T WORTH A CENT
BUY HERE AND
SAVE MONEY.

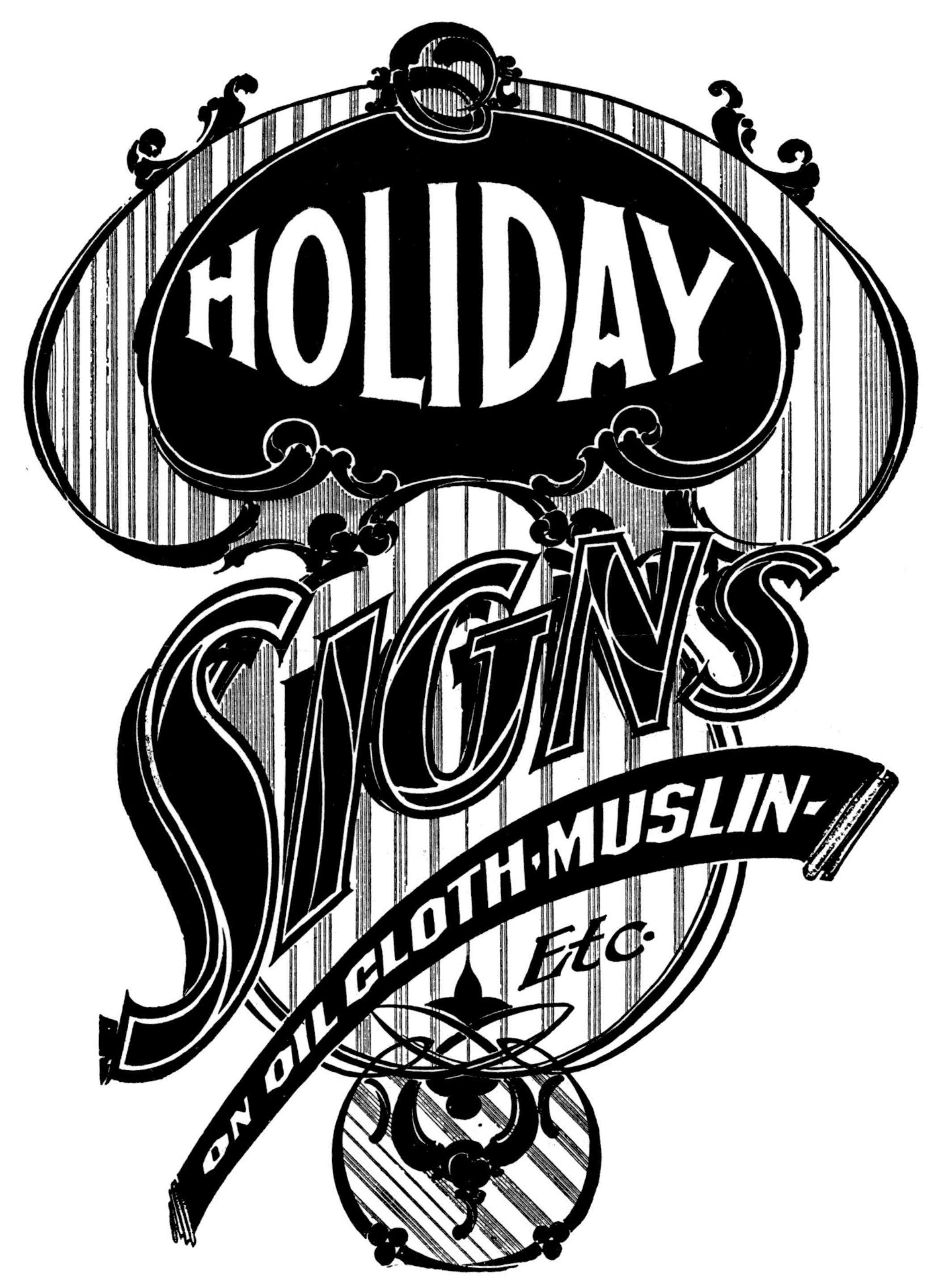
HOLIDAY
SIGNS
ON OIL CLOTH·MUSLIN·
Etc.

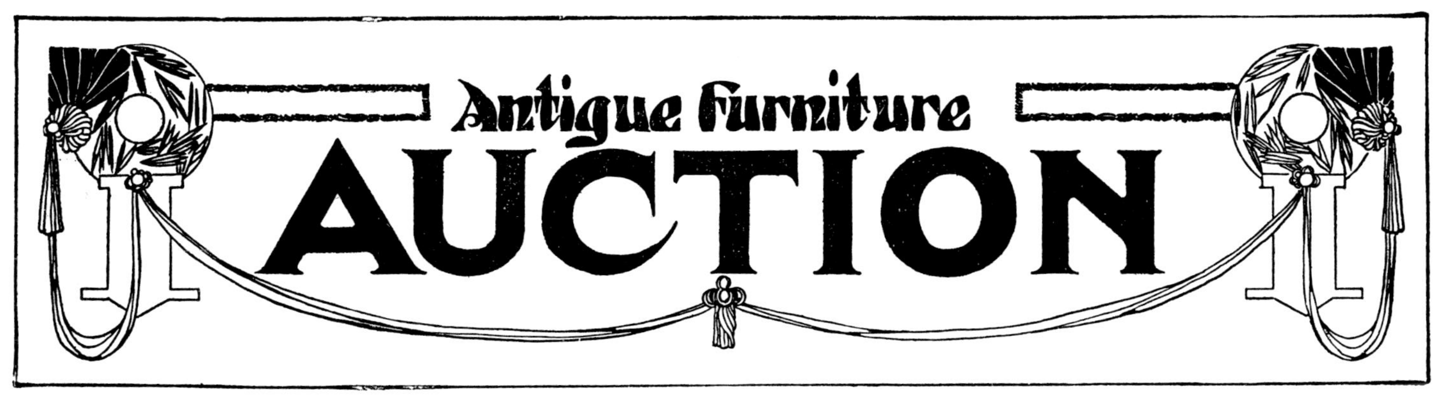
Antique Furniture
AUCTION

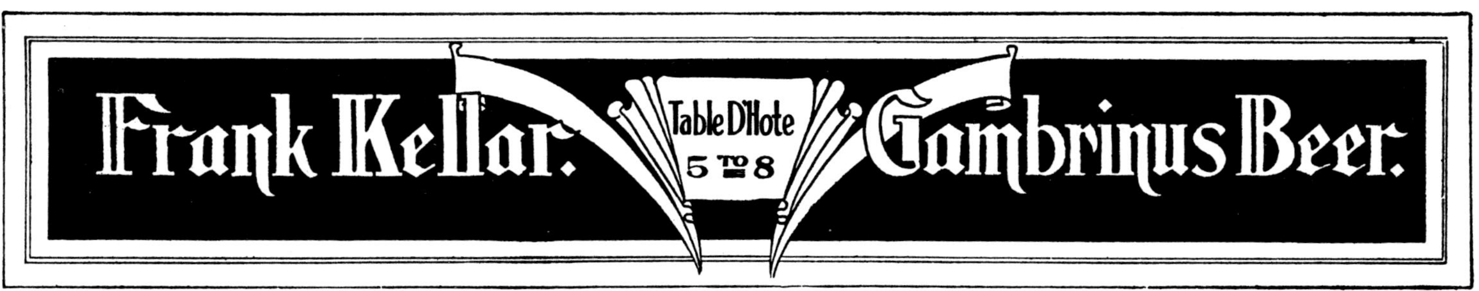
Frank Kellar.
Table D'Hote
5 TO 8
Gambrinus Beer.

ABCDEFGH
PQRSTUV
abcdefghijk
stuvwxyz 12

HALF·CLASSIC·ROMAN·

IJKLMNO
WXYZ&
lmnopqr
3456789

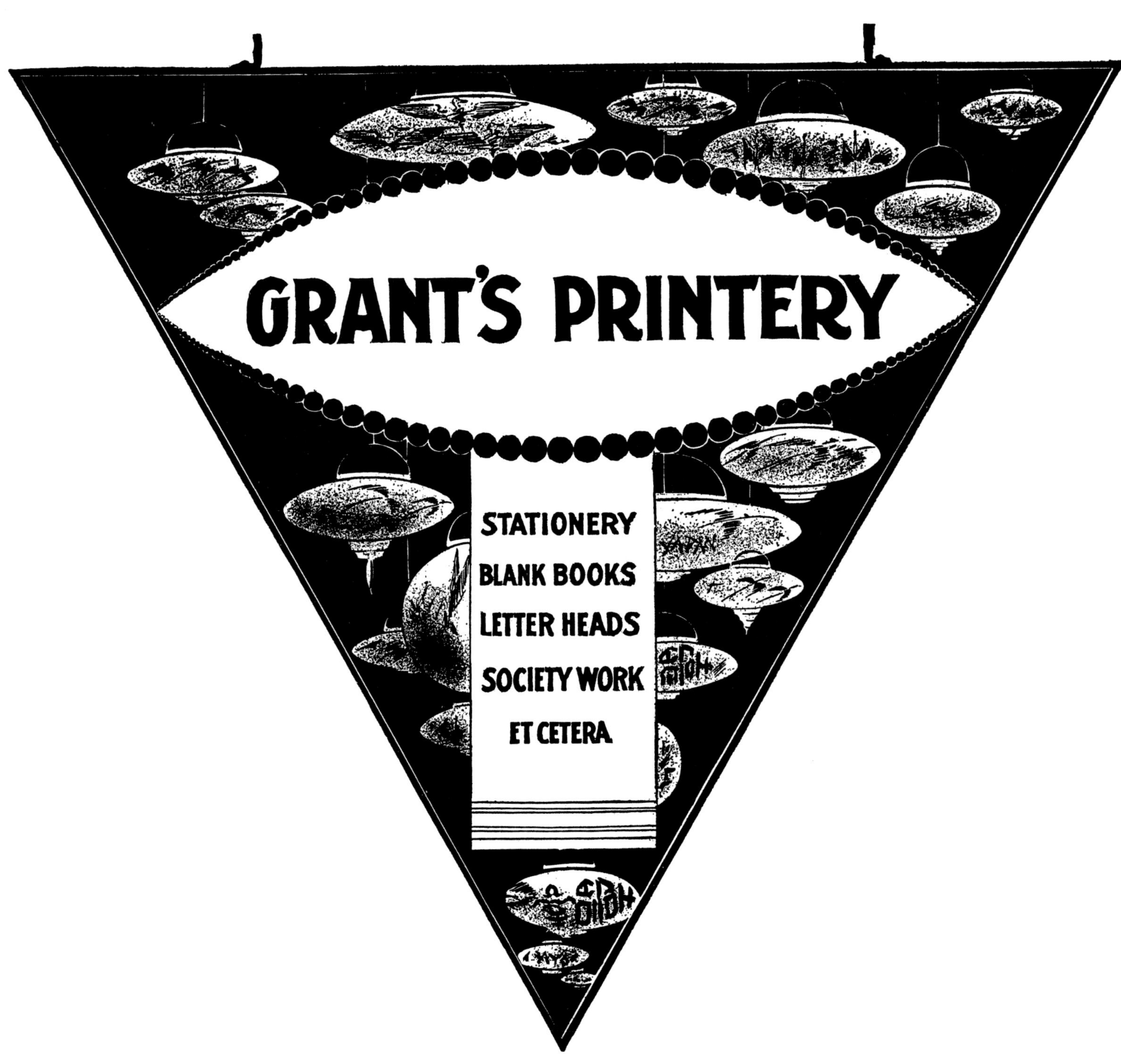
GRANT'S PRINTERY
STATIONERY
BLANK BOOKS
LETTER HEADS
SOCIETY WORK
ET CETERA

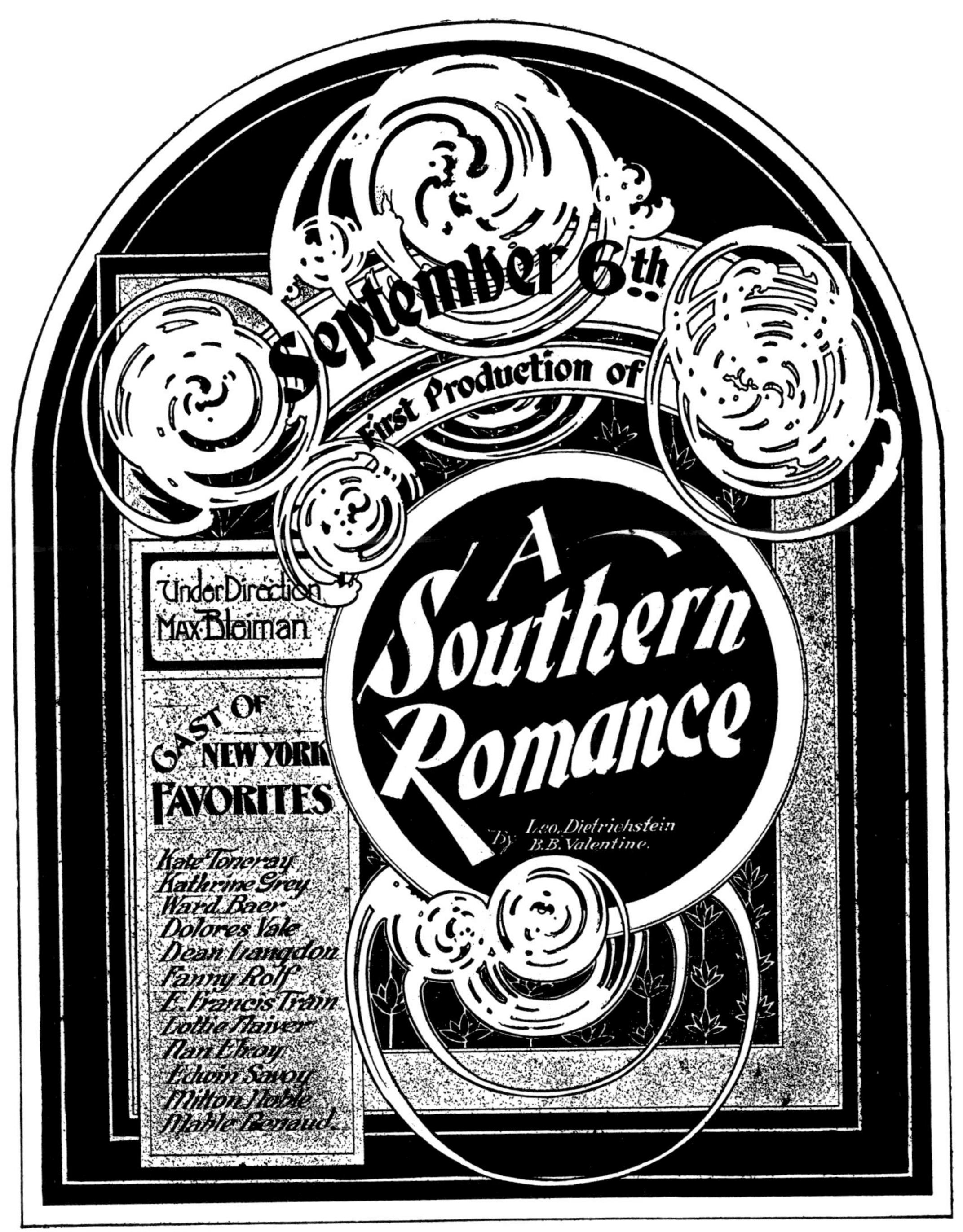
September 6th
First Production of
A Southern Romance
By Leo. Dietrichstein
B.B. Valentine.
Under Direction
Max Bleiman
Cast of New York Favorites
Kate Toneray
Kathrine Grey
Ward Baer
Dolores Vale
Dean Langdon
Fanny Rolf
E. Francis Train
Lottie Naiver
Nan Elroy
Edwin Savoy
Milton Noble
Mable Renaud.

"CHICAGO" TUSCAN ROMAN

A B C D E F G H I J K L M N O
P Q R S T U V W X Y Z & 1 2 3
4 5 6 7 8 9 a b c d e f g h i j k l
m n o p q r s t u v x w z y

MODIFIED TUSCAN ROMAN

A B C D E F G H I J K L M N O P Q R
S T U V W X Y Z & 1 2 3 4 5 6 7 8 9
a b c d e f g h i j k l m n o p q r s t u v w x y z

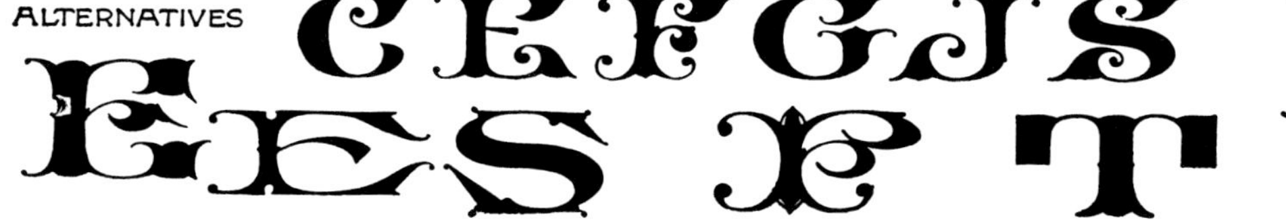

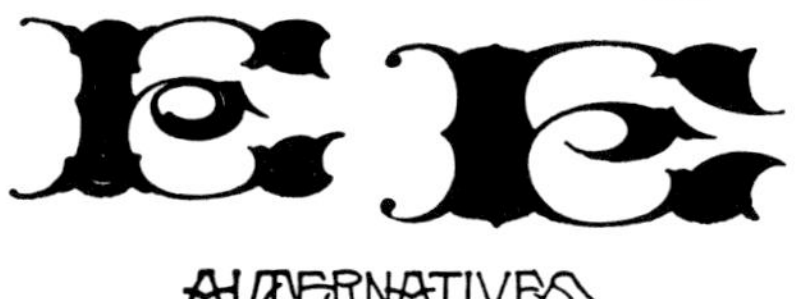

Sign Painters' Plymouth

ABCDEFGHIJKLM
NOPQRSTUVW
&XYZ&
abcdefghijklmnopqr
gstuvwxyz
1234567890

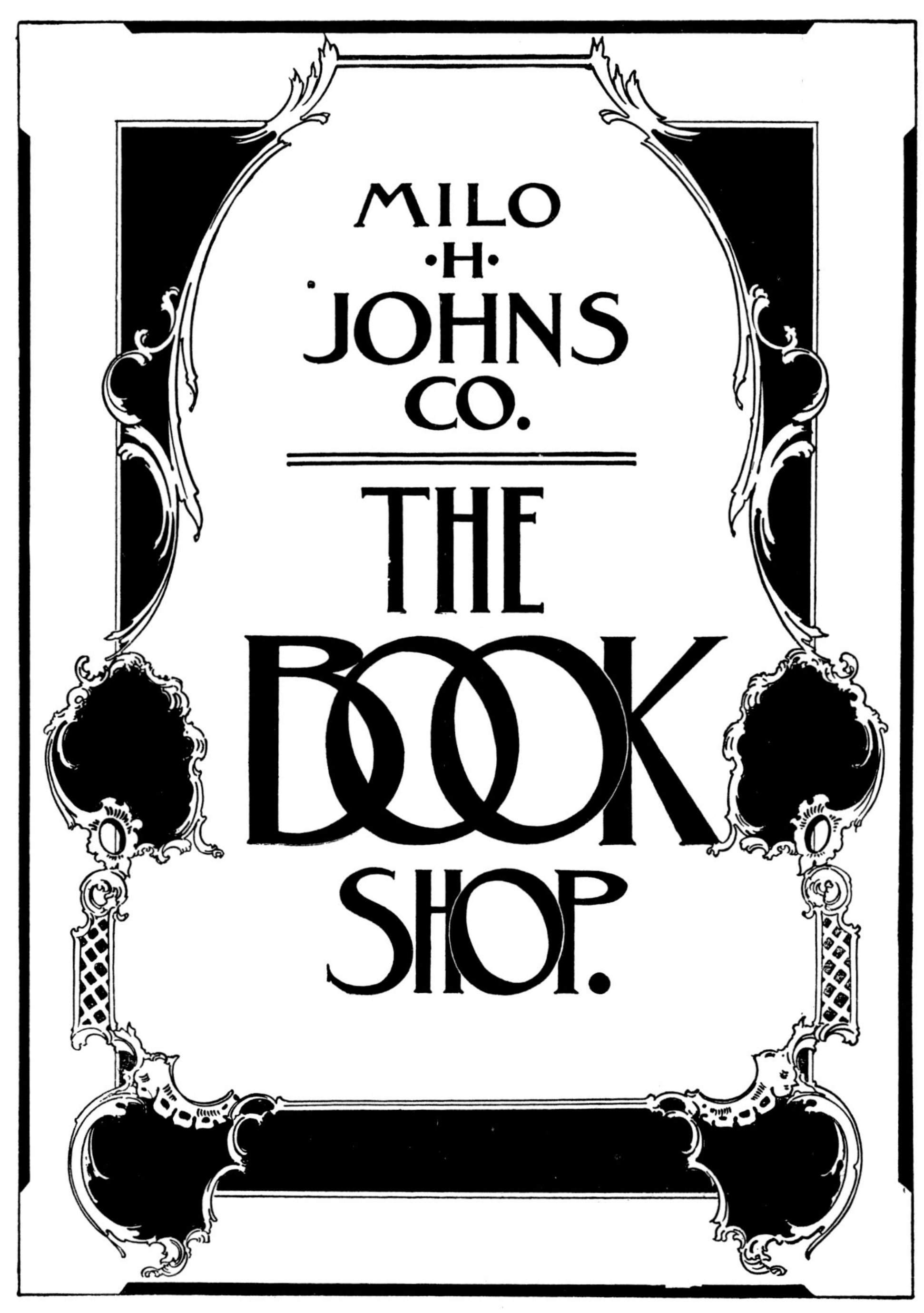
MILO
·H·
JOHNS
CO.
THE
BOOK
SHOP.

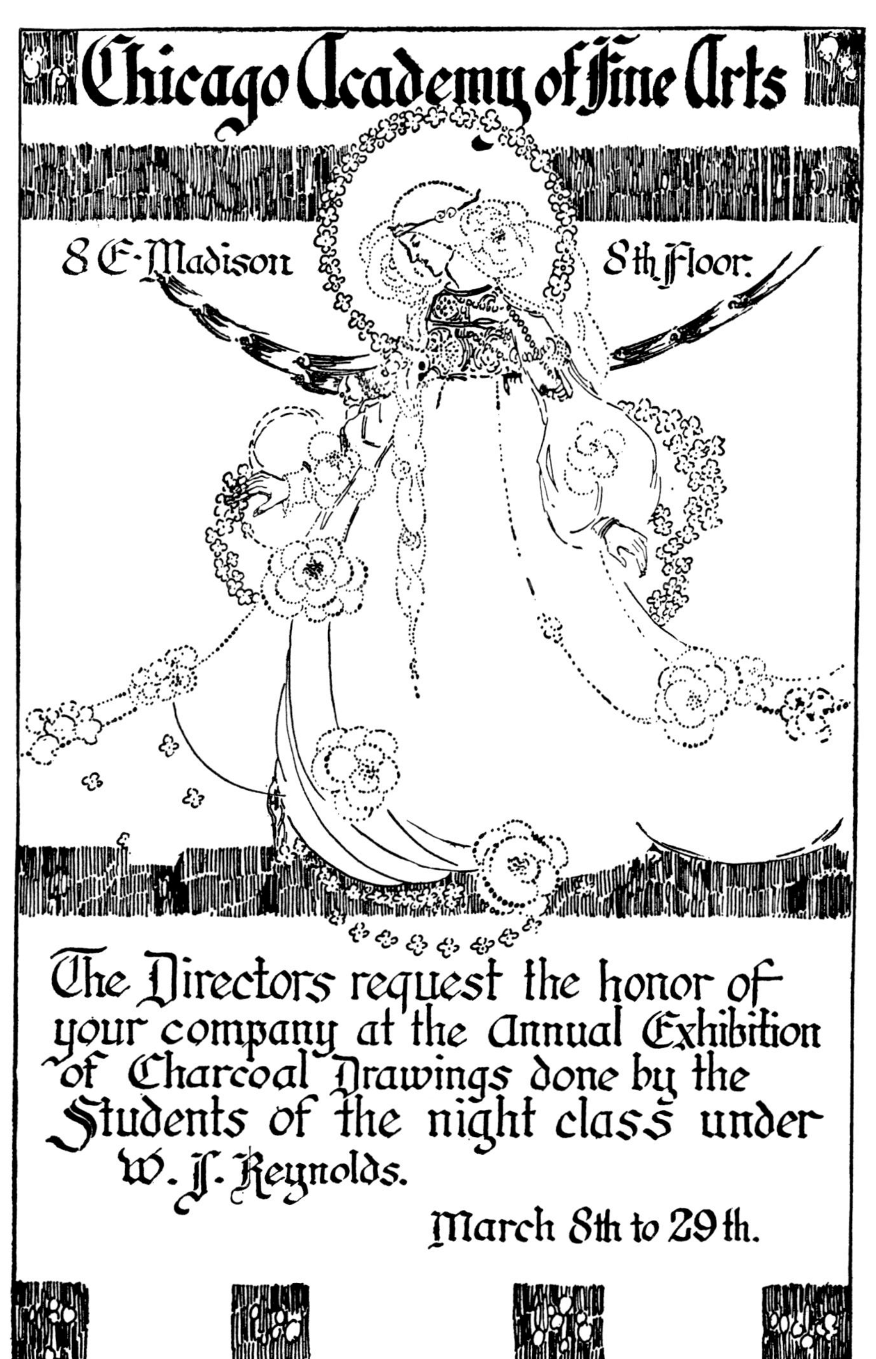
Chicago Academy of Fine Arts
8 E. Madison
8th Floor.
The Directors request the honor of your company at the Annual Exhibition of Charcoal Drawings done by the Students of the night class under W. J. Reynolds.
March 8th to 29th.

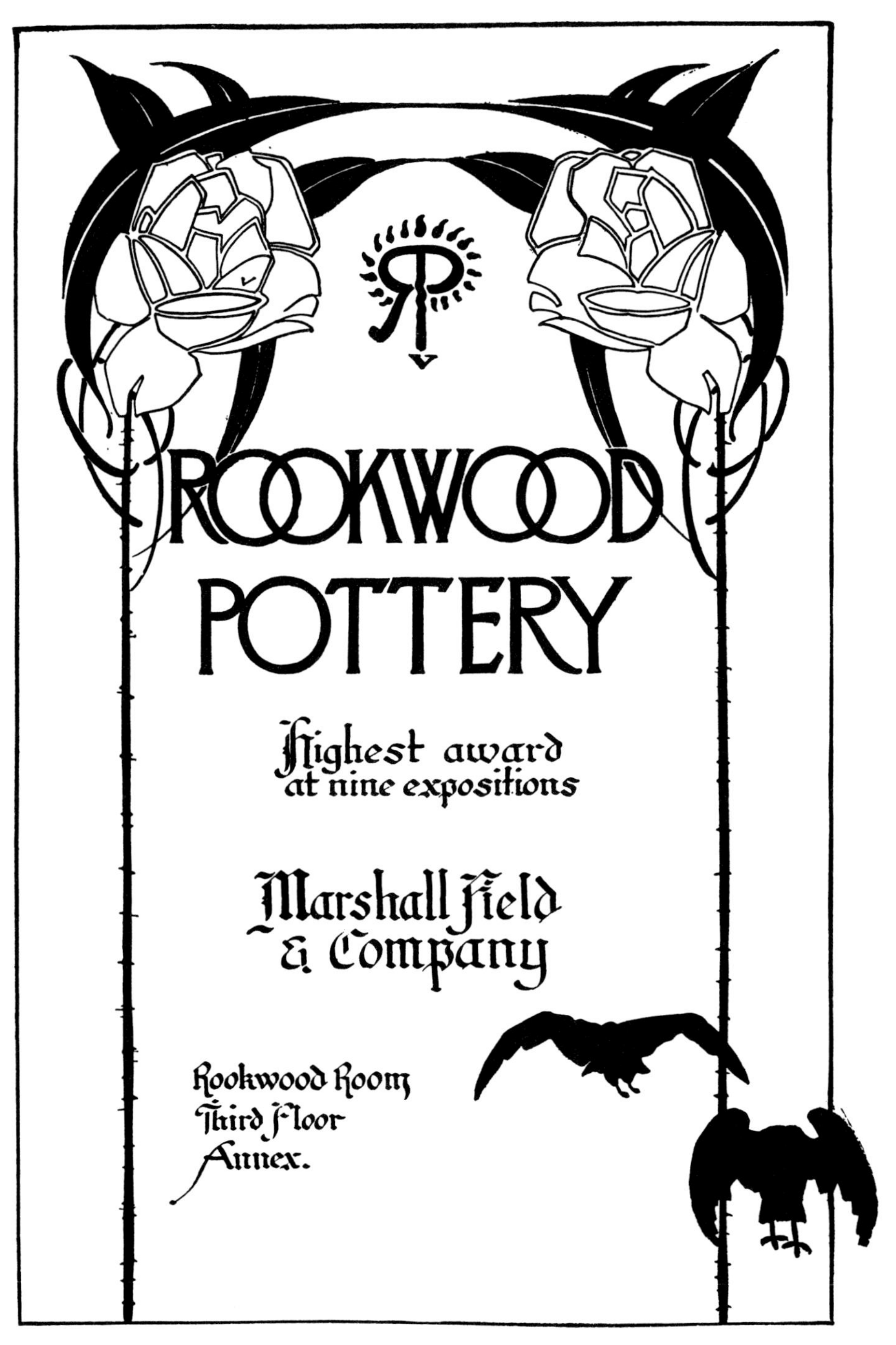
ROOKWOOD
POTTERY
Highest award
at nine expositions
Marshall Field
& Company
Rookwood Room
Third Floor
Annex.

"ADVERTISERS" "THICK & THIN PLUG"

A I a

BC 23 dcb

DEF 4 efg

GHIJK 5 hijlmnok

LMNOPQR qrstp

STUV 6 uv

WXY 78 w

Z 9 xy

& z

Broken Poster

ABCDEFGHIJKLM
NOPQRTUVWXY
Z&
abcdefghijklmnopqr
stuvwxyz
123456789

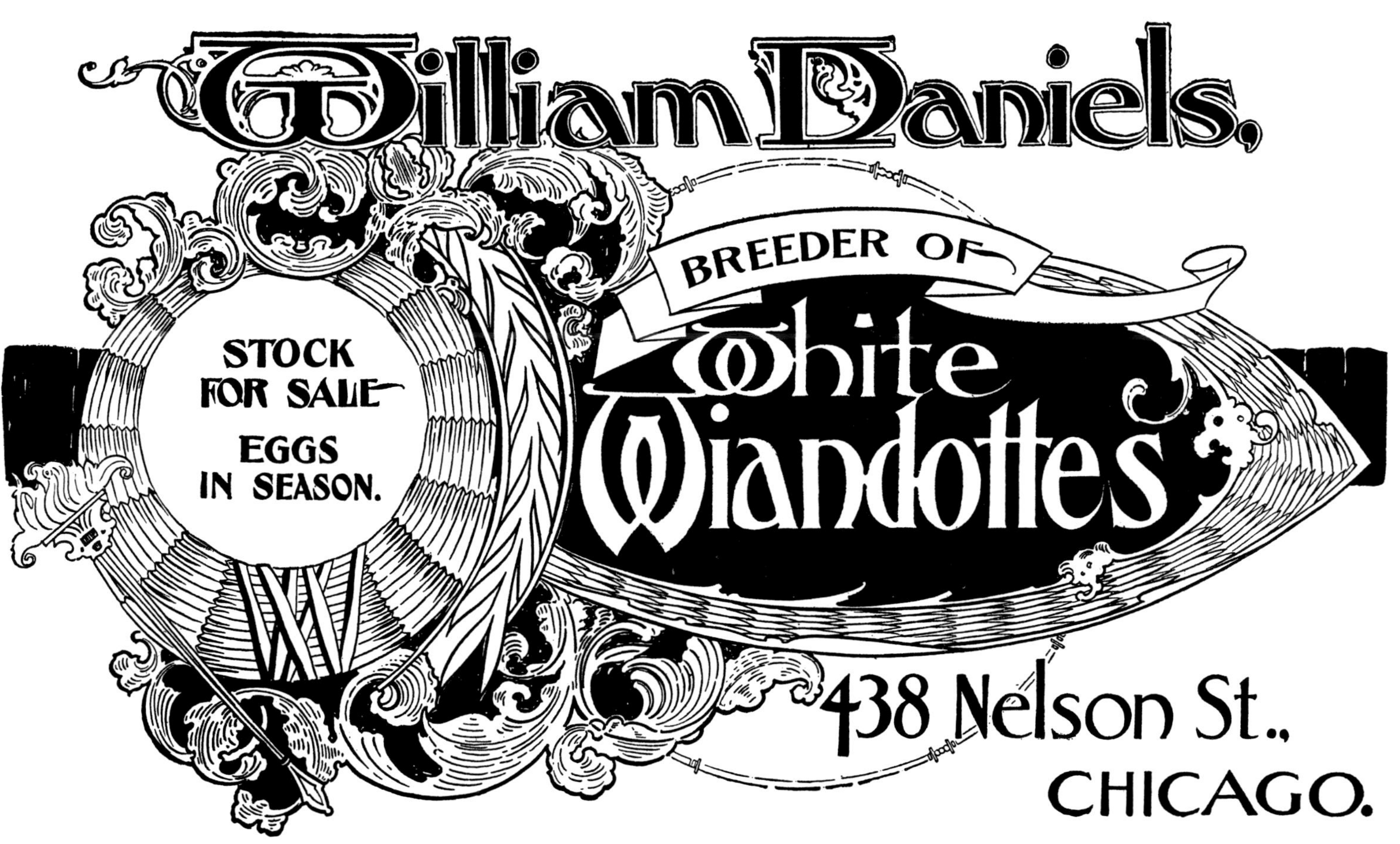
William Daniels,
BREEDER OF
White Wiandottes
STOCK
FOR SALE
EGGS
IN SEASON.
438 Nelson St.,
CHICAGO.

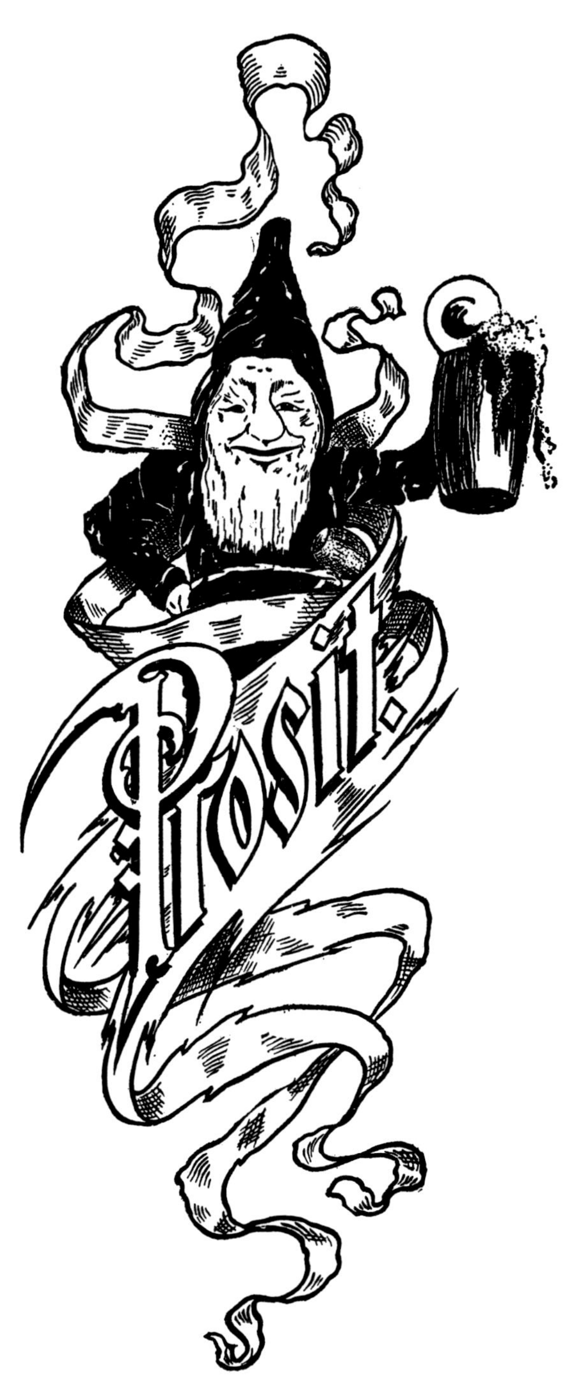

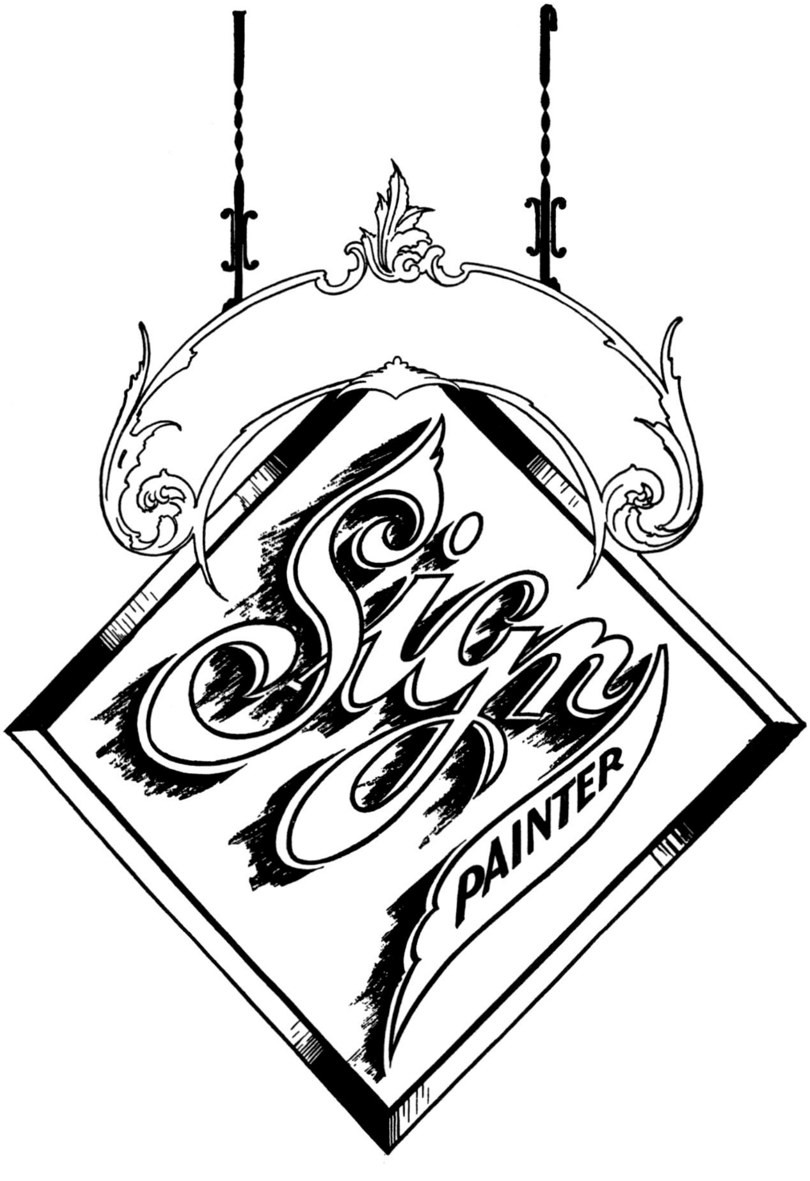

Sign
PAINTER

(heavy) FRENCH ROMAN

A 24567 a

BG 319 dcb

DEF R efg

GHIJK R hijlmnok

LMNOPQR R qstp

STUV uv

WXY 8 R w sp

Z E R xy

& z